"Gha-ra-bagh!"

"Gha-ra-bagh!"

The Emergence of the
National Democratic Movement in Armenia

Mark Malkasian

Wayne State University Press   Detroit

Library of Congress Cataloging-in-Publication Data

Malkasian, Mark.
   "Gha-Ra-Bagh!" : the emergence of the national democratic movement in Armenia /
Mark Malkasian.
      p.   cm.
   Includes bibliographical references and index.
   ISBN 0–8143–2604–8 (alk. paper).
   1. Armenia (Republic) — Politics and government.   2. Armenians — Azerbaijan —
Nagorno-Karabakh.   3. Nagorno-Karabakh (Azerbaijan) — History.   I. Title.
DK687.M35   1996
956.6′2 — dc20   96–20808

Design and cover art: Betty Pilon

Jacket photograph: Berge Ara Zobian

To the people of Armenia
May their strength sustain them

Contents

Acknowledgments

This book was written thanks largely to the contributions of others. From the earliest stages of conceptualization and organization, Tom Samuelian and Lucig Danielian were instrumental in getting the project off the ground. Drafts of the manuscript were conscientiously reviewed by Vahe Baloulian, Matthew Der Manuelian, Nora Dudwick, Tom Samuelian, and Galina Staravoitova. Many of those involved in the Karabagh movement graciously submitted to long, often tiring, interviews. Among those who deserve special gratitude are Levon Abrahamyan, Gurgen Boyajyan, Ashot Dabaghyan, Hambartsum Galstyan, Rafael Ghazaryan, Samson Ghazaryan, Vigen Hairapetyan, Ashot Manucharyan, and Hrair Ulubabyan. In addition, my thanks go to Daniel Karamanoukian for sharing his extensive notes on the mass demonstrations in Yerevan; to my mother, Anita Malkasian, for proofreading; to Bryan Bedrosian, George Bournoutian, and Barlow Der Mugrdechian for lending advice and encouragement; to Sergei Arutiunov for offering his insights into the ethnic divisions of Transcaucasia; to Matthew Der Manuelian, Salpi Haroutinian Ghazarian, Zaven Khachikian, Rouben Mangasarian, and Berge Ara Zobian for contributing photographs to the book; to Alice Nigoghosian, associate director of Wayne State University Press, for her helpful guidance; and to the staff of the Zoryan Institute for providing access to the institute's research materials. I am also indebted to Yerevan State University—in particular to Rafael Matevosyan, vice rector for international relations, and to Nika Babayan, the former secretary of the Armenian Republic Council for Foreign Students Affairs—for giving me the opportunity to study in Armenia during the 1987–88 academic year. Finally, and most significantly, I thank my chief adviser, editor, and unfailing source of support—my wife Deana.

Introduction

In 1988, the people of Armenia took part in a defining moment of history. Before that watershed year, the Armenian Soviet Socialist Republic had been viewed by both outside observers and long-time residents as a political backwater of the Soviet empire. That changed in February 1988, when Armenia suddenly emerged as a driving force of change in the Gorbachev era.

Armenia's transformation revolved around what came to be known as the Karabagh movement. At the core of the movement was concern for the fate of the Nagorno Karabakh Autonomous Oblast—an administrative unit within the neighboring Soviet republic of Azerbaijan populated mostly by Armenians. The Karabagh movement, however, extended well beyond the question of the oblast. Rather, it set into motion a revolution of Armenian society. In the upsurge of political activism that brought much of the republic's population into the streets, Armenia broke loose from its moorings. A self-image that had been molded over the course of the past century was reassessed.

The Karabagh movement was made by the people of Armenia. They shared in the mass rallies, celebrated their new-found ability to influence the political process, and agonized over the realization of their own limitations. Just as Americans who lived through the economic depression of the 1930s or the social turbulence of the 1960s were indelibly stamped by the temper of the times, so the Karabagh movement left a deep imprint on the collective consciousness of the people of Armenia.

The turmoil of the late 1980s and early 1990s marks a bridge between the Soviet period and a new era in Armenian history. The worldview that gradually coalesced among Soviet Armenians was demolished. The relative security that characterized the seven decades of Soviet rule melted away, as did the constraints of the Soviet political system and the central planning of the Soviet economy.

The Karabagh movement did not bring about these

1

changes. ~~Rather, the movement~~ shaped ~~the mindset through which~~ Armenians viewed the upheavals that swept away their ~~Soviet-made~~ universe. The movement created a fresh set of beliefs and values by which Armenians charted a new course in the wake of the Soviet Union's disintegration. It also fostered a sense of unity and purpose that was to continue flickering, albeit dimly, through the trials and deprivations that the Armenians were to suffer after 1991. The last time Armenian identity underwent such a metamorphosis, Josef Stalin was the agent of change. A generation earlier, the genocide of 1.5 million Armenians by Ottoman Turkey during World War I recast the Armenian self-image. In the case of the Karabagh movement, however, Armenians themselves were largely responsible for altering their assumptions about Armenia's position in the world. No wonder, then, that many Armenians drew a parallel between the Karabagh movement's significance and the impact of the Armenian revolutionary parties on national consciousness around the turn of the century.

This book offers the general reader an introduction to the aspirations, ideals, and frustrations of the Karabagh movement. It does not attempt to trace the ramifications of the Karabagh movement for Armenia in the post-Soviet era, nor does it analyze the role of policymakers in Moscow, Western Europe, or the United States in the movement's development. The scope is much more modest: to examine the Karabagh movement from the perspective of Armenia. The focus of the following chapters is limited to the events of 1988, and attention is fixed on Yerevan, or more precisely on the public squares and main boulevards of the Armenian capital that served as the stage for much of the Karabagh movement's drama. Above all, the aim of this book is to recapture the atmosphere, *Zeitgeist*, and mood that permeated the central core of Yerevan from the first mass rallies in February to the earthquake that struck northern Armenia in December.

Within the span of less than ten months in 1988, Armenia's political landscape was reshaped. From the initial euphoria generated by the outpouring of up to one million people in the streets of Yerevan, to the tentative efforts at influencing the political process, to the deepening disillusionment with the policies of the Kremlin, Armenians went from docile apathy to defiant politicization. The year 1988 also afforded a preview of the period that lay ahead. The chronology of events included huge rallies, meetings between popular spokesmen and Soviet officials, government crackdowns, grass-roots organizing efforts, special commissions, communal strife, transportation blockades, and massacre. The years that followed would witness further activism and crisis, but Armenians were by then treading over familiar ground.

In addition to presenting the events of 1988, this book seeks to clarify several issues surrounding the formative period of the Karabagh movement. Beyond the borders of Armenia, videotape of the vast crowds in the Armenian capital suggested to many that highly organized, malevolent forces were at work. Some imagined conspiratorial networks extending from Yerevan and Baku (capital of neighboring Azerbaijan) to the highest echelons of the Kremlin. In truth, the massive demonstrations that first took place in February 1988 were neither organized nor planned. The Karabagh movement flung open a window on Soviet and Armenian politics. For a brief period, the emphasis, if not the reality, was on the transparency of public life. A political culture long characterized by its opacity was shattered. Power belonged to the people in the streets. This book finds its purpose in exploring the meaning behind that spontaneous outpouring, not in probing the motivations of the Soviet Union's ruling elite.

This book also challenges those who contend that the activists at the head of the Karabagh movement in Armenia saw the campaign as a vehicle to gain power. Undeniably, the eleven-member Karabagh Committee that was formed in May 1988 served as a political launching pad for many of the leading figures in Armenia's post-Soviet government, including President Levon Ter Petrosyan. Political power, however, did not enter into their calculations in the early days of the Karabagh movement. In early 1988, the possibility that the Soviet Union would soon unravel was scarcely considered. Those choosing to take an active role in the Karabagh movement could hardly be accused of grasping for a higher rung on the Soviet career ladder. On the contrary, they were risking their livelihoods, if not their freedom. Some relished the celebrity and influence conferred by membership in the Karabagh Committee. Others viewed it as a burden. What united them was a gnawing fear that both the committee and the movement would eventually be the target of a government crackdown.

The account presented here of the Karabagh movement in Armenia offers neither fuel for conspiracy theories nor portraits of flawless heroes. From the outset, the movement set its own course, sweeping along the activists who positioned themselves at its vanguard. To its credit, the Karabagh Committee was guided by worthy principles. Committee members above all emphasized the democratic character and constitutionality of the movement. But they were also amateurish and inexperienced, even naive. Like other reformers in the last years of the Soviet Union, they were struggling to implant in their own society the norms and values of Western political culture, even as the framework of the Soviet system was crashing down around them.

The emphasis on democratic reform distinguished the movement in Armenia from its counterpart in the Nagorno Karabakh

Autonomous Oblast, or Mountainous Karabagh. As early as February 1988, the movements in Armenia and Mountainous Karabagh were headed in different directions. Karabagh Armenians were single-mindedly focused on one concrete objective: unification with Armenia. Their oblast, consisting of 1,694 square miles (less than the size of the state of Delaware), had been at the center of a territorial dispute between Armenians and Azerbaijanis that went back to the early years of the century. Karabagh Armenians, who made up 75 percent of the oblast's population of slightly more than 160,000 in 1988, saw Gorbachev's *perestroika* (restructuring) as their opportunity to assert their case for unification. In contrast to the Karabagh Committee in Armenia, the leadership of the movement in the oblast was dominated by factory managers, government officials, and other figures of authority. There was little interest in reforming the Soviet system, much less in overturning the rule of the Communist Party.

The movement in Mountainous Karabagh posed a counterpoint to the movement in Armenia and contributed to the philosophical tensions that ultimately shaped the political outlook of the Karabagh Committee and its members. Whereas nationalism inspired Karabagh Armenians, democratization was the touchstone for activists in Armenia. And while the movement in Mountainous Karabagh was closely bound to land and tradition, the temperament in Armenia was dominated by a search beyond the republic's boundaries for new ideas and models. During 1988, these distinctions were largely lost to the outside world. This book attempts to put them back into focus.

Chapter 1

Stepanakert

On 20 February 1988, 40,000 Karabagh Armenians gathered in front of the soviet of people's deputies in Stepanakert, the oblast capital. The crowd—quite literally the entire population of the town—had turned out to see that the legislature of the Nagorno Karabakh Autonomous Oblast vote to unify the oblast with the republic of Soviet Armenia. The resolution for which they rallied would set in motion a string of events that would reroute the course of Armenian history. On 20 February, however, the Armenians of Mountainous Karabagh had little idea of what the future held.

Theirs was a seventy-year struggle, spanning three generations. Virtually all the Armenians in Stepanakert were tied to the cause of unification in one way or another. Their collective effort to defend an outpost of the Armenian nation in hostile surroundings had hardened their outlook on life and given them a thorny outer shell. On that winter afternoon in the mountain air of Stepanakert, however, the bitterness was not apparent. Entire families had jammed into Lenin Square—stubble-chinned fathers with fur-lined *ushankas* covering their heads, grandmothers marked by weathered faces and faded kerchiefs, and rosy-cheeked children perched atop the shoulders of their older brothers. Portraits of Gorbachev, Lenin, and Stepan Shahumyan (Lenin's special commissar of Caucasian affairs during the Russian Revolution) swayed with the crowd. Banners spoke of unspoiled trust in *glasnost* (openness): "Justice will prevail"; "One people, one territory"; and "The Karabagh question should be decided by the Karabagh people." [1] Above all, there was a belief within the Karabagh Armenian community that the day when past injustices would be redressed was finally at hand.

5

Karabagh Armenians could be pardoned for their exuberance. Even many of those inside the chamber of the oblast soviet were less than savvy about the inner workings of Soviet politics. Several had walked ten miles or more through the rugged hills surrounding Stepanakert to avoid the roadblocks set up by Azerbaijani authorities. They had believed the optimistic reports of their representatives who had met with Moscow insiders during the past months. They had embraced the tools of do-it-yourself democracy: petitions, meetings of worker collectives, and letter-writing campaigns. And they had sized up Mikhail Gorbachev as a leader sympathetic to those who had been wronged by his predecessors. Most in attendance on 20 February were village folk. Graft and corruption were not unknown among them, but the oblast was too poor to provide most Communist Party members much more than a few extra kilos of meat and cheese at the end of the month. Indeed, many saw the marriage of party duties and national fealty as a compatible union.

Even on 20 February 1988, however, there were unmistakable signs that the hope springing up in Mountainous Karabagh would be in vain. Only two days earlier, a plenum of the Central Committee of the Communist Party of the USSR had rejected appeals to transfer Mountainous Karabagh from Azerbaijan to Armenia and had sent two candidate members of the Politburo, Georgi P. Razumovsky and Pyotr N. Demichev, to Stepanakert to voice Moscow's position. Mountainous Karabagh First Secretary Boris Kevorkov had joined his superiors from the Azerbaijani government in Baku in pressuring party members to fall in line behind the Central Committee statement. But the deputies were steadfast in their good faith. They were convinced that the Central Committee's decision had been based on ignorance, not Soviet policy. Once the facts were heard, they reasoned, the promise of *perestroika* and the Armenians of Mountainous Karabagh would prevail. The tenacity of the deputies did not come by accident. They were, after all, Armenians.

The Armenians are an ancient people. Their nation took shape in eastern Anatolia in the first millennium before the Christian era, a time when the Assyrians, Medes, Babylonians, and Persians were vying for power in the Fertile Crescent. The Armenian homeland is defined by mountain ranges. To the south, the Taurus Mountains separate Armenia from the lowlands of Mesopotamia. In the north, the Pontus range rises up close to the shores of the Black Sea. Further to the northeast, ancient Armenia's northeastern border is marked by the highlands of Mountainous Karabagh. Three lakes—Van, Sevan, and Urmia—also serve to frame the Armenian heartland.

The geography of Armenia dictated the fate of its people. Natural barriers guarded Armenia in the north and the south. From east to west, however, the route was open. Armenia through the ages was a crossroads for both commerce and conquest. The trade connection between the Mediterranean world and the riches of China and India passed through Armenia. So did the path for invaders, from the ancient Scythians to Timur-e Lang (Tamerlane). Because of its strategic highland position, Armenia has long been prized by the great empires that have come and gone in the region.

Armenia also was a powerful empire for a brief time in the first century B.C. Under Tigranes II, known as Tigran the Great, Armenia stretched from the Caspian Sea to the Mediterranean Sea, extending as far south as Damascus. Armenia's age of glory, however, was fleeting. As was often the case in Armenian history, Tigran's empire fell prey to ambitious neighbors. From the west, the Roman generals Lucullus and Pompey successively invaded Armenia, while the Parthians attacked from the east. By the time Tigran died in 55 B.C., Armenia had been reduced to a buffer state between Rome and Parthia. In the first century A.D., after more than a century of hostilities over Armenia, the two great empires reached an agreement whereby Armenia would be ruled by a Persian king to be crowned by Rome. The accord would be the first of many in which control over Armenia was to be divided between the powers of the region. Through the centuries, Armenia would be partitioned by Byzantines and Sasanids, Ottomans and Safavids, and finally Ottomans and Russians.

Armenians themselves were marked by the struggle over their homeland. Their culture combined features of both Greco-Roman civilization and ancient Persia. Developments in the fourth and fifth centuries A.D., however, stamped Armenian culture with an enduring distinctiveness. In the early fourth century, Armenia converted to Christianity, becoming the first state in the world to adopt the new religion. Roughly a century later, an Armenian monk, Mesrop Mashtots, created a unique alphabet for the Armenian language. In the following decades, the Bible was translated into Armenian, along with other Christian writings and many of the leading texts of Greco-Roman scholarship.

Armenia's faith was soon challenged. In the middle of the fifth century, zealous Sasanid rulers tried to convert everyone within their realm to Zoroastrianism. The Armenians rebelled. In 451, thousands of them organized under the command of Vardan Mamikonian to confront the Persian army. The outnumbered Armenian forces were destroyed almost to the last man. Their martyrdom, however, inspired a generation of their countrymen to continue the war of resistance. In 484, the Sasanids were forced to grant Armenians the right to practice Christianity.

The same year that Vardan Mamikonian was fighting the Persian army, the Fourth Ecumenical Council of the Christian church was meeting at Chalcedon to discuss the nature of Christ. The council decreed that the divine and human natures of Christ were each complete and yet united. Because of their struggle against the Sasanids, Armenian Church leaders did not review the canons of the council until forty years after they were issued. The Armenians rejected Chalcedon, affirming their allegiance to the decisions of the first three ecumenical councils. The Armenian position was not particularly significant in doctrinal terms, but it aggravated the growing political rift between the Armenian and Byzantine churches. Even before Chalcedon, Byzantium had begun pressuring Armenian clerics to recognize the authority of the bishop of Constantinople. Armenian Church leaders, however, jealously guarded their autonomy. In 609, they officially cut their ties with Constantinople and established a national church.

The invention of the Armenian alphabet and the creation of a national church set the Armenians apart from neighboring cultures and infused the nobility and the church hierarchy with the conviction that their separateness was worth preserving. The feeling was reinforced by the Islamic invasions of the seventh and eighth centuries. Islam swept over much of the Middle East, gaining millions of converts among followers of Zoroastrianism and Byzantine Christianity, but made few inroads among the Armenians. Under the rule of the Muslim Abbasid Empire, the Bagratuni clan emerged as the leaders of the Armenian people. Late in the ninth century, the Bagratunis took advantage of the decline of the Abbasids to fill the regional power vacuum and carve out a new Armenian kingdom. For nearly two centuries, Bagratuni rulers maintained their independence by deftly balancing relations among the Abbasids, Byzantines, and rival Armenian clans. Their most magnificent legacy was the construction of a new capital at Ani, city of 1,001 churches.

In 1045, pressure from Constantinople brought an end to the sovereignty of the Bagratunis. No other major Armenian kingdom would be established in historical Armenia. In the following decades, the conquests of the Seljuk Turks were to recast the political map of the Middle East. Not only was Armenia overrun, but also much of the Byzantine Empire in Asia Minor and many of the Muslim states.

The fall of Ani to the Seljuks in 1064 marked the beginning of a time of troubles in the Armenian homeland that lasted for centuries. The arrival of the Seljuk armies toppled the social order of Armenia. The Turks were nomads, and their pastoral lifestyle was ruinous for the local economy. During the course of the invasions, cities were pillaged and trade disrupted. Turkic tribal leaders claimed huge tracts of land from Armenian nobles. The decline of the Seljuks in the middle of the twelfth century permitted a brief revival of Armenian political fortunes. The Zakarian clan, vassals of the Georgian branch of the Bagratuni dynasty, united much of historical Armenia after a series of successful campaigns against Turkic nomads. More enduring was the establishment of an Armenian kingdom outside of the Armenian homeland in Cilicia, along the Mediterranean coast. The last Cilician king would not lose his throne until 1375.

The steppes of Central Asia, however, were to hold many more terrors for Armenia. Early in the thirteenth century, the armies of Jengiz Khan trampled over Armenia in search of greater conquests. Even more destructive were the forces of Timur-e Lang, which passed through Armenia several times from 1386 to 1403 to do battle against the Ottoman Turks and various Turkmen tribes. Streams of Turkic nomads followed the same routes into Anatolia.

For many Armenians witnessing the devastation of their homeland, the course of events seemed apocalyptic. One Armenian monk, living on the western shore of the Caspian Sea, entered the following observation as a colophon to the manuscript he copied in 1403:

> [copied] with much pain and labor . . . [and] in anxious, bitter and anguished times, for we were plundered, held in terror and trembling at the hands of the wretched and forerunner Antichrist T'amur [Timur-e Lang], which means *da mur* [he is soot], for wherever he goes he darkens and blackens, some by robbing, some by torture, some by slaying, some by carrying off into captivity, and also by separating the father from his child and the child from his father, and so forth. Those who escaped and [took refuge] in caves and crevices, in fortresses and castles did not enjoy freedom, because some died from famine and others from the heat and of thirst, some, who were struck by fear, threw themselves down into the precipice. And there were numerous other evils, which I hesitate to relate in order not to cause tedium to you readers.[2]

Armenia yet again served as a battleground from 1501 to 1639, as the Ottoman Turks and Safavid Persians struggled for control of the Caucasus. The Safavids employed a scorched-earth defense, laying waste to a swath of land nearly fifty miles wide that cut Armenia in two. Shah Abbas the Great contributed to the desolation by deporting 250,000 Armenians from the plain of Ararat, Van, and Nakhichevan to Persia.

The turmoil from the fall of Ani in 1064 to the end of the Ottoman–Safavid war in 1639 transformed the Armenian people. The physical damage could be repaired, but the destruction of Armenia's social structure was complete. By the middle of the 1300s, Armenians no longer constituted a majority in Eastern Armenia.[3] Armenia's aristocracy was gone. Many of Armenia's nobles had been wiped out by warfare. Others had converted to Islam. Still others had sought refuge in Cilicia, the Crimea, or Constantinople, laying the foundations of the Armenian diaspora.

The Armenian homeland was left largely defenseless without the presence of Armenia's landowning nobles, or *nakharars*. Outside of Karabagh and a few other areas, control over the land was in the hands of Muslim *khans* and *beks*. Muslim law accorded members of the faith political and social superiority, even if the great majority of them were lowly nomads and peasants. Among the Armenians, political leadership passed from clans of warriors to a subjugated clergy. By necessity, a new national character took shape under Ottoman rule: obsequious, compliant, fatalistic. In the Ottoman Empire, the Armenian community became known to the royal clan as "the loyal *millet*" (religious community) for its obedient role within the imperial system.

Thus, the Armenian people entered the modern era politically weak and divided. A cultural renaissance, however, began to gather momentum in the early 1800s. The revitalization of the Armenian language, new literary styles, and advancements in education placed Armenians at the forefront of Westernization among the peoples of the Middle East. For Armenians under Ottoman rule, the main influences were French, British, and Italian. In Eastern Armenia, the entry of the Russian Empire into the region was to redirect Armenia's destiny.

In 1801, Russia officially annexed Georgia. Tiflis (modern Tbilisi) emerged as the commercial and cultural hub of Transcaucasia. Armenians responded by migrating from areas of their homeland to make Tiflis the center of Eastern Armenian life. In 1813, the Treaty of Gulistan concluded the Russo–Persian war of 1804–13, awarding Russia much of eastern Transcaucasia. The heavily Armenian regions of Karabagh, Zangezur, and Ganja were incorporated into the Russian Empire along with the Caspian lowlands. Not until the Treaty of Turkmenchai ended the Russo–Persian war of 1826–28 was the remainder of Eastern Armenia added to the Russian Empire. As a result, the regions of Yerevan and Nakhichevan were administered separately from other Armenian lands.

As had occurred with the triumph of the Seljuks in the eleventh century, the conquests of Christian Russia completely overturned life in the Transcaucasus. First came a substantial realignment of population. Although Armenians had fared well under the benevolent administration of Hosein Qoli Khan, the governor of the Yerevan khanate in the final two decades of Persian rule, they represented only 20 percent of the population.[4] Under the 1828 Treaty of Turkmenchai, Armenians were given a one-year window to move from Persia to Russia. More than 30,000 migrated. A similar provision the following year within the Treaty of Adrianople between the Russian and Ottoman empires prompted approximately 20,000 more Armenians to become subjects of the tsar.[5] Russia also created an Armenian province, centered around Yerevan. Although some Armenians were disappointed that Tsar Nicholas I rejected appeals to proclaim himself monarch of an Armenian kingdom, just as he wore the crown of Poland, Armenia nonetheless became a political entity in Transcaucasia for the first time since the thirteenth century.[6] In addition, the central government granted the Armenian Church freedom of worship and wide-ranging autonomy in the *Polozhenie* (Statute) of 1836.

Still more portentous was the economic impact of Russian expansion. Armenians were the first among the peoples of Transcaucasia to take advantage of the trade opportunities within the Russian Empire and beyond. Paradoxically, a long history of calamities had provided Armenians with a few unsolicited benefits.

The commercial diaspora that had largely been forged by Persian-Armenian merchants in the seventeenth and eighteenth centuries offered a ready-made network of contacts. Unlike the Georgians and Azerbaijanis, Armenians had no landed nobility to brake migration to the new economic centers of the Transcaucasus.[7] Furthermore, centuries of second-class status in Muslim empires had pushed Armenians into occupations that were better suited to an urban environment.

Politically, however, there was a downside. The Armenian population of Transcaucasia was becoming still more widely dispersed just as the notion of the compact nation-state was trickling down into the minds of intellectuals in Eastern Europe and the Middle East. As late as the turn of the century, Muslims constituted a majority of Yerevan's residents.[8] At the same time, tsarist officials were increasingly taking notice of the potentially disruptive political activism among the growing Armenian intelligentsia. In Saint Petersburg, the tsar's advisers were divided between those who sought to impose strict centralized authority in line with the expanding bureaucratization of other European states and those advocating greater regional autonomy.[9] During most of the Romanov dynasty's final century, the centralists were at the helm. Four years after the *Polozhenie* of 1836, for example, a broader decree brushed aside local laws and customs throughout the empire and ordered that all official business be conducted in Russian by Russian administrators.[10]

Particularly significant for Armenia were the Transcaucasian redistricting plans of the mid-1800s. The *Armyanskaya* (Armenian) oblast was erased in 1840, when Russia reorganized its territory south of the Caucasus Mountains into two administrative units. Boundaries were redrawn shortly thereafter to placate local concerns, and in 1849 the Yerevan province was created. By 1868, the political divisions of tsarist Transcaucasia were more or less finalized. The Yerevan *guberniya*, or province, roughly matched the original Armenian province of the 1830s. A substantial chunk of historical Armenian land in Transcaucasia and most Armenians in the region, however, remained outside of the *guberniya*. Most critical in this regard was the creation of the Elizavetpol *guberniya* between the provinces of Yerevan and Baku. The new *guberniya* included Zangezur and Mountainous Karabagh, combined the highlands of the Armenian plateau with Caspian lowlands, and left a hopeless ethnic tangle of Armenians, Azerbaijanis, Georgians and other groups. As late as 1917, there were 419,000 Armenians in the province, comprising 33 percent of the total population.[11] Moreover, Mountainous Karabagh became linked to the transportation and communication system of Baku rather than to that of Yerevan, especially after the construction of the Baku to Batum railroad in 1893.[12] (A rail line from Tiflis to Kars was completed in 1902, with a branch reaching Yerevan soon thereafter.)

Russian imperialist policy, of course, was hardly interested in promoting the national aspirations of its subject peoples. On the contrary, the formation of the Elizavetpol *guberniya* was illustrative of the divide-and-rule principles that tsarist officials put into practice throughout the Romanov Empire. But as imperial tacticians everywhere inevitably found out, the spirit of nationalism could be kept at bay for only so long. By the late 1800s, nationalism had reached Transcaucasia, and the seeds of ethnic conflict planted in the Elizavetpol province began to bear bitter fruit.

The Armenian Revolutionary Federation (ARF), founded in Tiflis in 1890, espoused essentially the same doctrine of national liberation, socialist utopianism, and means-to-an-end violence that characterized most political parties formed by subject peoples in the Romanov, Ottoman, and Habsburg empires.

Initially, the growing politicization of educated Armenians in the Transcaucasus was focused exclusively on elevating the political rights of Armenians in the Ottoman Empire. Armenian intellectuals borrowed liberally from the tactics and spirit of revolutionary Russian populism, but few joined the struggle to overthrow the tsar.[13] Meanwhile, the emergence of Marxist social democracy in Tiflis around the turn of the century added another kink in the ethnic politics of Transcaucasia. The Social Democrats began as a movement aimed at mobilizing the growing working class around Tiflis, and among the most conspicuous villains were members of the city's prosperous Armenian middle class. As World War I approached, the Social Democrats increasingly came to be identified as a Georgian national party, with little room available for the participation of Armenian socialists.

The establishment of the ARF coincided with a reactionary twist in tsarist policies following the assassination of Alexander II in 1881 and the subsequent dismissal of the Armenian chief minister, Count Loris–Melikov. Nationalism and socialism had emerged as the two biggest threats to Saint Petersburg, and the Armenians were viewed as active in both movements. As a result, Armenians and other non-Russian nationalities found themselves subject to a punitive Russification campaign. Armenian Church schools came under strict government control after 1885 and were closed altogether in 1896. (Ironically, the minister of education who implemented the tsar's Russification policy from 1882 to 1897 was an Armenian, I. V. Delianov.)[14] The pressure against the Armenians intensified under the administration of Prince Grigorii Golitsyn, the governor-general of Transcaucasia from 1896 to 1905. Golitsyn saw to it that Armenians were cut from the ranks of the civil service. Most provocative, though, was the decision in 1903 to rescind the *Polozhenie* of 1836 and place the property of the Armenian Apostolic Church, including its network of schools, under the control of Saint Petersburg.[15] ARF leaders resolved to strike back for the first time against the tsarist authorities.

Elsewhere in the empire, the conflict over the Armenian Church might have remained a clash between the center and the periphery. But in the ethnic crazy quilt of Transcaucasia, the dispute spilled over into intercommunal hostilities. A Western writer traveling through Transcaucasia in 1905 remarked on the volatility of the region:

No part of Russia at the present moment is more full of acute problems of great interest for the students of politics than the Caucasus. There, side by side with Nationalist claims and bitter racial and religious animosities, we see attempts to realize the conceptions of Social Democracy; together with evidences of medieval barbarism we find men actually putting the theories of Marx into practice.[16]

In and of itself, the confrontation between the ARF and Golitsyn resulted in something of a victory for the Armenians. As a response to the 1903 decree, demonstrations broke out in Armenian communities throughout the empire and the ARF directed a terror campaign against tsarist bureaucrats, even wounding Golitsyn himself. Russian police occupied Echmiadzin, but could do nothing to slow the rise of popular resistance. In 1905, the tsar was compelled to remove Golitsyn and rescind the decree.[17] By that time, much of Russia had been caught up in the

political turmoil that began with the "Bloody Sunday" massacre of protesters in Saint Petersburg in January 1905.

Armenians did not have a chance to savor their political
success. Armenian–Azerbaijani violence broke out in Baku in February
1905 and soon spread throughout eastern and central Transcaucasia, eventually reaching Mountainous Karabagh, Nakhichevan, Zangezur, Yerevan,
Elizavetpol, and Tiflis. Although Armenian and Azerbaijani clerics in Baku
and Shushi worked together to stanch the violence, tsarist authorities made
few efforts to restore order. On the contrary, leaders of both communities
concurred that Saint Petersburg had touched off the bloodshed.[18]

Before the conflict ended in 1906, the ethnic and social
fabric of Transcaucasia had been torn asunder. As many as 10,000 were
killed on both sides. Thousands more were made refugees. As throughout
much of the Russian Empire during the strife-filled year of 1905, the
clashes cut along the lines of both class and nationality.[19] For example,
Armenians were well represented among the industrialists of Baku, while
the lowliest workers were predominantly Azerbaijani. At the same time,
Armenians were prominent within the upper echelons of the revolutionary
parties. Although Armenians and Azerbaijanis had joined in a successful
strike in December 1904, the bonds dissolved when pogroms against Armenians broke out in February 1905. Evidence suggests that Armenian
political leanings entered into the calculations of tsarist officials. For example, foreign diplomats testified to the role of the authorities in inciting
Azerbaijanis to attack Armenians. Just before the February violence, the
governor-general of Baku issued a large number of arms permits to his
Muslim subjects. Moreover, 130 secret police were sent to Baku to provoke
discord.[20]

The economic, social, and political fissures that had
opened up during nearly a century of Russian rule were clearly defined by
the violence of 1905–06. The Armenians had undergone the most striking
transformation, and the events of 1905–06 furthered the crystallization of
their political consciousness. Under the leadership of the ARF, Armenians
had fought back against Muslim forces and held their own. Resistance in
Shushi was especially impressive, repulsing a five-day Azerbaijani attack
in 1905 and again turning back Azerbaijani invaders after nine days of
fighting in 1906. In Baku, Azerbaijani mobs torched dozens of oil derricks
owned by Armenians but failed to overcome armed Armenian workers.[21]
The self-defense efforts boosted the stature of the ARF among the Armenians of Transcaucasia and established the party's credentials as a leading
force for revolution in the Russian Empire. In 1907, the ARF was admitted
to the Second Socialist International.[22] Until Armenia's sovietization, the
ARF held sway as the main political actor in Armenia.

The 1905–06 conflict proved to be a turning point among the Azerbaijanis as well. The interplay of class and nationality strengthened the incipient sense of Azerbaijani identity. Moreover, the rift with the Armenian community propelled Azerbaijanis into professions and crafts long dominated by Armenians.[23]

Meanwhile, the Russian authorities learned their own lessons from 1905–06. Readily exploitable resentments were identified and likely flashpoints became apparent. The power of the ARF was subsequently undercut by mass arrests, while restiveness among the Azerbaijani intelligentsia was kept under close watch. The events of 1905–06 clearly demonstrated that neither Armenians nor Azerbaijanis had the power to overwhelm the other. The forces of the central government were left right where they wanted to be, capable of tipping the balance to suit their interests.

In Western Armenia as well, the first decade of the twentieth century brought both political turmoil and cause for hope. Armenian resistance to Ottoman oppression had gained strength under the leadership of local guerrilla bands, or *fedayeen*, usually associated with the ARF or the Hunchakian Social Democratic Party. The ARF cooperated as well with other opponents of the regime, and played an important role in the Young Turk Revolution that deposed Sultan Abdul Hamid in 1908 and restored constitutional government in the Ottoman Empire.

The overthrow of the sultan placed power in the hands of the Committee of Union and Progress (CUP). The CUP's personality, however, was itself not fully defined. Armenian forces had allied themselves with the wing of the movement that stressed progress, Westernization, and modernization. The CUP's other face—the side that emphasized union—was turned toward the east and the creation of a vast Turkic empire. The proponents of pan-Turkism hoped initially to establish ties with the Azerbaijanis and then to reach across the Caspian Sea to the Turkic peoples of Central Asia. The position of the Armenians in eastern Anatolia and the Transcaucasus was viewed as an obstacle to their goals.

The Ottoman Empire's humiliating defeat in the First Balkan War of 1912 strengthened the hand of the pan-Turkic ultranationalists. As a result of the war, the Ottoman presence in the Balkans was reduced to a precarious toehold west of Constantinople. More than 500,000 Turkish refugees were resettled in Anatolia. The ultranationalists saw an opportunity in the debacle. In January 1913, they seized control of the government and put the country on a more militaristic, authoritarian course.

The outbreak of World War I raised the possibility of realizing the pan-Turkic vision. After the Ottoman Empire's declaration of war against the Allies in October 1914, strategists in Constantinople focused their attention on the Transcaucasus. In the winter of 1914–15, an Ottoman army under the command of Enver Pasha, a member of the Young Turk triumvirate, launched an offensive against the Russians designed to reach Baku. The Turkish forces suffered a crushing defeat. The Young Turk leaders then turned toward another element of the pan-Turkic agenda: the extermination of the Armenians.

The first steps of the genocide began shortly after the failure of the winter campaign in the Transcaucasus. The more than 100,000 Armenians serving in the Ottoman military were disarmed, assigned to labor battalions, and later killed. In March and April 1915, the Turkish army attacked the areas of Zeitun and Van—established centers of Armenian resistance and political activity. Except for the Armenian quarter of the city of Van, Armenians in both regions were killed or deported. Meanwhile, the Turks arrested more than 200 Armenian community leaders and intellectuals in Constantinople on 24 April. Almost all were murdered within a few days.

By May 1915, the Young Turks were ready to complete the annihilation of the Armenians. Secret orders were sent to Turkish officials and military commanders throughout Anatolia to carry out the plan of extermination. Massacres of Armenians in the Ottoman Empire were hardly a new development. As recently as 1895–96, 100,000 to 200,000 Armenians had been slaughtered under Sultan Abdul Hamid, and in 1909 roughly 20,000 Armenians had been massacred in Cilicia. The 1915 genocide, however, was unprecedented in its scope and level of organization. The Young Turks sought nothing less than the extirpation of the Armenian people from their homeland.

The pattern varied little in the Armenian-populated towns and villages of Anatolia. First, the few able-bodied men were rounded up and shot. Then women, children, and the elderly were driven toward the deserts of northern Syria. Most died along the deportation route, often at the hands of the criminals who had been released from prison to shepherd the death march. Others were dragged away by local Turks and Kurds to serve as concubines or household servants. Still others perished in the barren deserts at the end of their journey. Eight hundred thousand to 1 million Armenians died in 1915. In addition, hundreds of thousands of other deportees succumbed from disease and starvation in 1916–18.

The Armenian genocide came at the expense of the Ottoman Empire's war effort. By the middle of 1916, the Russians had gained control over much of Western Armenia. The region, however, was largely a wasteland. The elimination of Armenian peasants had crippled local agriculture. Moreover, the rotting corpses of thousands of genocide victims had triggered epidemics of cholera and typhus.

Pan-Turkic ambitions were revived by the Russian Revolution. The abdication of the tsar in March 1917 undermined discipline among Russian soldiers along the Transcaucasian front. Soon after Lenin's seizure of power in November, the Russian army was withdrawn altogether. The Treaty of Brest–Litovsk in March 1918 marked the official end of Russia's participation in the war and forced Armenians in the Transcaucasus to craft a new strategy to counter the advancing Turks.

In April 1918, Armenians joined with Georgians and Azerbaijanis to form the Transcaucasian Federation. The makeshift republic was doomed from the start. Behind the scenes, the Georgians were seeking protection from the Germans while the Azerbaijanis openly sided with the Ottoman Turks. Within a month, Armenian troops (mostly members of the tsarist forces and a few volunteers from Western Armenia) found themselves confronting an invading Ottoman army alone. On 28 May, Armenia issued a tentatively worded declaration of independence in the wake of the Transcaucasian Federation's collapse. More important were events on the battlefield just a few miles outside of Yerevan. At Sardarabad, Kara Kilisa, and Bash Abaran, a desperate Armenian army rallied to throw back the Turks. A peace treaty was signed with the Ottoman Empire a few days later, but the Turkish threat did not recede until the Ottoman surrender to the Allies in October 1918.

The end of World War I brought hope to the leaders of the Armenian Republic, but scarcely improved the horrific conditions in their newly created state. Of the republic's nearly one million people, one-third were refugees from Western Armenia. Most of the infrastructure of the country had been destroyed during the war. The winter of 1918–19 was especially severe, contributing to the deaths of nearly 200,000 people. At the same time, Armenia was embroiled in border disputes with Georgia and Azerbaijan.

Armenians looked toward the international community for deliverance. Among the three Transcaucasian republics, only Armenia had remained steadfast to the Allied cause during the last months of the war. When the Paris Peace Conference convened in January 1919, Armenian delegations representing the newly independent republic and Western Armenia pressed the Allies to create an Armenian state stretching from the Transcaucasus to the Mediterranean. But the Armenian claims were overshadowed by the larger issues of the conference. Ultimately, the British and French foisted responsibility for Armenia on President Woodrow Wilson. Although Wilson was personally disposed to accepting a mandate for Armenia, his vision for the postwar world was in political trouble at home by the time he returned from Paris. Republicans in the U.S. Senate were indignant that they had not been involved in the negotiations of the Versailles Treaty.

The centerpiece of the treaty in Wilson's mind—the establishment of the League of Nations—was the target of especially deep suspicion. Months of debate only led to a hardening of positions, culminating with the Senate's vote against the treaty in March 1920. Less than three months later, the Senate rejected a U.S. mandate over Armenia by a wide margin.

While the great powers discussed Armenia's fate, the situation on the ground in the Transcaucasus was turning against the tiny republic. In Russia, the Bolsheviks had gained the upper hand in the civil war and were determined to spread their revolution into the southern tier of the old Russian Empire. In April 1920, the Red Army moved into Azerbaijan. Meanwhile, a Turkish army under the command of nationalist leader Mustafa Kemal was marching toward Armenia from the west. Kemal's offensive advanced rapidly through the Armenian districts of Kars and Ardahan during the fall of 1920, while Bolshevik forces gathered along the Armenian–Azerbaijani border. Faced with a hopeless dilemma, Armenia's government chose to surrender its independence to the Red Army rather than deal with the Turks. On 2 December 1920, Armenia was sovietized.[24]

The arrival of the Bolsheviks in Armenia ended a crucial chapter in Armenian history, and at the same time introduced a new wrinkle into perhaps the most intriguing subplot of the Armenian saga—the story of the Karabagh Armenians. Armenians in general are obsessed by their history. Armenians in Karabagh embody it, and have long occupied a unique place in the Armenian nation. They are mountain folk—proud, self-sufficient, suspicious of outsiders, and intractably headstrong. Their culture has been held together by strong rulers and a distinctive dialect that is virtually unintelligible to other Armenians. Nowhere else have Armenians clung to their native soil with such ferocity, and with such success. Within a nation that has suffered nearly a millennium's worth of loss and defeat, the Armenians of Karabagh have been the only real winners.

Karabagh ("black garden"—*kara* from Turkish and *bagh* from Persian) did not acquire its name until the invasions of Timur-e Lang in the late 1300s. Before that, the upland area rising from the plain west of the Caspian Sea had been known as the Armenian province of Artsakh. In ancient times, the province constituted one of the fifteen regions of Armenia. After the Persian Sasanids put an end to the Armenian Arshakuni (Arsacid) dynasty in 428, the local chieftains of Artsakh developed an unbreakable commitment to independence. Artsakh's Armenian identity was consolidated during the seventh century after the ruling class of another ancient people, the Caucasian Albanians, adopted the culture of the local Armenian population.[25] Even when the Armenian Bagratuni kingdom arose in the ninth century, Artsakh Armenians clung to their sovereignty. Loyalty in Artsakh revolved around the clan, with feudal bonds governing relations among landowners, monasteries, and peasants. Sizable towns did not emerge in the region until the nineteenth century, and even then the economy remained almost entirely agricultural.

Waves of Turkic and Mongol invaders redrew the political map of the Middle East beginning in the eleventh century, and yet Mountainous Karabagh Armenians held onto their autonomy. With the fall of the Armenian kingdom of Cilicia in 1375 and the onslaught of Timur's horsemen, only four areas—Mountainous Karabagh, Zangezur, the villages around Lake Sevan, and the highlands of Sasun and Mush near Lake Van— remained in which Armenians exercised some degree of self-rule. Of these bastions, Karabagh was the largest and most well-developed. The region served as the see of a separate catholicosate in the Armenian Church.

Mountainous Karabagh's autonomy was formalized in the mid-1400s, when the Turkmen chieftains who succeeded Timur recognized Armenian rulers in the region as *melik*s (an Arabic word for "king") in exchange for their allegiance. Eventually, five clearly defined *melik*-doms were established under Karabagh Armenian leadership, defending their birthrights from highland fortresses. All of the *melik* clans traced their origins to the house of Khachen, the last remnant of Armenian nobility to retain a foothold on historical Armenian lands.

Although rocky, Mountainous Karabagh was fertile, and since ancient times the land had been noted for its well-tended mulberry orchards, vineyards, and fine silk. The decorative carpets of the area gained fame along the caravan routes of the Middle East and beyond. As nomadic Turkic tribes came to dominate the southern Caucasian lowlands bordering the Caspian Sea, they too were integrated into the economy. Flocks of sheep were led up highland pastures to graze during the summer months, giving rise to trade between the Karabagh Armenians and the Muslim nomads.

Karabagh's unique status proved especially important as the Ottoman Turks and Safavid Persians struggled for control of the Caucasus from 1501 to 1639. When the two Muslim titans finally reached a peace settlement, most Armenians in Eastern Armenia fell within the boundaries of four Persian khanates. Only Mountainous Karabagh was granted autonomy outside of the khanate system.

Armenians in Safavid Persia prospered. They served the shah as a privileged class of merchants and extended Persia's silk trade to the far corners of Asia and Europe. By the end of the seventeenth century, however, the Safavid dynasty was faltering as British traders asserted their dominance in the Indian Ocean and the Arabian Sea. A power vacuum was developing in the Caucasus. Persian-Armenian merchants were among the first within the Armenian world to appreciate the global shift engendered by the rise of European nation-states and the technological advances spawned by the gathering scientific revolution in the West. To usher Armenian national aspirations into the modern age, they took the lead in uniting the financial resources of the Persian-Armenian community with the political stature of Karabagh's ruling families. The most noteworthy product of this collaboration was a freelance diplomat known as Israel Ori.

Israel Ori was the scion of one of Mountainous Karabagh's five princely clans. His entry into the world of diplomacy came in 1678, when he accompanied a delegation of clerical leaders and Karabagh notables bound for a meeting in Rome with the pope. The mission was the brainchild of Catholicos Hakob IV, the head of the Armenian Apostolic Church and previously the Armenian bishop of New Julfa in Persia. Hakob IV's exposure to European diplomats and merchants in Persia had convinced the catholicos that Armenia's salvation lay in establishing firm ties with the Roman Catholic West. Hakob IV never made it to Rome, however. The aged catholicos died in Constantinople, prompting his traveling companions to decide to return to Armenia. Only the 19-year-old Ori pushed onward. In the course of the twenty-year odyssey that followed, Ori went into business in Venice, joined the army of Louis XIV, fought the British, was captured and released, and eventually found himself in the service of Prince Johannes Wilhelm of the Palatinate. He offered the German prince the crown of Armenia and promised to raise an army of 200,000 infantrymen and 10,000 cavalry soldiers. Nothing came of Ori's efforts, but Ori was encouraged to embark on a second mission after returning to Karabagh. Ori's new plans led him to the court of the Habsburg Emperor Leopold I in Vienna and then to Tsar Peter the Great of Russia. Again, Ori was disappointed, although he did receive the post of Russian envoy to Persia. He died in 1711 while on his way to Saint Petersburg with another proposal for the tsar.[26]

While Israel Ori was testing the waters of diplomacy, other Karabagh Armenians were being called upon to take up arms in defense of their homeland. Among the most remarkable was Davit Bek.[27] An officer in the Georgian army originally from Zangezur, Davit Bek shared the noble blood of Mountainous Karabagh's *meliks*. He united Armenians of the Caucasus into a formidable force by introducing his troops to firearms and other advances in warfare. Davit Bek was joined by the commander of Karabagh's nearly 40,000-man army, Avan (or Hovannes) Yuzbashi, from the *melik*dom of Dizak, and Mkhitar Sparapet.[28] When the fall of the Safavids in 1722 prompted Russian and Turkish forays into the region, Davit Bek offered to assist Peter the Great's campaign along the eastern shore of the Caspian Sea. After the tsar signed a truce with the Ottomans in 1724, Davit Bek spent the remaining four years of his life defending Armenian lands against Turkish intrusions. In gratitude, Shah Tahmasp, himself displaced from the Persian throne by invading Afghans, recognized Davit Bek as supreme commander of the southern Caucasus. After Nader Shah imposed his rule over Iran in 1736 and drove the Ottomans back to the boundaries of 1639, he rewarded the Armenian *melik*s by exempting them from tribute payments and recognizing their autonomy.[29]

When Armenian nationalism began to take a more coherent form in the late 1800s, Israel Ori and Davit Bek served as historical icons. Ori represented one of the first diplomatic contacts between Armenia and the West. Generations of Armenian suppliants in the nineteenth century would, in the fashion of Ori, direct their own elaborate appeals to Russia, Britain, France, and the other great powers. Their often naive hopes and unrequited expectations seeped into the historical consciousness of Armenians in Mountainous Karabagh under Soviet rule. Davit Bek also looked northward and westward, but was adept at navigating his way through the shifting alliances of the Persians, Turks, Russians, Georgians, and other forces in the Caucasus. In the process of defending his homeland, he and Avan Yuzbashi rekindled a proud martial tradition. Like many of his modern-day countrymen, Davit Bek saw himself as guarding the frontier of Christendom in a struggle of cosmic proportions.

Neither Israel Ori nor Davit Bek lived to see Christian rulers lay claim to their homeland in the early 1800s. On the face of things, the Russian conquests should have been the answer to Armenian prayers of centuries past. But the quirks of history proved unkind to the Armenians. As was noted earlier, Eastern Armenia was annexed by Russia in two chunks, leaving the Armenians of Karabagh, Zangezur, and Ganja separated by provincial boundaries from their fellow Armenians in the regions of Yerevan and Nakhichevan.

For most of the period up to the Russian Revolution, the divisions did not mean much. The tsar's empire-builders ran roughshod over national interests in Transcaucasia, all but extinguishing the proud *melik* clans of Mountainous Karabagh by the 1830s. What Armenians could not foresee, of course, was that the rather arbitrary lines on the map would serve as the basis for national homelands in the twentieth century.[30]

When Russian authority did in fact disintegrate in 1917–18, the administrative divisions of the Transcaucasus became one of the few tangible reference points for asserting national claims. With the collapse of the Transcaucasian Federation in May 1918, the Azerbaijanis and the Georgians fell back on tsarist provincial boundaries to justify the outlines of their national republics. The Georgians made Tbilisi (known earlier as Tiflis) their capital while Ganja (known as Kirovabad in Soviet times and Elizavetpol under the tsars) became the governing center of the new Azerbaijani state. Azerbaijan also staked its claim to Mountainous Karabagh.

Throughout the summer of 1918, Armenians in Mountainous Karabagh resisted the Ottoman army. In August, they set up an independent government in Shushi, the administrative center of the region. Ottoman troops responded by razing the Armenian villages between Mountainous Karabagh and Zangezur, thus further isolating the Armenian community. In October, a 5,000-man Turkish force reached Shushi after fierce fighting. From there, however, the Ottoman army was repeatedly thwarted in efforts to extend Turkish authority to outlying areas. Around the same time that Ottoman representatives agreed to the Mudros Armistice, the Armenian militia decimated an Ottoman unit trying to advance to the Varanda River. A few days later, Turkey's surrender to the Allies resulted in the evacuation of Ottoman forces.[31]

Seizing the opportunity, Karabagh Armenians called upon a legendary guerrilla fighter, General Andranik Ozanian, to lead his band of irregular troops into the heart of Mountainous Karabagh from his base in Zangezur. In late November 1918, Andranik set out along the road to Shushi. Azerbaijani resistance pinned down his forces for three days, but eventually Andranik broke through to take the commanding heights. Shushi was only 26.5 miles away—a day's rapid march—and the route lay open. But just as Andranik's forces set out, they were met by an automobile bearing a French and a British officer. The pair delivered an urgent message from British Major General William M. Thomson, commander of the 2,000 Allied troops in the eastern Transcaucasus. The communiqué instructed Andranik to return to Zangezur, emphasizing that Armenian concerns would be taken up by the peace conference in Paris. Like many of his countrymen, Andranik had placed his faith in Allied pledges to grant justice to Armenia. He dutifully withdrew to Zangezur. In a sharp about-face, Thomson later recognized temporary Azerbaijani jurisdiction over both Mountainous Karabagh and Zangezur, and approved the appointment of an Azerbaijani as provisional governor-general of the regions. Armenia was given control over Nakhichevan, thus denying Azerbaijan a link to Turkey. As for Andranik, he was to die an embittered exile in Fresno, California.[32]

The British military representative to Yerevan, Lieutenant Colonel John C. Plowden, well understood the significance of his country's Transcaucasian policy. In August 1919, as British forces withdrew from Azerbaijan, he reported:

The handing over of Karabagh to Azerbaijan was, I think, the bitterest of all. Karabagh means more to the Armenians than their religion even, being the cradle of their race, and their traditional last sanctuary when their country has been invaded. It is Armenian in every particular and the strongest part of Armenia, both financially, militarily and socially.[33]

As might have been expected, the issue of Mountainous Karabagh did not quietly fade away. Karabagh Armenians were compelled to recognize provisional Azerbaijani rule in August 1919 in exchange for official assurances of cultural autonomy. But the failure of an Azerbaijani military thrust into Zangezur in November bolstered the spirits of Armenian rebels. With aid from the Armenian republic, Karabagh Armenians were on their way to ousting Azerbaijani forces by the spring of 1920.

The arrival of the Red Army in Azerbaijan and the subsequent sovietization of Armenia ended the fighting over Mountainous Karabagh, but the question of the region's future remained unsettled. Lenin himself had made self-determination for non-Russian peoples a key weapon in his propaganda arsenal during the Russian civil war. For Lenin's commissar for foreign affairs, Grigorii V. Chicherin, that meant that Mountainous Karabagh belonged to Armenia.[34] Initially, the sentiment was shared by leading communists in Azerbaijan, most of whom were not ethnic Azerbaijanis. On 30 November 1920, the day after the Bolsheviks declared Armenia to be a Soviet Socialist Republic, the authorities in Soviet Azerbaijan announced that Mountainous Karabagh, Zangezur, and Nakhichevan—the three focal points of Armenian–Azerbaijani conflict and all claimed by Azerbaijan during its two years of independence—were integral parts of the Armenian Soviet Socialist Republic. The proclamation was hailed by Stalin in the 4 December issue of *Pravda* (Truth) and cited by the leading Bolshevik in the Transcaucasus, Grigorii K. (Sergo) Ordzhonikidze, as proof of Bolshevism's power to heal national disputes.[35]

In fact, the proclamation was too good to be true. Nariman Narimanov, chairman of the Azerbaijani Revolutionary Committee, raised the specter of an anti-soviet revolt among Azerbaijanis if Mountainous Karabagh were left to Armenia.[36] Less than three weeks after the newspaper *Sovetakan Haiastan* (Soviet Armenia) announced that authorities in Armenia and Azerbaijan had agreed to attach Mountainous Karabagh to Armenia, the party's Caucasian Bureau convened to examine the issue. On 4 July 1921, a plenum of the bureau voted by a 4–3 majority to place Mountainous Karabagh within Soviet Armenia. The following day, however, Ordzhonikidze and an Armenian communist from Tbilisi, Hmayak Nazaretyan, called on the Caucasian Bureau to reconsider the resolution. Without further discussion, the bureau voted (four in favor with three abstentions) to reverse its decision, making Mountainous Karabagh an autonomous oblast under Azerbaijani jurisdiction.[37]

The next act of the drama was played out in the Azerbaijani Communist Party, which was assigned the task of delineating the oblast's borders. By the time the boundaries were submitted, the administrative center of the oblast had been transferred to the largely Armenian town of Khankendi (Stepanakert). The outline of the oblast, however, had been gerrymandered to exclude Shamkhor, Khanlar, Dashkesan, and Shahumyan, districts in northern Mountainous Karabagh with Armenian populations of 90 percent.[38] From the beginning, the oblast was an anomaly. Elsewhere in the young Soviet state, autonomous republics, oblasts, and eventually districts were formed as a concession to the national identity of ethnic groups denied their own union republic. Mountainous Karabagh, as well as Nakhichevan, reflected Soviet foreign policy interests.

In the context of the early 1920s, the oblast was part of a larger game involving the viability of the communist revolution, Kemalist Turkey, and geopolitics. In 1921, Kemal was still an unknown quantity. The Bolsheviks saw him as the key to spreading their revolution across the Muslim East. Kemal's vision was on a more practical level. He wanted to weaken Armenia and create a link with Azerbaijan. In March, his envoys met Soviet representatives in Moscow to decide, among other issues, the borders of Soviet Armenia. The Turks pressed for the inclusion of Mountainous Karabagh within Azerbaijan. They also demanded that Nakhichevan be detached from Armenia and placed under Azerbaijani jurisdiction as an autonomous republic.[39] Another dimension in Ankara's designs was the acquisition of the Surmalu district, which had been held by the Ottomans only briefly during the chaos of the eighteenth century. In the cession of Surmalu, Armenia lost Mount Ararat and the town of Igdir, while the Turkish frontier crept closer to Nakhichevan. In the 1930s, Turkey exchanged territory with Iran to gain a contiguous border of a few miles with Nakhichevan.[40]

Moscow's sole concession to Yerevan—the inclusion of Zangezur in Armenia—also figured into Soviet calculations. The thin strip of mountainous terrain served as a wedge between Nakhichevan and Azerbaijan and also discouraged any possible ambitions on Kemal's part to drive toward the Caspian Sea. The arrangement was formalized with the establishment of the Nagorno Karabakh Autonomous Oblast in 1923 (with Armenians comprising 94 percent of the population) and the Nakhichevan Autonomous Soviet Socialist Republic in 1924.

The behind-the-scenes horse trading left future generations of Armenians with a clear villain: Stalin. As a member of the Caucasian Bureau and a climber in the Communist Party bureaucracy, he had orchestrated events in Transcaucasia to serve both the revolution and his own career. Lenin himself became increasingly mistrustful of his underling in the last two years of his life. In January 1923, already crippled by a series of debilitating strokes, Lenin wrote from his sickbed that Stalin should be removed from the newly created post of general secretary.[41] Many Armenians also saw a malicious streak behind Stalin's actions, tracing Stalin's anti-Armenian feelings to his boyhood in Georgia.

After Lenin's death in January 1924, Stalin steadily accumulated power over the Soviet bureaucracy and systematically crushed national movements throughout the country. Karabagh Armenians were just one of many groups to be silenced. A "Karabagh to Armenia" society briefly surfaced, distributing thousands of leaflets in 1927 that demanded unification with Armenia and branded servile Armenian communist officials as "lackeys." There was also muffled discontent when the land bridge that had originally connected Mountainous Karabagh to Armenia by way of Lachin was snipped after 1929. Armenia's first secretary, Aghasi Khanjyan, reportedly raised the matter of Mountainous Karabagh at the time Stalin's 1936 constitution was about to affirm the borders of the Transcaucasus. Shortly thereafter, Khanjyan, himself a young protege of Stalin, was shot to death in the Tbilisi office of Lavrentii Beria, first secretary of the Transcaucasian Communist Party and chief of the NKVD (People's Commissariat of Internal Affairs) for Stalin after 1938.[42]

The question of Mountainous Karabagh emerged again in 1963, when 2,500 Karabagh Armenians directed a petition toward Nikita Khrushchev. The document brought to light that no new construction or repair work had been performed on roads leading from Stepanakert to outlying Armenian villages in forty years. The petition also noted that the administrative centers for many of the oblast's enterprises had been transferred to nearby Azerbaijani towns.[43] In the case of Mountainous Karabagh's legendary silk, the appeals of Stepanakert Armenians to control the final output—the dyeing and decorating of silk cloth—were repeatedly denied by Baku. Meanwhile, according to the petition, Azerbaijani authorities set quotas on wool that compelled Karabagh Armenians to remove stuffing from their mattresses. In 1965, Armenians sent another document to the Central Committee, accompanied this time by 45,000 signatures.[44] Both appeals, however, were ignored. Thirteen prominent Karabagh Armenians addressed a letter to Moscow in 1968. Within a few years, the signatories had been hounded out of the oblast. Likewise, a letter of protest in 1977 by a prominent Armenian novelist, Sero Khanzatyan, was received with official silence and unofficial threats. Even the recitation of a patriotic poem in 1975 cost the Komsomol (the communist youth organization) secretary of Mountainous Karabagh his job and brought on official pressure that forced him to leave the oblast.[45]

By and large, however, the cause of Mountainous Karabagh's Armenians was generally forgotten outside of the oblast. Economically and socially, the forces of modernization reached Mountainous Karabagh well after making inroads in major urban centers of the Transcaucasus. In the early 1920s, most of the population of the oblast was engaged in small-scale agriculture—growing wheat, rye, Persian rice, cotton, and tobacco, as well as tending their vineyards, orchards, and livestock. Industry was absent and transportation poor. Stone houses, typically characterized by flat roofs and earthen floors, accommodated large extended families. Although the patriarch was at the top of the family hierarchy, he and other adult men were often forced to work as migrant laborers in distant cities. Women acquired the responsibility of holding together the household.

The culture and character of Mountainous Karabagh were not easily bent, even under the weight of Stalinism. Long centuries of holding out against Muslim encroachment produced a defiantly martial tradition that continued into the Soviet era. The oblast's remarkable record during World War II added to the Karabagh mystique. More than 15 percent of Mountainous Karabagh's population—22,000 men—died at the front during the war. Fifteen thousand of the oblast's soldiers earned orders and medals. Twenty Karabagh Armenians were decorated with the highest honor—Hero of the Soviet Union. All four of Transcaucasia's marshals and admirals (the highest ranks in the Soviet armed forces) had their roots in Karabagh's Armenian community.[46]

Mountainous Karabagh's lack of contact with Armenia during the Soviet period deepened the sense of isolation among Karabagh Armenians. For inhabitants of the area, the relative decline of Mountainous Karabagh's importance was not readily accepted. It constituted an affront to the Karabagh psyche. There was scant consolation in the fact that transplants from the oblast made up a substantial segment of Armenia's population. Even as their numbers dwindled, Karabagh Armenians could not quite let go of the conviction that the heart of the Armenian nation beat with them, and they could not easily forgive their countrymen in Yerevan for largely overlooking their plight during nearly seven decades of Soviet rule.

Thus, the Mountainous Karabagh question made its way inconspicuously into the Gorbachev era. Dormancy is not the correct description for what had been happening in the oblast after the 1920s. Rather, an odd slow-motion war had been taking place between Armenians of the oblast and officials in Baku. The casualties were tallied in terms of demographic statistics and economic development, and the Armenians saw themselves as losing a conflict of attrition. From the 1926 census to the 1979 census, their proportion of the population in the oblast had dipped from 89 percent to 76 percent, while the Azerbaijanis had increased from 10 percent to 23 percent.[47] By the 1970s, the great majority of high school graduates were leaving the oblast to seek their fortunes elsewhere.

Armenians contended that Mountainous Karabagh's economy and cultural development had been deliberately sabotaged by Baku. Indeed, in March 1988 Soviet officials acknowledged that many of the Armenian complaints were justified. Among their conclusions: transportation and communication links between Armenia and Mountainous Karabagh had been neglected; Baku officials had limited cultural exchanges between Karabagh Armenians and their countrymen outside of the oblast; young people were forced to leave Mountainous Karabagh in pursuit of educational and employment opportunities.

In a state where industrialization and progress were synonymous, Mountainous Karabagh had been left to rely on agriculture. Capital investment in the oblast lagged well behind the rest of Azerbaijan. By 1970, only 10 percent of the work force was employed in industry, compared to the USSR average of 24 percent. Furthermore, over half the oblast's industrial production was accounted for by the processing of grapes.[48] Just as in Azerbaijan as a whole, grapes came to dominate farming in Mountainous Karabagh to the detriment of grains, potatoes, and other staple food crops. Gorbachev's anti-alcohol campaign, which resulted in the uprooting of thousands of acres of vineyard in 1985 and 1986, hit the local economy particularly hard. In the area of administration, there was a concerted effort to bring more Azerbaijanis into the oblast. Jobs in law enforcement and economic planning were largely filled by Azerbaijanis after a 1975 plenum of the local party recommended doing more to promote "representatives of all nationalities."[49] Karabagh Armenians asserted that they were also the victims of more overt discrimination. In Shushi, for example, the mostly Azerbaijani residents were able to buy meat without restrictions, while a few miles away in Stepanakert townspeople were limited to one kilogram per person. The infrastructure in some Armenian villages was so backward that the nearest source of potable water was one or two kilometers away.[50]

Baku had also kept up the pressure on the cultural front. As part of Stalin's assault against religion, the authorities in Azerbaijan closed Mountainous Karabagh's 118 functioning Armenian churches and arrested 276 clerics in the 1930s.[51] Textbooks teaching Armenian history were banned from schools. In 1957, the Azerbaijani legislature decreed that

Azerbaijani was to be the main language throughout the republic.[52] Beginning in the 1960s, Azerbaijani authorities whittled away the oblast's education budget and closed twenty-eight Armenian schools. Each Armenian language class was forced to make do with two aged, tattered workbooks.

Over the years, Azerbaijani historians dealing with Mountainous Karabagh had quietly removed references to Armenians. A book on tourism in the republic made no mention of the many well-known examples of Armenian architecture in and around the oblast, such as the renowned thirteenth-century monastery at Gandzasar, the see of the catholicosate serving Mountainous Karabagh, and the Gaghivank complex, whose foundation went back to the first century of Christianity. Under Soviet rule, 167 churches, 18 monasteries, and 120 cemeteries in Mountainous Karabagh were destroyed either through negligence or state planning.[53] Even a number of distinctive, antique Karabagh Armenian rugs were removed from the oblast and displayed in Baku as examples of Azerbaijani artistry.[54]

And yet, as events were to prove, Baku's efforts to snuff out the spirit of resistance among the Armenians of Mountainous Karabagh had failed. From the first whispers of reform, Karabagh Armenians were ready to renew their struggle. When Gorbachev invited criticism of the Soviet system through his policy of *glasnost* at the landmark Twenty-Seventh Congress of the Communist Party in February 1986, Armenians in Transcaucasia and in Moscow marked the occasion by petitioning for the unification of Mountainous Karabagh with Armenia. Thousands of individual letters followed, along with more petitions from scientists, intellectuals, and senior military officers in Armenia. The party organization of the History Institute of the Armenian Academy of Sciences passed a resolution on Mountainous Karabagh. Reports on cultural repression and discriminatory administrative practices were compiled. The pace quickened throughout 1987, when local writers and other intellectuals undertook a petition drive that gained 80,000 signatures (31,000 from Mountainous Karabagh). The more than forty deputies of the oblast soviet who signed the petition were also backing efforts to convene their legislative body for a special session.[55]

Although the campaign on behalf of Mountainous Karabagh caused scarcely a ripple in Moscow, Armenians nonetheless chose to find signs of encouragement. In the fall of 1987, a trusted economic adviser to Gorbachev and native of Karabagh, Abel Aganbegyan, expressed hope while visiting Paris that the Mountainous Karabagh issue would be resolved under *glasnost*. In speaking to a group of French-Armenian World War II veterans, Aganbegyan referred to Mountainous Karabagh and Nakhichevan as "historic Armenian territory." Two other prominent Armenian figures within the Soviet intelligentsia—writer Zori Balayan and scholar

Sergo Mikoyan (son of long-time Politburo member Anastas Mikoyan)—
also raised the issue while in the United States early in 1988.[56]

Three separate Armenian delegations from Mountainous
Karabagh discussed their grievances with Central Committee officials in
Moscow. Armenian representatives arriving in November 1987 were given
scant attention, but in January 1988 another delegation was received by
Politburo candidate member Pyotr Demichev. Balayan reported that the
group had been lauded as "patriots" by Vladimir Mikhailov, head of the
Central Committee's newly created commission on nationalities problems.
A third delegation traveled to Moscow in early February and returned to
Mountainous Karabagh on 18 February with a still more favorable im-
pression.[57]

On 6 February 1988, Gorbachev issued a statement on
the situation in Mountainous Karabagh that the Karabagh Armenians inter-
preted as another positive sign. Although warning against "the power of
spontaneity and emotion," the general secretary acknowledged that "not a
few shortcomings and difficulties have accumulated in the Nagorno Karabakh Autonomous Oblast." Gorbachev urged that Mountainous Karabagh's
problems be solved "in the spirit of the policy of *perestroika*." [58]

At the grass-roots level in Mountainous Karabagh, the
hints of progress trickled down to nudge the movement forward during the
winter of 1987–88. More signatures were gathered. Worker collectives
passed resolutions calling for unification. Leaflets were distributed reporting
that negotiations in Moscow were making headway. Communist Party meetings were given over to the Mountainous Karabagh question. Meanwhile,
efforts by Baku to reassert party discipline only provoked protests. The
republic's second secretary, V. N. Konovalov, was defied at a special meeting
called on 12 February 1988 in Stepanakert. The next day, 7,000 demonstrators were waiting for him in Lenin Square, demanding an explanation of
Baku's policies. Konovalov did not appear, signaling to many of the demonstrators that the authorities were no longer in control of the streets.

Attempts by Mountainous Karabagh First Secretary
Boris Kevorkov to break up the meeting and close the square were frus-
trated on 14 February, when teachers and students from a Stepanakert
vocational school led organizing efforts to persuade more city residents to
join the protest. For the next week, the square would be the site of an
around-the-clock demonstration. Campfires were built in front of the oblast
soviet building. The total number of protesters never dipped below 1,000,
even with nighttime temperatures falling well below freezing.[59]

In the Hadrut district of southern Mountainous Kara-
bagh, a gathering in front of the local Communist Party headquarters on 12
February debated the language of a declaration on unification well into the

night. The crowd was still there the next morning, not dispersing until the party's district executive committee endorsed the document.[60] The decision by the party committee in Hadrut, soon lost in the surge of events, was unprecedented in Soviet politics. Never before had public pressure overridden Communist Party discipline. By 16 February, soviets in three of the other four districts of Mountainous Karabagh had followed Hadrut's lead by passing resolutions in support of unification and appealing to the Central Committee to resolve the issue. As the work week began on Monday, 15 February, the sense of momentum was fueled by the growing number of demonstrators. Schoolchildren walked out of classes and students at the pedagogical institute staged a boycott. Hundreds of telegrams were fired off to Moscow.[61]

Baku was ruffled. Attempts to assert control through the party had failed. After the first demonstrations in Stepanakert, Kevorkov harangued the city party committee for a full day and most of the evening. As the hour turned late, the discredited party boss even hinted that "100,000 fanatics" might enter the city, presumably from Azerbaijan, if demonstrations continued.[62] Although Kevorkov summoned 750 officials to the party committee building, his tactics did little to snuff out the movement. Likewise, his decision to dispatch local party bureaucrats to outlying towns and villages backfired. Instead of convincing Karabagh Armenians to condemn the initial demonstrations, many of Kevorkov's emissaries were besieged by local residents and forced to turn back.

A stronger dose of intimidation was called for. Hundreds of extra Azerbaijani police were sent to ring the oblast's borders while criminal charges were filed against demonstrators in Hadrut. The Baku media also tried to deflate Armenian hopes, announcing that the Central Committee would not take up the case of Mountainous Karabagh. Even the statement against unification issued at the Central Committee plenum on 18 February, however, did little to dampen the defiant mood. Instead, Armenians took heart in Gorbachev's pledge to hold a special Central Committee meeting on nationalities problems. That same day, the authorities went so far as to block the roads to Stepanakert in order to prevent the meeting of the oblast soviet.[63] It was no use, however. News had already traveled mouth-to-mouth throughout Mountainous Karabagh. The groundwork for convening an extraordinary session of the oblast soviet was completed.

On 20 February, Lenin Square in Stepanakert was full by dusk. Legislative deputies continued to enter the city, many on foot. A quorum was reached at 8 P.M. By that time, Azerbaijani First Secretary Kyamram Bagirov, a representative from the Central Committee, and members of Azerbaijan's politburo had arrived in Stepanakert. Bagirov immediately convened the bureau of the oblast central committee. The Azerbaijani

first secretary offered to organize a meeting between Armenian party officials in Mountainous Karabagh and their counterparts in Baku to discuss the
oblast's problems, but first, Bagirov insisted, the Armenians would have to
accept a resolution stating that the oblast central committee was entirely
responsible for the unsettled situation. The bureau members refused.[64] Next,
Kevorkov and Bagirov telephoned the legislature and ordered party members to report to the oblast executive committee. Again, they were rebuffed.
Regardless, the crowd outside would not have let the deputies leave.

In a final attempt to preempt the extraordinary session of
the legislature, Kevorkov, Bagirov, and the other officials proceeded en
masse to the oblast soviet. Once inside, Bagirov offered economic reforms
as a solution to the oblast's problems. The primary responsibility for defusing the meeting, however, fell to Kevorkov. From the podium, he tried to
soothe the deputies by acknowledging the oblast's problems, but also force-
fully denied the soviet's right to press for unification. The deputies patiently endured Kevorkov's speech. Vardan Hakobyan, head of the writers'
union in Mountainous Karabagh, then rose from his seat to advise
Kevorkov that he was invited to participate in the session. Otherwise, there
was no need for further speeches. Kevorkov left in anger.

Shortly before midnight, the vote to unify with Armenia
was passed by a margin of 110 to 7, with 13 abstentions (30 Azerbaijani
deputies did not attend). Although Kevorkov had made sure that the official
Communist Party seal was not available to certify the resolution, the deputies went home satisfied that their decision had met the necessary legal
requirements.

The offices of *Sovetakan Gharabagh* (Soviet Karabagh)
had remained open so as to include the resolution in the next day's edition.
Until 3 A.M., a handful of the deputies worked on polishing the final
document. Other examples of territorial transfers in the Soviet Union (including the 1954 decision to grant Ukraine jurisdiction over the Crimean
peninsula) were examined to ensure that the language of the Mountainous
Karabagh resolution conformed to legal precedent.

Toward dawn, newspaper typesetters filled the hole they
had blocked out on the front page. The resolution read as follows:

> Supporting the desires of the laboring masses of the NKAO
> (Nagorno Karabakh Autonomous Oblast), we petition the Supreme
> Soviet of the Azerbaijani SSR and the Armenian SSR to demonstrate
> a deep understanding of the sincere aspirations of the Armenian
> population of Nagorno Karabakh and to resolve the issue of the
> transferral of the NKAO from the Azerbaijani SSR to the Armenian
> SSR. Concurrently, we petition the Supreme Soviet of the USSR for

an affirmative decision regarding the transferral of the NKAO from the Azerbaijani SSR to the Armenian SSR.[65]

A copy of the resolution was given to a young courier with instructions to get through to Armenia. Despite the roadblocks, he managed to reach Goris, in southeastern Armenia, by morning.[66]

When news from the central square of Stepanakert reached beyond Transcaucasia, many of the questions raised by outsiders focused on timing. Why had the issue of Mountainous Karabagh been quiet for so long? Why had Karabagh Armenians made their stand in February 1988? The answer, as Karabagh Armenians would gladly explain, was that they had been making a stand since 1918. Like the alpine flower that clings to the rocky mountainside, the cause sprouted anew even through the most inauspicious cracks in the political structure. For the most part, officialdom tolerated little beyond letters and petitions, and often those means prompted arrests and persecution. But the Karabagh Armenians were always willing to test the leadership, to push the system until it pushed back. In that sense, 20 February was inevitable. The demonstrations were simply the logical next step in the campaign for unification.

Perhaps not so logical, however, were the events that followed. The movement that had been nurtured so patiently in Mountainous Karabagh spread to Yerevan like a wildfire that final week of February, and with it came a much larger forum for the Armenian story.

Chapter 2

Yerevan

*T*he twentieth of February 1988 arrived in the Armenian capital of Yerevan without fanfare. News of the events in Mountainous Karabagh had reached the city, but interest in openly supporting the demonstrators in Stepanakert was largely confined to a handful of intellectuals. More immediate were the rallies of the two previous days against the construction of a chemical plant in Abovyan, ten miles to the northeast of Yerevan. A march from the town, led mostly by women, had drawn the participation of more than 2,000 people. Many expected the protests to continue through the weekend, especially as word spread about developments in Mountainous Karabagh.

Yerevan, however, was not Stepanakert. By noon Saturday, the fate of Mountainous Karabagh and the Abovyan chemical plant had attracted no more than 3,000 people to the circular plaza outside of Yerevan's imposing, stone opera house. Most of those in Theater Square were veterans of past political gatherings—young scientists involved in the ecology movement, schoolteachers and professors, well-educated transplants from Mountainous Karabagh, rebellious artists and journalists, and students from Yerevan State University, particularly budding historians. Many frequented the cafés and restaurants that dotted the city's center, talking politics over demitasses of gritty Middle Eastern coffee or plates of gristly spiced meatballs and fried potatoes. Their collective memory told them to proceed with caution.

The last attempt to raise the issue of Mountainous Karabagh on 18 October 1987 had ended in a show of police force. The abortive Karabagh protest occurred the day after an officially sanctioned demonstration of environmental activists had been held. With overhead banners at

33

the environmental rally declaring, "We Want Healthy Children!" and "Shut Down Nairit (a chemical factory) So the Armenian People Will Survive!" thin, inconspicuous strips of paper were distributed among the crowd of 4,000 calling for a noon gathering to discuss Mountainous Karabagh near the Central Committee building, headquarters of the Communist Party in Armenia. A phalanx of Armenian policemen arrived early that Sunday morning in front of the Marshal Bagramyan subway stop to make certain the demonstration never took place. Those venturing too close to the subway entrance were roughed up before being sent home, usually minus their homemade placards and portraits of Gorbachev.

A few of the same policemen were undoubtedly stationed around Theater Square on Saturday, 20 February, trading glances with members of the crowd. Nonetheless, they did not pounce. Instead, there was a chilly unease in the air to complement the February weather. The stubborn low clouds that blanket the plain of Ararat during much of the winter sealed off the sun, rendering the sky as grey as the basalt façade of the opera house.

Tentatively, the gathering took on the form of a demonstration. A few impromptu speeches were made with the help of a bullhorn. Most concentrated on recounting the past week's events in Mountainous Karabagh. The Armenian government was called upon to support efforts for unification. The ecology theme was sounded again. And all the while, the crowd waited anxiously for the crackdown that never came. Only four days earlier in Lithuania, officials had gone to great lengths in squelching efforts to commemorate the seventieth anniversary of the declaration of independence issued by the Lithuanian National Council. Unofficial meetings had been banned in Vilnius and supporters of the regime had patrolled the streets.[1] In Yerevan, however, the police milled about the square, observing, but showing no signs of intervening. As the afternoon progressed, the sky gradually cleared. Hundreds of additional protesters entered the square, mostly alerted by telephone calls from friends participating in the meeting. The demonstration did not end until 9 P.M., and only after those present had vowed to spread the news about their cause.

The following day, the demonstrators returned at 2 P.M., this time double in number. Information on the resolution passed by the Mountainous Karabagh oblast soviet was greeted enthusiastically. Later came news that the Central Committee in Moscow had scheduled a meeting that evening to deal with the question. Speakers seemed emboldened by the course of events. A forbidden song celebrating the exploits of turn-of-the-century Armenian guerrilla fighters, or *fedayeen*, was sung. The mood still was not that of Stepanakert, but those on hand in Theater Square at least felt that they were playing a supporting role in what they hoped would be a historic victory. They dispersed late in the afternoon in anticipation of a positive decision from Moscow.

The response they received that Sunday night from the Central Committee was unexpectedly brusque. Not only was the appeal for unification rejected, but the Armenians themselves were denounced for the "breaching of public order" and heeding "irresponsible calls by extremist individuals." [2] The rebuke struck Yerevan like a slap in the face. The Armenians were not floored, though, only stung. Among the thousands of living-room pundits who dissected Moscow's statement well into the night, a consensus emerged that anti-*perestroika* forces in the Kremlin had distorted the cause of Mountainous Karabagh. The reformers had somehow been deceived. (In fact, the Central Committee's declaration echoed the report that Azerbaijani First Secretary Bagirov and Azerbaijani Second Secretary Konovalov had made after returning from Stepanakert.)

Telephone conversations the next morning devised what seemed like a logical strategy: turn up the volume. University students called for a boycott of classes. Participants in the weekend rallies roused their family and neighbors. Many Yerevanis who had paid scant attention to the movement were now incensed. Altogether, nearly 150,000 of them turned out in Theater Square on Monday, 22 February, and the Karabagh movement was born.

The sheer enormity of the 22 February demonstration stunned even those present. The first emotion was awe. No one quite believed that a people best noted for cynicism and dark humor would suddenly join hands in solidarity. For much of the afternoon, heads swiveled with incredulity. The vast sunken square was almost full, stretching back more than a hundred yards to a clump of shade trees and pines. A tranquillity almost unknown in Yerevan seemed to settle over the multitude. The belief of Alexander Tamanyan, the architect of modern Yerevan, that a pagan temple "of song and love" had once stood where the crowds now gathered at last seemed validated.[3]

Absent were the normal unpleasantries of social intercourse in the Armenian capital—no shrill shouting matches, no jostling for a better view, no poison-dipped insults. People long accustomed to elbowing their way through lines for a kilo of chicken or a movie ticket shared, at least for the moment, an inexplicable bond. The students and intellectuals from the weekend rallies were still there, but now they stood shoulder-to-shoulder with a few factory workers, department store clerks, and others representing the first signs of working-class involvement. Unspoken that Monday afternoon was the realization that Yerevan had grown up.

Although Yerevan's origins predate the founding of Rome, the modern city is very much a Soviet creation. For most of the nineteenth century, Yerevan was a sleepy backwater. The old town remained within the confines of the deep gorge cut by the Hrazdan River and the surrounding hills. Once the Persians were defeated, the city lost its strategic value. Russia's wars with Ottoman Turkey in 1853–56 and 1877–78 elevated Alexandropol (present-day Gyumri) above Yerevan in terms of vitality and importance. Up until World War I, Yerevan had been an overgrown village of 30,000 people, roughly half Muslim. The one-story, flat-roofed houses were mostly of adobe and stone, roads were narrow and dusty, and camel caravans were an essential means of commerce. The remains of a walled fortress, first built by the Ottoman Turks in the sixteenth century, stood out as the city's most prominent architectural feature long after giving way to Russian cannons in 1827. Also dating from centuries of Muslim rule were eight mosques, as well as six Armenian churches. Beyond the city, the Hrazdan River watered lush gardens and bountiful orchards.[4]

Under Soviet rule, Yerevan was methodically transformed into a republic capital by the same brute power that recast other towns and cities throughout the USSR. The first urban plan drawn up by Tamanyan in 1924 envisioned a city of 150,000. Fifteen percent of Yerevan's total area was set aside for beltways of greenery and tree-lined boulevards. New buildings made use of stone indigenous to Armenia—tufa, basalt, trachyte, granite, and marble. By 1959, the city's population had topped 500,000. Urban sprawl had climbed into the northern hills of Nor Arabkir and Kanaker, and claimed the high ground of Nork and Sari Tagh to the east.[5]

The Armenian genocide brought the first of many demographic changes in the twentieth century, as tens of thousands of refugees from Western Armenia poured into the city. The refugees continued coming after sovietization, and increasingly they were joined by educated Armenians squeezed out of their middle-class lifestyles in Baku and Tbilisi. Meanwhile, a massive migration of peasants into the city was engineered by Stalin's collectivization of the countryside and forced industrialization in the 1930s. After World War II, the Soviets directed a repatriation campaign at Armenian diaspora communities in the Middle East and Europe, settling many of the approximately 150,000 immigrants in the capital to work in the chemical industry.[6] By the 1970s, Yerevan's population had topped one million, and even with the Soviet melting pot at full boil, the mix of dialects, cuisines, and customs did not readily blend. Eastern Armenians were pitted against Western Armenians. Urbanites from Tbilisi, Baku, and elsewhere looked down on native Yerevanis. Repatriates resented their Sovietized countrymen. And everyone despised the peasants.

Beneath the fractured surface, however, a coherent Yerevani identity quietly took shape. Intermarriage forged links between otherwise clannish communities. Patronage networks created new loyalties by providing secure jobs and access to consumer goods. The Soviet experience gradually supplanted old divisions based on regional ties. Finally, Yerevan itself unleashed its own array of forces.

As a Soviet city, Yerevan had become the first truly Armenian metropolis in history. The major nineteenth-century urban centers of Armenian life—Constantinople and Tiflis—had been polyglot cities on foreign soil. On the other hand, the Armenian heartland had produced architectural splendor at Ani, Van, and elsewhere, but the populations were relatively small. Yerevan was a new page in Armenian history. And along with numbers came other features of modern urban life: heightened political awareness, a substantial educated class, a standardized national literature, the homogenizing effect of mass media, and the development of common values and beliefs. All of this occurred under a government at least nominally in the hands of Armenians.

The 150,000 people in Theater Square the afternoon of 22 February clearly understood that they were part of something unprecedented. As darkness fell, many remained where they had stood nearly the entire day, unwilling to return to their otherwise mundane lives. The speeches continued. One activist suggested the demonstrators march through the city to inform residents of plans to launch a city-wide strike. A legion of volunteers came together, and within minutes more than 15,000 set out into the streets. Their ranks quickly grew as others left their apartments to join the stream of demonstrators. Before they came to a symbolic halt in front of the Pantheon of Heroes at 4:30 A.M., they had walked eighteen miles. The march had set its own course, with the old pushing the young onward each time the crowd reached a crossroads. They chanted, they sang, they tiptoed softly past hospitals, some even wept. "People marched without feeling tired," journalist Meri Yuzbashyan later wrote. "We forgot about our injuries and impotence." [7]

By Tuesday morning, the march had become the stuff of legend. Those who had spread the word took credit for the outpouring of workers into Theater Square that distinguished Tuesday's rally and boosted the size of the crowd to nearly 300,000. Strikes shut down many of the city's factories and offices. University students stayed away from classes. The demonstrations had begun to acquire a distinct character. More homemade banners appeared in Russian and Armenian. "Karabagh Is a Test of Perestroika" took hold as the unofficial slogan of the movement. Others stood out as well: "There Is No Brotherhood without Justice"; *"Perestroika Is Not Extremism;"* and "One Nation, One Republic." More prominent was the ubiquitous image of Gorbachev—hundreds of leaflet-size portraits waving above the crowd, as well as a few that stood a meter tall.[8] A rhythmic chant gained acceptance: *Gha-ra-ba-ghe mer ne!* (Karabagh is ours!), with the accent falling on the possessive pronoun. The demonstrations even generated their own theme songs.

The microphone, powered now by an electrical generator, was still open to anyone with something to say, but the attention of 300,000 onlookers tended to discourage the more faint-hearted. For others, the vast audience was exhilarating. Vatche Sarukhanyan, a theater director and native of Mountainous Karabagh, was among the early crowd favorites. With his oratorical eloquence and poet's eye for the nature and people of his birthplace, Sarukhanyan lent Mountainous Karabagh an almost heavenly quality. Aside from a few well-turned phrases, however, Sarukhanyan had little to say of significance. Ashot Manucharyan, one of the movement's most astute participants, later analyzed the rhetorical evolution of the February demonstrations:

> The boldest, the most emotional speakers became the recognized leaders. It was whoever made the strongest impression on the crowd. Sarukhanyan and others played the role of actors. What they said was often not important. The danger, of course, is that actors use appeals to emotion, shifts in the direction of their ideas, simply to boost the emotional level of the crowd without appreciating the consequences.[9]

Indeed, much of what was heard from the speaker's platform pressed well-known emotional buttons. There were allusions to the glorious past of Karabagh, persecution under the Turkish yoke, and longing for the snow-capped peaks of Mount Ararat. But along with the boilerplate lamentations, a few speakers also criticized the lethargy of the Armenian government. From the first day of the demonstrations, activists Hambartsum Galstyan, Vazgen Manukyan, and Levon Ter Petrosyan had challenged Armenian party and government leaders to lend their support to the movement in Mountainous Karabagh. A few days earlier, Armenian officials had received telegrams from organizers of the movement in Mountainous Karabagh urging them to organize rallies in solidarity with Karabagh Armenians. On Monday, however, the leadership of the Armenian Communist Party dutifully approved the resolution of the Central Committee condemning the Karabagh movement. Armenian First Secretary Karen Demirchyan spoke gravely of the dangers posed by the Karabagh question. "The actions and demands," he said, "oriented to the review of the existing national-territorial system in this region, contradict the interests of the workers of the Armenian and Azerbaijani SSRs." Speakers in Theater Square, however, were not deterred. Rather, they called on the Armenian Supreme Soviet to convene an extraordinary session.[10] Manukyan went so far as to suggest launching a labor strike to exert leverage on the Kremlin.

The twenty-third of February brought an acknowledgment from Moscow that the demonstrations were serious business. In Mountainous Karabagh, First Secretary Boris Kevorkov was replaced with oblast soviet First Deputy Chairman Henrik Poghosyan, an official better attuned to Armenian concerns. (Poghosyan's lineage was tied to one of Mountainous Karabagh's *melik* families.) Meanwhile, Politburo candidate member Vladimir Dolgikh and Central Committee Secretary Alexander Lukyanov were dispatched from Moscow to Yerevan to meet with Armenian First Secretary Demirchyan, as well as with protest organizers.

There had been previous demonstrations in the non-Russian republics during the Gorbachev era. In December 1986, 3,000 Kazakh students had clashed with police during protests over the replacement of First Secretary Dinmuhammad Kunayev by an ethnic Russian.[11] The summer of 1987 had also witnessed a rally by the Crimean Tatars in Moscow and public commemorations in the Baltic republics of the 1939 pact between Hitler and Stalin. In size and scope, however, the Yerevan demonstrations opened a new chapter in Soviet history.

Upon hearing of the Politburo delegation's arrival, much of the crowd in Theater Square spilled into the streets and surged toward the Central Committee building, located less than a mile away. Once stationed before the towering wrought-iron fence that separated the well-tended grounds of the party headquarters from Bagramyan Prospekt, the protesters waited until 9 P.M. before Lukyanov appeared. The Kremlin spokesman's comments were brief. Speaking into a microphone that had been set up across the street from the Central Committee, Lukyanov noted that the Soviet Union faced many nationalities problems. He promised a more studied response the next day after talking with leaders of the movement.[12]

The arrival of Dolgikh and Lukyanov was shaded with an irony few appreciated. The Kremlin representatives had come to Yerevan to meet with popular leaders, and yet there were no leaders with whom to meet. Only after Lukyanov's remarks in front of the Central Committee on 23 February was the Karabagh Organizing Committee in Armenia formed. Igor Muradyan, an iron-willed economist who had devoted much of his energy after 1985 to the unification campaign in Mountainous Karabagh, dominated the selection process that extended into the early hours. To present the Armenian case at the 24 February meeting, Muradyan chose a few articulate intellectuals, most of them historians. Manucharyan inserted himself into the delegation at the last minute by arguing that a political analyst was needed to place the movement in the context of *perestroika* and *glasnost*. Equally important was the task of designating several trustworthy activists to collect relief supplies and money for Armenians in Mountainous Karabagh's Armenian community, which was already feeling the effects of retaliation from the Azerbaijani government in Baku. Muradyan's two closest associates were Gagik Safaryan, a native of Mountainous Karabagh, and Manvel Sargsyan. Both men had worked with Muradyan in coordinating petition drives on behalf of Mountainous Karabagh. Before the night of 23 February was over, seven or eight others had also received Muradyan's approval—but it was hardly the entrenched underground network that Dolgikh and Lukyanov expected.[13]

Hrair Ulubabyan, a schoolteacher and one of the early committee members, offered a simple explanation for the lack of structure:

> No one expected this movement to escalate so quickly, and as a result no one paid much attention to the question of leadership. From the start, this was meant to be a real popular movement. We only tried to gauge the feeling of the people.

The truth, however, was hardly what Moscow (or even many Armenians) wanted to hear. Much more appealing to Kremlin propagandists and armchair theorists were the various cloak-and-dagger conspiracies that emerged in the wake of the huge demonstrations. Perhaps most widespread was an imagined web linking Politburo conservative Yegor Ligachev, KGB (Committee for State Security) chief Viktor Chebrikov, and other hard-liners in a plot to discredit Gorbachev's reforms by instigating nationalist unrest. There was also a local Armenian angle pointing to beleaguered First Secretary Demirchyan. Demirchyan had been publicly chastised by Gorbachev in 1987 for lagging behind in implementing *perestroika*. According to rumors circulating in early 1988, Demirchyan was hoping to save his own career by stirring up trouble in Transcaucasia. The disturbances, so the line of analysis went, would allow Demirchyan to play the role of peacemaker. Finally, Moscow was playing up speculation that Armenian political parties in the diaspora had somehow orchestrated the demonstrations from abroad.

The conspiracy theories, however, all failed to account for the phenomenon that made the Karabagh movement a historic event. The KGB or Demirchyan might have been able to bring 5,000 people into the streets, even 10,000. However, no behind-the-scenes conspiracy could have possibly enticed hundreds of thousands of average Yerevanis to join their neighbors in Theater Square. The numbers, eventually approaching one million, were awe-inspiring. None of the Yerevan activists, much less the authorities, imagined that the populace would turn out with such force. In a very real way, the people defined the movement.

Even Muradyan, himself inclined to backroom deals, conceded that, "We never had any idea it would get this big."[14] A tall, burly, almost intimidating figure, Muradyan had been born in Baku and lived there for the first twenty-six years of his life before moving to Armenia. His political efforts began soon after he completed his doctorate in economics and settled in Yerevan, working as a researcher at the Armenian Economic Planning Research Institute. Muradyan first took aim at Haidar Aliyev, the long-time first secretary of Azerbaijan who was dismissed from the Politburo in 1987.[15] Single-handedly, Muradyan documented Aliyev's record of corruption, sending the file initially to the prosecutor general of the USSR, then to the Supreme Court, and finally to President Andrei Gromyko. Each time, the dossier was returned.[16] Mountainous Karabagh, however, was Muradyan's true obsession. After 1985, Muradyan became the point man of the movement, shuttling between Stepanakert and Yerevan, cultivating support among well-placed Armenians in Moscow, and arranging meetings with Soviet officials. The cause of Karabagh also led Muradyan to hold talks with Marius A. Yuzbashyan, head of the KGB in Armenia and a native of Karabagh.[17]

When the Yerevan demonstrations began, Muradyan quickly asserted himself before the crowds as the leader of the movement. Despite a slight stutter and limited knowledge of Armenian, Muradyan was blessed with a powerful voice and a quick wit. Initially, the crowd in Theater Square was disappointed to hear Muradyan address them in Russian. Muradyan, however, managed to turn his language deficiency into a strength:

> A [Armenian Communist Party] Central Committee secretary [Robert Arzumanyan] addressed you before me from the tribune. He was speaking Armenian. And what did he say to you? Nothing. I may be speaking in Russian, but I'm speaking of our common grief.[18]

Muradyan likewise held sway at the early meetings of the Karabagh Committee, again conducting business in his native Russian. He chose not to include Sarukhanyan in the committee, perhaps wary of the theater director's popular appeal. More important, he set the parameters of the committee's focus. Muradyan warned against raising issues that would detract from the goal of unifying Mountainous Karabagh with Armenia. He disapproved in particular of criticism directed at the corruption and stagnation of the government in Armenia. In Muradyan's view, the demonstrations were a vehicle for expressing the commitment and discipline of the Armenian people. Antagonizing the authorities with barbed political commentary and calls for labor strikes were seen as counterproductive. For Muradyan, Mountainous Karabagh was a singular struggle. Other problems and other people might be means to an end, but Mountainous Karabagh was the sole item on Muradyan's agenda.

The 24 February meeting among the Kremlin representatives, Armenian officials, and six members of the newly formed Karabagh Committee was uneventful. Astrophysicist and chairman of the Armenian Academy of Sciences Viktor Hambartsumyan provided the occasion's most noteworthy moment by following up the long string of titles attached to the introduction of Dolgikh with his own personalized credentials: "Viktor Hambartsumyan, extremist, nationalist." [19] Otherwise, the Karabagh Committee members complained of the paucity and bias of Soviet media coverage, while the authorities, from Moscow and Yerevan alike, pressed for an end to the demonstrations.

In Theater Square, the crowds were still growing. Columns of marchers, some numbering into the thousands, arrived on foot from villages and provincial towns, and received salutes of acknowledgment before merging with the mass. Some had walked from as far away as Leninakan (present-day Gyumri), a distance of seventy-five miles. Following his meeting, Dolgikh appeared on Armenian television and called on demonstrators to return to work. That evening, two speakers from the Armenian Central Committee tried lamely to convince the gathering in Theater Square that the government was on the people's side. Robert Arzumanyan, secretary of the Central Committee in charge of ideology, made the first faux pas by remarking, "We hear your problem and we are studying it." The response: "Our problem!" Minister of Higher Education Ludwig Gharibjanyan followed: "You think that we do not have sentiments like you?" The answer: "No!" [20]

The next day, 25 February, the government presented its case more resolutely. Nearly 5,000 Ministry of Internal Affairs (MVD) troops were flown into Yerevan to guard government buildings. (Until 1988, MVD troops had been used mainly to protect prison camps and other high-security facilities, not for crowd control.) At the same time, access to long-distance telephone service was restricted and foreign journalists were banned from traveling to Armenia. (The ban on foreign journalists would not be lifted until September, and then only temporarily.) After the nighttime march of 22–23 February, the Yerevan city soviet had imposed an 11 P.M. to 9 A.M. curfew, claiming that the measure was in response to citizen complaints. Enforcement of the curfew, however, was largely overlooked.[21]

Theater Square had by now become a world unto itself. Nearly half a million people ringed the opera house and spilled over behind the artificial pond called Swan Lake. Dazzling sunshine punctuated by snow flurries heightened the drama of the day. Those close enough to the speaker's platform cheered as veterans of the Afghanistan war renounced their medals and declared their readiness to fight in Mountainous Karabagh in "the spirit of internationalism." The 123rd anniversary of the birth of General Andranik was marked by appeals for construction of a memorial statue. A Russian journalist condemned distortions in the Soviet media and pledged solidarity. Later in the day, thousands of protesters walked a few blocks from Theater Square to voice their complaints at the television/radio building in Yerevan.[22]

The demonstrations, in effect, had taken the form of a general strike. Even the most apathetic Armenians found themselves drawn into the square. Some were driven by a sense of curiosity, others by a desire to stake their claim in history. In and around Theater Square, however, individual motives counted for little. The crowd did what crowds do everywhere, forming a new entity that in turn shaped those who were a part of it; 26 February was remembered in those terms. Numerically, the turnout was at its peak, totaling nearly one million and covering much of the city's center, while the day's events befitted the national forum that had assembled in the Armenian capital.

Gorbachev was the first to address the crowd. At noon, his fifteen-minute statement was read over television and radio by Dolgikh in Armenia and Georgi Razumovsky in Azerbaijan. In Yerevan, loudspeakers broadcast it live to the crowd in Theater Square. Gorbachev warned against "the power of spontaneity and emotion," and called on listeners to "return to normal life and work, and observe social order." At the same time, though, he conceded, "not a few shortcomings and difficulties have accumulated in the Nagorno Karabakh Autonomous Oblast," and committed the Central Committee to closely monitoring the fulfillment of its recommendations to improve conditions there.[23]

The crowd's reaction was far from unanimous. In fact, with people spread out over half a dozen blocks between Lenin Prospekt and Abovyan Street, the crowd was more a quilt of discussion groups than a single audience. The microphone set up at the rear of the opera house reached only those within the cement boundaries of the square. Beyond the range of the amplifiers, hundreds of smaller debates offered various interpretations of Gorbachev's address as information passed from ear to ear.

Early in the afternoon, another piece of news grabbed the crowd's attention. Unexpectedly, the Armenian Central Committee had recommended that Moscow establish a commission to examine the future of

Mountainous Karabagh.[24] At 2:30 P.M., First Secretary Demirchyan made his first appearance before the demonstrators to take credit for the Armenian Central Committee's decision and to pronounce an end to the rallies. Demirchyan's only other public comment on the Karabagh movement had come 22 February during a brief statement on local television, when he endorsed Moscow's decision against the unification of Mountainous Karabagh. This time he sought to cast himself as a national leader.

But the crowd saw him differently. Demirchyan appealed in a paternalistic tone for an end to strikes and for trust in the government. He was answered by piercing whistles. Flustered, the Armenian first secretary turned threatening: no work, no pay. An anonymous voice shot back: "It's all the same. We can't buy anything anyway."[25] Demirchyan retreated from the encounter without accomplishing his mission. Whatever fence he had imagined himself to be straddling between the interests of the Kremlin and Armenia had obviously given way.

With Demirchyan deflated, the news that Zori Balayan and poetess Silva Kaputikyan had flown to Moscow for a meeting with Gorbachev was greeted with open enthusiasm. (Balayan and Kaputikyan were both well-connected members of Armenia's intelligentsia.) The afternoon of 26 February represented a high-water mark in the optimism of the Karabagh movement. No one actually came forth to say it, but underlying the popular mood was a conviction that Armenia had achieved something. The euphoria that settled over Theater Square that Friday also said much about the difference between Mountainous Karabagh and Armenia. The movement in Stepanakert was clearly defined from the start, with an objective, a battle plan, and a population ready for its marching orders. In contrast, most of the demonstrators in Yerevan came to Theater Square looking for a purpose.

Hambartsum Galstyan, a young ethnographer and member of the Karabagh Committee, recognized that for most in Armenia the issue of Mountainous Karabagh's unification was:

> a pretext for expressing the discontent which has been accumulating over decades in the face of social injustice, corrupt leaders, the degradation of the environment, [and] the decline of cultural and moral values.[26]

Justified or not, Soviet Armenians often characterized themselves as a nation of deep thinkers. Their ruminations focused especially on their nation's history of past glories and modern disappointments,

turning downright morose as they approached the 1980s. After de-Staliniza-
tion, life in Armenia had acquired a dull (albeit merciful) stability, with the
bleak monotony of the Soviet state weighing heavily on the collective mind.
Three or four generations earlier, Armenians were at least able to find
inspiration in the nineteenth-century utopian revolutionary philosophies that
sprouted up in the final decades of the Russian and Ottoman empires. Even
the early years of communism held out promise for some. But Stalinism
crushed whatever hope had survived into the 1930s. By the time life resumed a more routine pace under Nikita Khrushchev and Leonid Brezhnev,
Armenia had become a dreary place for many of its inhabitants.

At the most basic level, Soviet Armenians viewed them-
selves as expecting more from life than their neighbors. As was frequently
said, a loaf of black bread and a tin of sardines might be sufficient for the
stereotypical Russian, but not for Armenians. Not only were there more
private automobiles per capita in Armenia than in any other republic of the
Soviet Union, but Yerevan was also the place to find Japanese electronics,
fine jewelry, brand-name sneakers, and dozens of other consumer items in
high demand. The often crass materialism, however, masked a deeper mal-
aise.

Armenians reveled in telling their national story to outsiders. The presentation typically began some 3,000 years earlier with the
kingdom of Urartu in Asia Minor, then moved on to the empire of Tigran
the Great and highlighted Armenia's decision to become the first nation to
accept Christianity. If given the opportunity, Armenians would also ex-
pound on their unique alphabet, distinct religious architecture, rich literary
tradition, and instrumental role in the empires to which they were subject.
The hearty pride, however, usually sputtered to a halt in the Soviet period.

Armenia's status as a tiny, peripheral Soviet republic
never meshed with its past grandeur. Indeed, the incongruity drove many
Armenians to look beyond the borders of their republic. Nearly 30 percent
of Soviet Armenians lived outside of the Armenian republic, half in Transcaucasia and half in more distant republics.[27] The approximately 80,000
Armenians in Moscow and smaller communities in Leningrad (present-day
Saint Petersburg), Kiev, and elsewhere in the Soviet Union attested to the
forces that for centuries had drawn many of Armenia's most highly educated sons and daughters away from their homeland. In the 1970s and
1980s, tens of thousands of repatriates from the post-World War II period
emigrated to the West.

The diaspora served as a ready yardstick for Armenians
to measure their discontent. Air routes connecting Yerevan with Armenian
communities in the Middle East brought waves of newly prosperous tour-
ists to Armenia beginning in the 1960s. Soon after, increasing numbers of

Armenians from Europe and the Americas also started visiting. Khrushchev and Brezhnev tolerated homeland–diaspora contacts. Dance ensembles, choral groups, and trustworthy literary figures toured abroad, while from the diaspora young people came to attend Armenian summer camps, clerics participated in church synods, and sympathetic community leaders were feted by local officials. Beginning in 1962, university students from the diaspora were invited to study in Armenia, and limited repatriation was resumed.[28] While most of the Soviet Union remained isolated from the outside world, Armenians learned the truth of their system's failures with each planeload of their diaspora cousins. The bulging suitcases that stocked Yerevan's thriving black market also led much of the younger generation to aspire to a standard of living that could not be attained in Armenia.

As Yerevan awoke in February 1988 and complaints about the problems of pollution, corruption, cultural stagnation, and political repression grew louder, Galstyan's reading of the Karabagh movement was affirmed. The February demonstrations assumed the characteristics of a national renaissance—a metaphor quickly adopted by intellectuals of a literary bent. Kaputikyan's language, for example, is that of the poet:

> During these demonstrations our people arose and were reborn; they rid themselves of the mire and mustiness of the years of stagnation and of the temporarily acquired traits of selfishness, greed, and of national and social indifference. During these demonstrations our people assumed their fate and, proudly leading the way of their glorious history, stood assembled and imposing as is characteristic of an ancient nation that has recovered the remnants of its lost biblical origins.[29]

Nora Dudwick, an American anthropologist conducting field research in Yerevan at the time of the demonstrations, also recorded the shift in temperament. She was most struck by the "transcendental" quality of the week—a sense that the laws governing human nature had been temporarily suspended. By February, Dudwick had been observing Armenian society at close range for four months at a grade school on the outskirts of Yerevan. The demonstrations not only redirected the focus of Dudwick's research, but also recast the personalities of the teachers and students around her. Dudwick recalled that many of the teachers returned to their classrooms as if they had visited another planet, while students grew overnight from protected children to political activists.[30]

Perhaps the most compelling testimony to the transformation of consciousness was found in anecdotes and popular lore. The small events were best remembered: hundreds of thousands of people squatting in Theater Square in deference to a legless speaker; the sudden appearance of thousands of bottles of Pepsi, passed hand-to-hand in an orderly fashion into the center of the huge crowd; old women offering baskets of bread and cheese brought from home; drivers in private cars shuttling food to the multitude.[31]

Order, self-discipline, and compassion in Theater Square became a matter of national honor. A few words were sufficient to open pathways through the throng to accommodate first-aid workers administering to demonstrators taken ill after long hours of standing. As the crowds grew, organizers at the speaker's platform were unable to police the occasional scuffles that the authorities were suspected of instigating. Instead, the crowd itself acted to smother the disturbances by closing in tightly around the participants. When a teenager seized the microphone and testified that Azerbaijanis had killed his father and burned the corpse, the crowd had already learned its lesson. The overwhelming response was: "Provocation!" Even Yerevan's underworld seemed to have been affected by the movement. One story, related to the crowd in Theater Square by an MVD officer, told of how the city's MVD office had been contacted by the ringleader of local thieves, who promised that his men would not practice their trade during the demonstrations. One criminal reportedly passed out money to strangers, beseeching, "I hope this will redeem me in the eyes of my people." Whatever the cause, there were in fact no crimes registered in Yerevan during the last week of February.[32]

Rafael Ghazaryan, an elder statesman of the Karabagh Committee, described the events in political terms:

> The Karabagh movement has awakened the masses in the republic to the terrors of feudalism in all organizations. The nation started to believe that such a struggle is possible and is not hopeless.[33]

For the hundreds of thousands in Theater Square, the politics of the movement trickled down into their personal lives. As one average Yerevani said:

> We are so proud of ourselves. No matter what happens, we are standing on our feet now, instead of being on our knees. For the first time in my life, I feel like a human being.[34]

For all the euphoria in Armenia, however, the prickly question of Mountainous Karabagh was what the authorities saw when they looked at the Karabagh movement. And at the practical level, the issue was becoming pricklier with each day. Violence had already marred the peaceful protests in Mountainous Karabagh. Armenians in the oblast had been attacked as early as 21 February, the day Azerbaijani First Secretary Bagirov had sternly rejected territorial changes in a televised address.[35] Clashes later in the week led to the first deaths blamed on the movement. At the same time, roads between Stepanakert and outlying districts of Mountainous Karabagh remained blocked. As a general strike among Armenians in the oblast took hold, representatives from Baku and Politburo candidate members Razumovsky and Demichev leaned more heavily on threats and intimidation to choke off the protests. Baku authorities, including Armenian party officials, were dispatched to Stepanakert to stamp out popular participation in the movement. Darkening the atmosphere further was the broadcast of *Bloody Sunday* on 26 February. The film, which preempted regular programming, depicted tsarist police gunning down peaceful protestors in the streets of Saint Petersburg in 1905.

In Moscow, the discussion Gorbachev held with Balayan and Kaputikyan on 26 February represented another dimension of the Kremlin effort to plug the hole in the dike. Alexander Yakovlev, Gorbachev's closest Politburo ally in 1988, had summoned the two reform-minded writers to Moscow to convince them of the danger that the Karabagh movement posed to *glasnost* and *perestroika*. Both over the telephone and in a three-hour conversation at his Kremlin office, Yakovlev emphasized the need "to put out the fire" in the streets of Armenia. Later in the day, Gorbachev hammered away at the same point. The only glimmer of hope for the Armenian representatives came as Gorbachev worked to charm Kaputikyan by recalling how he had memorized her poems in the 1950s. Kaputikyan seized the literary allusion to note that "Secret Ballot"—Gorbachev's personal favorite—told the story of a Communist Party member facing up to a difficult choice in a party election during the Khrushchev era, or, as Kaputikyan put it, "when there was a little renaissance." Gorbachev carried the theme further, promising to create the conditions for a little renaissance in Mountainous Karabagh. According to the general secretary, the Politburo would look after the problem.[36]

Otherwise, Gorbachev rebuffed a proposal to send a commission to Mountainous Karabagh. Unification was dismissed as out of the question, Gorbachev said, lest it stir up the country's eighteen other pressing nationalities problems. Gorbachev even remarked obliquely on the vulnerability of the more than 200,000 Armenians in Baku, prompting a response of "So what?" from Balayan.[37]

The Kremlin meeting was hardly the breakthrough that had been anticipated in Theater Square, but the two Armenian representatives had at least been granted a hearing by the Soviet leader. They left the Kremlin with a feeling that something had been achieved and were more than willing to serve Moscow's cause in ending the demonstrations. The next day in Yerevan, Balayan went to Theater Square while Kaputikyan recorded an interview for local television. Back in the small pond of Armenia, the pair reveled in the celebrity status that their Kremlin meeting had bestowed upon them. Both Balayan and Kaputikyan belonged to a nimble-footed stratum of the Armenian intelligentsia. For decades they had tightroped along a fine line between Armenian nationalism and official Soviet internationalism. On the Karabagh question, the genocide issue, and other matters dear to the Armenian soul, they spoke with the voice of their people. At the same time, they kept themselves in good stead with Moscow and reached the upper crust of the Soviet intelligentsia.

Balayan was best known as a correspondent of *Literaturnaya gazeta* (Literary Newspaper), one of the Soviet Union's most prestigious periodicals. He was also a native son of Mountainous Karabagh, whose father oversaw education in the region until he was purged in 1937. Balayan was a natural leader among the thousands of transplants from the oblast who had established themselves within the educated class of Armenia. As Balayan saw it, their growing influence was the driving force behind the Karabagh movement in Armenia. Balayan's Karabagh side came out in his fierce dedication to the Armenian community's political cause and often ferocious denunciations of the Azerbaijanis. On the other hand, Balayan's status in the Soviet elite led many younger intellectuals to accuse him of protecting Moscow's interests.

Kaputikyan's story was similar, although she trod along the path of success more cautiously. Born in 1919 in Yerevan, Kaputikyan learned the dos and don'ts of career advancement under Stalin. She published her first poem in 1933 and by 1945 was a member of the Armenian Central Committee. In 1952, she received the USSR State Prize for Poetry, largely for glorifying the sovietization of Armenia. And yet, like Balayan, Kaputikyan managed to carve out a niche for herself as a spokesperson on Armenian national issues. From her position of privilege, Kaputikyan lashed out against officialdom on a number of occasions. In 1966, she cited the indifference of Armenia's government toward the genocide as the key factor in inciting an unauthorized demonstration held 24 April 1965 in Yerevan to commemorate the fiftieth anniversary of the genocide. In 1980, she fretted that Armenian parents felt compelled to send their children to Russian-language schools to broaden their career opportunities. And in 1987, given the chance to be the first non-Russian under *glasnost* to analyze nationalities issues in the pages of *Pravda*, Kaputikyan accused Moscow of steadily expanding the sphere of Russian-language usage at the expense of Armenian, and suggested indirectly that Russian chauvinism continued to mar relations among the peoples of the Soviet Union.[38]

Kaputikyan was satisfied that she was serving the role of both loyal party member and good Armenian on 27 February. During her interview with local television, broadcast that evening, Kaputikyan conveyed Gorbachev's call for Armenians to get back to work. More significantly, she termed the meeting a triumph for the Armenians. Kaputikyan had applied a generous measure of poetic license to her report, but for most Armenians and Azerbaijanis her proclamation of victory was taken quite literally.[39] Earlier that day, Balayan had likewise raised expectations in Theater Square. With the late afternoon chill settling over a crowd of half a million, Balayan also called on Armenians to heed Gorbachev's appeal. In fact, Igor Muradyan and a number of other speakers had already suggested that the demonstrations be suspended and that the republic work Sunday shifts to make up for lost production. Balayan formalized the consensus, composing a letter in his own hand at the microphone while the crowd below waited silently. Again with a flair for the dramatic, Balayan rejected the "V" for victory sign a few orators had flashed and gave the movement a new symbol. He held up an open hand and instructed his audience. "To demonstrate unity, we must raise our hands in a clenched fist," Balayan said as he curled his thick fingers toward the base of his palm, "because if we fight with open fingers we run the risk of breaking our bones."[40] With night falling, Balayan ordered the crowd to disperse in an orderly fashion; the demonstrators along the rim of the huge semicircle were the first to turn around and head for their homes. Before more than a handful had left, however, Muradyan stepped forward and announced that the next rally would be held on 26 March. Although the date was picked randomly, the hope was that Armenia would be gathering to celebrate a favorable decision by the Politburo.

For many in Yerevan, the evening of Saturday, 27 February, was itself an occasion for celebration, or at least thanksgiving. Most went home sincere in their commitment to give up their Sundays in exchange for Gorbachev's pledge to consider their demands. More important, they left Theater Square secure in the belief that the Armenian people had regained control over their destiny, that once again they belonged to a nation of actors rather than passive spectators.

Less than 200 miles away in Stepanakert, the mood was starkly different. Protestors there had drawn inspiration from events in Moscow, but they were hardly prepared to bring their demonstrations to a halt. On the contrary, the Armenians of Mountainous Karabagh were determined to set the pace of their struggle. When the appeal of Balayan and Kaputikyan to end the protests reached Stepanakert, the reply was fittingly defiant: "We did not ask you when to begin. You cannot tell us when to stop. We will stop when our demand is met."[41]

Chapter 3

Sumgait

*T*he city of Sumgait hugs the shoreline of the Caspian Sea twenty miles north of Baku. As an industrial center mapped out by Soviet central planners under Stalin, its population boomed from 6,000 in the 1940s to 223,000 by 1988.[1] Huge factories producing synthetic rubber, steel pipe, aluminum, superphosphate, and petrochemicals went into operation.[2] Along with the growth came polluted marshes and squalid slums. The poorer neighborhoods were inhabited mostly by peasants who had migrated from the Azerbaijani countryside. During the sultry summer months, the city proved especially insufferable. Noxious fumes and a film of gritty white powder cut residents off from the sea breezes of the Caspian. Acrid reminders of one of the city's most well-known products— "Sumgait" laundry detergent—were never far away. One macabre example of local humor raised the possibility that Sumgait's horrendous air pollution had enabled the city's residents to survive gas chambers.[3]

On the evening of 27 February, however, Sumgait gained another sort of notoriety. A rally in Sumgait's Lenin Square had attracted thousands of participants, most of them young Azerbaijani men. The theme of the gathering was Mountainous Karabagh's campaign for unification with Armenia. The mood was angry. Many of the speakers tried in vain to calm the crowd. One of the republic's leading poets, Bakhtiar Bagab-Zade, was spurned. A historian and the director of the republic's Institute of Political Education counseled reasoned discussion and were shouted down. More inflammatory orators emerged, ranging from a high school principal to a well-known actress. Their message was venomous. Armenians were blamed not only for taking the issue of Mountainous Karabagh to the streets, but were accused of committing atrocities against Azerbaijanis in

51

Ghapan, a town in southeastern Armenia. The Soviet and Azerbaijani media later condemned the rumors as false, but the charges fueled calls of "Death to the Armenians" and served to transform the crowd into a mob.[4] With bottles of vodka being handed out from the back of a supply truck, emotions boiled over into violence by nightfall.

Much of what happened over the next three days in Sumgait will never be fully known. Soviet prosecutors and eyewitness court testimony, however, established that a massacre against the city's 19,000 Armenians took place. Official sources claimed 26 Armenians died. Many Armenians insisted that dozens more were killed. Regardless of the death toll, Sumgait was more than a massacre. Even as the victims were being mourned, Armenians were calling the events a pogrom, a conspiracy, and, most significantly, a watershed.

The violence that had occurred a week earlier in and around Mountainous Karabagh had already tarnished the peaceful nature of the Karabagh movement. Most ominous were the incidents that had taken place at Askeran, near the oblast's eastern border, on 22 February. Two days after the special session by the oblast soviet of Mountainous Karabagh, as many as 8,000 Azerbaijanis from the town of Aghdam crossed into the oblast, heading down the railroad toward Stepanakert. Along the way, offices, equipment, and vehicles at factories inside Mountainous Karabagh were destroyed. Azerbaijani women threw down their headdresses in front of the column's path. Some in the crowd heeded the traditional admonishment to avoid conflict and returned home. Others continued onward. A few miles from Askeran, the mob was met by a detachment of Azerbaijani and local Askeran police. The militia forces, however, lacked the manpower to block the marchers. Instead, the mob spilled onto the main road passing through the oblast. After ransacking two other factories and demolishing a militia post, the crowd collided with residents of Askeran. Twenty-five people on both sides were injured in the clash. Troops from a nearby garrison of the Soviet army were ultimately called in to restore order. More important, two Azerbaijanis, the younger only 16 years old, were killed. Later investigations showed that one of the dead had been shot by a Soviet soldier.[5]

The deaths at Askeran fanned local tensions, but the real impact came on 27 February when news of the Askeran incident was broadcast on Soviet television by the deputy prosecutor general of the USSR, Alexander Katusev. Mountainous Karabagh First Secretary Henrik Poghosyan had previously warned of the dangers involved in disclosing the nationalities of the two youths without fully explaining the circumstances surrounding their deaths, but Katusev disregarded the advice. Instead, he suggested that lives were lost as a result of "crimes committed by isolated hooligan elements." Hundreds reacted to the announcement by joining the mob assembled in Sumgait's Lenin Square.[6]

Katusev's broadcast is but one element in an intricate conspiracy theory Armenian activists constructed after the Sumgait massacres. As with theories on the origins of the demonstrations in Yerevan, the main actors in Moscow were again KGB heavies seeking to undermine reform. Those with the most at stake, however, were Azerbaijani party bosses, especially the officials tied most closely to the republic's notorious mafia. As Armenian activists probed deeper, they uncovered a trail of evidence that indeed seemed to lead back to Baku.

The starting point was apparently the sizable Azerbaijani community that lived in Ghapan before 1988. Armenian activists believed that four busloads of young Azerbaijani men were recruited from the area and then crossed into Azerbaijan. By late February, rumors about Armenian massacres of Azerbaijanis—even stories of rail cars filled with Azerbaijani corpses—were circulating in the republic. Members of the caravan fanned the rumors as they drove deeper into Azerbaijan, exhorting their compatriots in small towns and villages to join them in the trek to Sumgait. "You do not know what is being done to your brothers and sisters in Nagorno Karabakh," one of the ringleaders reportedly shouted. "They [the Armenians] will kill us as well." [7]

The young men arrived at the city bus depot on 26 February, setting off the first round of anti-Armenian demonstrations. They were joined by 14- to 17-year-old students from a Sumgait vocational school, most of whom were housed in dormitories, and unemployed youth from the city's outlying districts. Local Armenians reacted by alerting Moscow of the danger, placing dozens of phone calls to the MVD, the KGB, and other governmental offices to request protection. Their pleas were uniformly ignored.[8]

The next day's rally served as a staging ground for the pogroms that followed. Court testimony later confirmed that hundreds of marauders were armed with sharpened steel rods and heavy clubs. In addition, they were given the addresses of Armenian residents—a necessity in a city where Armenians were widely dispersed. Threatening leaflets had already been posted on apartment buildings housing Armenian families. From 27 February to 1 March, telephone service was cut off for much of Sumgait. Finally, the local law enforcement body—the Sumgait militia—made no effort to bring the massacres to a halt.[9]

Many of the Azerbaijanis who had been forewarned of the violence provided sanctuary for their Armenian neighbors, often at great risk to their own lives. Individual MVD soldiers also intervened to stop the attack, but the overall response of the Soviet authorities fueled

Armenian suspicions. Two battalions arrived in Sumgait on 29 February, two days after the massacre had begun. More puzzling, the troops came unarmed and without orders to confront the mob. Many saw their armored personnel carriers overturned and were subject to beatings by club-wielding attackers. By 1 March, however, Sumgait fell eerily calm. Garbage trucks swept through the ransacked neighborhoods during the night, clearing away debris and hosing down the streets before the arrival of investigators from Moscow.[10]

Conspiracy or no conspiracy, the impact of Sumgait was devastating. The agenda of the Karabagh movement was derailed. What had begun as a campaign for political change and human rights was recast overnight in the context of an ethnic feud. Armenia was numb. Whatever the intent, Sumgait failed to provoke eye-for-an-eye retribution. On a day-to-day level, activists busied themselves with recording the eyewitness accounts of Sumgait survivors and organizing relief aid for the refugees. The massacre, however, sent many desperately groping for explanations. Vazgen Manukyan, a prominent voice in Theater Square, found an answer in the Soviet fear of popular democracy:

> The government is genuinely scared of our unity. They just wanted to intimidate us—to stop the demonstrations from happening. They thought it was all being directed from somewhere; they just couldn't imagine that half a million people would interrupt the day-to-day business of their lives to express their bitterness at how they had been treated.[11]

Even before Sumgait, the central media had launched a counterattack against the Karabagh movement. Two stalwart clichés of Soviet domestic policy—"friendship between peoples" and "internationalism"—were immediately pressed into service. Interviews by the dozen were conducted with Azerbaijanis and Armenians alike. From common peasants to state farm directors, gushing enthusiasm came for the official multinational harmony of the Soviet system. One letter condemning the movement in Mountainous Karabagh carried signatures of Armenian and Azerbaijani geophysicists.

In Sumgait, workers blamed the violence on outsiders and noted proudly that the production of mineral fertilizer had not been interrupted.[12] Moscow's official pronouncement on the Sumgait massacres attributed the events to "hooligan elements." Rather than sinister motives, TASS found "wavering, immature people who fell under the impact of false rumours concerning the developments in Nagorno Karabakh and Armenia." The death toll was put at 31 initially, and ultimately rose to 32. The victims, however, were described as belonging to "various nationalities." Finally, in a concluding bit of dark irony, Sumgait residents were lauded for demonstrating "self-discipline and sentiments of internationalism." [13]

The first informative account of the Sumgait massacre by the Soviet media came nearly two months after the fact, when a young, *glasnost*-era journalist, Genrikh Borovik, narrated a television documentary titled *Pozitsiya* (Position). For the first time, Soviet viewers saw video footage of rioters racing through the streets of Sumgait.[14] During the course of the broadcast, Borovik castigated the Azerbaijani press for inflaming passions and compelled Deputy Prosecutor General Katusev of the USSR to admit that no Azerbaijanis had been killed by Armenians at Sumgait.

Whether calculated to smear the Karabagh movement or simply Moscow's knee-jerk reaction, the central media's emphasis on Soviet internationalism did indeed serve to blur the political issues Armenians had raised. In Yerevan at the time, there was little doubt that the media was under the thumb of Yegor Ligachev, Gorbachev's conservative Politburo rival, and doing its part to stamp out the first sparks of democracy. A published statement issued by the Institute of Philosophy and Law in Yerevan on 11 March 1988 succinctly presented the Armenian interpretation:

> It remains a fact that for the entire eight days of the Yerevan demonstrations, the principle of friendship between peoples was not once placed in doubt by any act or word from the demonstrators. The issue was righting an historical wrong. The Azerbaijani people bore no responsibility for past ill deeds during the times of Stalinism. The substitution of the real issue by formulas of friendship between peoples was nothing less than a serious and artificial distraction for both of the friendly peoples.[15]

The public relations jousting was taken up by hundreds of Armenian intellectuals, but they also understood that the deepest wounds of Sumgait could not be completely appreciated by outsiders. In the Armenian mind, Sumgait was about genocide. And genocide became the burial shroud for each of its victims.

For Armenians, genocide was more living reality than historical fact. The persecution in the Ottoman Empire that culminated with the extermination of 1.5 million Armenians during World War I constituted a layer of collective memory that rested just below the surface of everyday life. With Sumgait, the memory reemerged. American anthropologist Nora Dudwick watched the process take place. Genocide, she observed, became the prism through which Armenians viewed their struggle:

Hence, the "de-Armenization" of Nakhichevan is referred to as "white genocide," the severe air pollution of Yerevan is "ecological genocide," and the assimilationist policies of Azerbaijan are considered "cultural genocide." The massacre at Sumgait became simply "genocide." It seemed that every social and political problem took on additional significance as containing a threat to the Armenians' continued existence as a people.[16]

Most Soviet Armenians traced at least one branch of their family tree back to the genocide that began in 1915. Eyewitness accounts of rampaging mobs, gang rapes, and frenzied acts of butchery sank into the common culture. The Armenian genocide lacked the inhuman precision of the Jewish Holocaust or the cold indifference that accompanied the annihilation of native peoples in the Americas. On the contrary, it was a slaughter of knives and clubs, starvation and fire. Bullets were often judged too valuable to be expended on the victims. As with other massacres of the Middle East, death during the genocide was only one dimension of the suffering. Degradation and humiliation were also central to the atrocities. There were cases of crucifixion, disemboweled pregnant women, and violated children.

The perpetrators of the Sumgait massacre seemed bent on reawakening nightmares of the past. The first tales of brutality came from refugees fleeing to Armenia and were often discounted. As evidence was collected and trials organized, though, the worst was confirmed. Court testimony from Azerbaijani and Russian witnesses left Armenians shaken:

The top part of one man's body was on the bonfire, but his legs were sticking out. He was still showing signs of life, trying to get out of the fire, but some fellow was holding him down with an iron bar so he couldn't get out. (Witness M. Mamedov)

From entrance No. 3 they dragged a man of about 30.... When they had dragged him out, they began to hit him. Then they took him away to a wooden walkway outside block 5V and started to beat him again. After that a man of between 23 and 28 years old went over to him as he lay on the ground and threw a burning rag over his chest. The man jumped up screaming and ran around the back of block 26. I didn't see the man again. Later, I saw them dragging Irina from the second doorway of block 26. I knew her. The mob dragged her to a transformer hut. What they did to her I did not see. When the crowd dispersed, I saw that she was lying naked on the ground and a youth of about 14 or 15 was hitting her on the back with a spade. He struck her on the back full force about five or six times. (Witness E. Salamov)

He was surrounded by fifteen to twenty men and they started to attack him with axes, knives, and bars. They hit him about the body and the head. Then one of them pulled over a burning mattress and smothered the man with it. (Witness D. Zerbaliev)[17]

"Sumgait exacerbated everything," Ashot Manucharyan reflected three months later. "It was as if someone had hit us over the head with a rock. Now we hear more extreme demands from both sides." Manucharyan and most others in the Karabagh Committee were quick to stress the distinction between the perpetrators and the Azerbaijani people as a whole. Inescapable, though, was the collective déjà vu that swept over Armenia. Again, Manucharyan:

The genocide of 1915 is always in front of our eyes, a reason for our seriousness. The road toward massacre is always a possibility. It has sunk into our psychology, made us cautious. But that's a terrible mistake, that we can never raise our heads for fear of massacre.[18]

Ottoman persecution during the last decades of the empire deepened the Armenian people's sense of vulnerability. As a result, many Armenians under tsarist and Soviet rule placed their faith in Russia. Incidents such as the Sumgait massacre seemed only to reinforce the notion that Armenia had no choice but to look north. Kaputikyan drew from a seemingly bottomless reserve of resignation when she noted in a television interview that Armenians were "doomed to believe the Russians. We are doomed to trust Moscow." [19] Among Communist Party members of Kaputikyan's generation, allegiance to the Soviet system and trust in Russia had gone hand in hand. Of course, the flip side of Russophilia was Turcophobia. As the argument went, Armenia was an island of Christian civilization in a sea of Islam. Without Moscow's protection, Armenia would be instantly devoured.

But even after Sumgait, many within the Karabagh Committee were looking for a new standard on which to base Armenian–Azerbaijani relations. Manucharyan, for one, placed hope in open dialogue:

Azerbaijanis first must accept responsibility for Sumgait. After that, I'm ready to sit down with them and discuss anything. Then let that exchange be broadcast on television. Part of the problem is that the press has led Azerbaijanis to believe they are correct, that history justifies their attitudes. Aside from the Karabagh issue, though, there has at least been a sense of neighborliness in areas where Armenians and Azerbaijanis live together. They have lived side by side, helped each other, attended each other's weddings. Coexistence is possible.[20]

So long as Armenians blamed the government for Sumgait, rather than the Azerbaijani people, coexistence was possible. In March of 1988 at least, most Armenians were willing to hear talk of reconciliation. The Baku media in fact bemoaned the violence in Sumgait. An Azerbaijani Muslim leader expressed regret and called for peace. Privately, many liberal Azerbaijani intellectuals were hoping for a stronger condemnation of the massacre. Following Moscow's lead, however, Azerbaijani spokesmen attributed the events to "a group of hooligans."[21] The official apology to the Armenian people never came. Unrealistic or not, many Armenians would settle for nothing less. As Armenian–Azerbaijani relations grew more strained in later months, Sumgait for many Azerbaijani journalists became a symbol of the republic's environmental, economic, and social degradation at the hands of Moscow. Ironically, an Azerbaijani television documentary on Sumgait that aired the following year was entitled "Death Zone." The broadcast probed the human cost of the city's industrial pollution while making no mention of the massacre in 1988.[22]

Hambartsum Galstyan understood that few Azerbaijanis could risk acknowledging the anti-Armenian nature of Sumgait in such a supercharged atmosphere. Voices of conciliation had little choice but to keep quiet. Three months after the massacre, Galstyan reported:

Now I can't even call my Azerbaijani friend in Moscow because of the blood that has been spilled. Another Azerbaijani intellectual told me that he can no longer sleep at night because of what has happened. He can't shake the hand of an Armenian. But in the future, we have no choice but to share this land together.[23]

Without recognition of Sumgait by Azerbaijanis, Armenians were not capable of granting forgiveness. Without forgiveness, there was no healing. Instead, Sumgait proved to be only one of many wounds. The Karabagh movement would recover, but the euphoria of February could not be summoned again.

Chapter 4

Dormancy

*O*n 8 March 1988, the Soviet Union celebrated International Women's Day. Throughout the country, women were honored with official pronouncements and bouquets of flowers from family and friends. In Armenia, however, the occasion served as an opportunity to mourn the victims of Sumgait. More than half a million people followed a phalanx of prominent women up the path that led to the genocide memorial at Tsitsernakaberd. The procession filed silently by the monument, ringing the eternal flame with red and white carnations. Solemn, stoic, almost lifeless—the commemoration made plain the impact of the recent massacre.

The Karabagh movement was not dead, however, only silent in anticipation. Ad hoc committees were forming to funnel aid to Mountainous Karabagh and Sumgait refugees. Rumpled ruble notes were passed from hand to hand and were stuffed into envelopes that wound up at the Karabagh Committee's relief center inside the Writers' Union. Political activists were collecting signatures from deputies of the Armenian Supreme Soviet on a petition calling for an extraordinary session of the legislature. Nearly 100 deputies endorsed the initiative before Karen Demirchyan quashed the effort. (Officially, signatures from one-third of the 340 members of the Armenian Supreme Soviet were needed to convene an extraordinary session.) Meanwhile, Yerevan was working overtime to make up for production lost during the February demonstrations. The sorrow of Sumgait had steeled the people's determination. If anything, the massacre had demonstrated that Azerbaijan could not responsibly govern Mountainous Karabagh. The Kremlin leadership, popular wisdom held, would surely agree. In the meantime, the Karabagh Committee made sure that there were no unruly protests to distract the Politburo's attention.

Thus, Moscow's March blitzkrieg against the Karabagh movement slammed into Armenia all the more furiously. Igor Muradyan had set 26 March as the target date for the Kremlin's response, and for the first three weeks of the month Armenians scavenged the media for clues to Moscow's disposition. The small circle of Armenian intellectuals in the capital relayed scraps of information to Yerevan by telephone. Suspense was peaking when the official answer finally came in a *Pravda* article published 21 March 1988.

There was nothing subtle about "Emotion and Reason," an ironically entitled commentary that laid out the Soviet position. Rather than being hailed as the first flowering of *glasnost*, the February demonstrations were dismissed as "street democracy" and the organizers branded as enemies of *perestroika*. The article went on to state Moscow's case against reviewing nationalities problems: "What if the rest of the regions, at the expense of other peoples, similarly start satisfying their own interests? What will then become of the fraternal union of the peoples, the country's economy?"[1] If the text itself were not enough, the commentary bore the name of an Armenian author, Yuri Arakelyan, along with Russian and Azerbaijani collaborators.

The *Pravda* article proved only to be the first strike in a concerted offensive. That night, a TASS commentary read on *Vremya* (Time), the union-wide television news program, accused Muradyan of seeking foreign support for the Karabagh movement. In the harshest assault yet against the demonstration organizers, TASS said: "Cynically and perfidiously, they are prepared to make capital on the difficulties of *perestroika*, [and] exploit the emotions of people for provocative aims so as to reverse society's development."[2]

By noon the next day, a few thousand Yerevanis had gathered outside the city's media headquarters to shred their copies of *Pravda* and to demand that the republic's newspapers defy Moscow's order and not translate the article into Armenian. A delegation representing the media eventually emerged and assured the crowd that no translation would be published. The following day, though, the translation indeed appeared in the pages of *Sovetakan Haiastan*. Elsewhere in the city, a smaller group was clustered around a small bonfire of *Pravda* dailies burning in front of the apartment of the newspaper's Yerevan correspondent, Yuri Arakelyan. The outcry against the article was sufficient for Arakelyan to publicly disavow his role as author. Later, his family claimed that he had suffered a heart attack because of the stress.[3]

As Silva Kaputikyan put it, the *Pravda* article was a "spiritual Sumgait."[4] Given her penchant for hyperbole, Kaputikyan was not far from the mark. The Karabagh movement had staked out a claim for justice in political and moral terms, and in the end the unification of Mountainous Karabagh depended on Moscow. In the *glasnost* era, that meant winning over the hearts and minds of thinking people across the Soviet Union. Armenians could unfurl banners hailing *perestroika* and give speeches steeped in democratic principles, but they needed the Soviet media to carry their message beyond the republic's borders. Needless to say, the word was not getting out.

In reality, the Karabagh movement had first faced an information blockade in February. Armenian television crews began recording the Yerevan demonstrations almost from the outset, but official policy kept the footage off the airwaves. Only after journalists throughout the republic threatened a walkout on 26 February were scenes of the mass meetings shown on Armenian television.[5] Of course, the central media in Moscow was impervious to popular pressure in Yerevan. Instead, Armenians consoled themselves with the belief that the opinions voiced by *Pravda* and *Vremya* reflected the partisan wishes of Yegor Ligachev and his hardline cronies. The media's condemnation of the Karabagh movement had coincided with the publication of a combative defense of Stalinism in *Sovetskaya Rossiya* (Soviet Russia) on March 13.[6] The fact that Gorbachev was out of the country at the time raised fears of a palace coup. Most Yerevan activists felt that the fight for Gorbachev's reform program was reaching a critical stage, and assumed that the general secretary and the Karabagh movement were on the same side. This indeed was the basic premise underlying the boycott of the central media launched by Muradyan on 2 March, and later in the month spurred a flurry of letters to the editor of *Sovetskaya Rossiya* from Armenian intellectuals. Sure enough, the supposition gained credibility with the publication of a relatively sympathetic article in the purportedly reform-minded *Izvestia* (News) on 24 March. While brushing off calls for border changes, *Izvestia* at least validated Armenian claims of Baku's heavy-handedness in the cultural and economic spheres.[7]

In retrospect, no single statement by the Soviet media definitively presented the Kremlin's stance on the Karabagh movement. Rather, the real story of Moscow's makeshift strategy emerged only over long months of coverage. Above all, the solution to the problem was portrayed as economic and administrative rather than political—a refurbished factory here, a new sports complex there, maybe an added dose of local control—but unification was not part of the debate. Second, according to Moscow's interpretation, the events of early 1988 had been spurred by hot-blooded Caucasian passion. Whether in Yerevan, Stepanakert, or Sumgait, those in the streets during February were somehow stirred by the same unbridled emotions. Finally, the official line left no alternative but for Moscow to step in as a dispassionate mediator. On the Mountainous Karabagh question, intransigence was a characteristic that afflicted both Armenians and Azerbaijanis alike in the media.

By early April, the media campaign had also linked the Karabagh movement to a familiar villain: the West. Gorbachev himself set the tone of Soviet allegations, charging that news accounts from the West had played an inflammatory role in the Karabagh movement. "They are trying to interfere in our internal affairs," he claimed, "to exacerbate problems from the outside and engaging in provocations."[8] Journalists for *Pravda* and *Argumenty i fakty* (Arguments and Facts), however, turned back the clock to the pre-*glasnost* era in launching the most rabid attacks against the British Broadcasting Corporation (BBC) and the Voice of America (VOA). *Pravda* made a point of taking a swipe at both the Karabagh Committee and the Western media with the same brush:

> Like Siamese twins, foreign and domestic instigators cannot exist without each other, and they pursue identical goals. They both dislike the system existing in the USSR. They would both like to pervert our democratization and restructuring to the point where our country's territory turns into an arena of persistent and fierce internation and social conflicts. Our ideological adversaries, even though forced to camouflage themselves as democrats and champions of justice, actually reject altogether the desire and will of all soberminded people for mutual understanding, friendship, and cooperation, for the quest for sensible ways to solve pressing complex problems.[9]

The media blitz was not the only element in Moscow's offensive against the Karabagh movement. The centerpiece of the Kremlin's response came in the form of a seven-year, 400-million ruble package of economic and cultural reforms for Mountainous Karabagh. Announced on 24 March, the twenty-one-point resolution dovetailed with the official diagnosis of the oblast's problems. The economic measures included plans to boost overall industrial output by 50 to 60 percent, to increase housing construction by 40 percent, and to improve water supplies by building two new reservoirs. On the cultural and social side, there were provisions for renovating historical monuments, enhancing Armenian language education, rebuilding the road linking Stepanakert with Goris in southeastern Armenia, broadcasting Armenian television in the oblast, and constructing a 400-bed hospital, as well as nine or ten new schools.[10]

On paper, the reform package appeared to be a major concession on the part of Moscow. At least that was the desired impression. Within Armenia, however, the resolution won scant praise. Central to the Armenian critique was Baku's control over the seven-year plan. Armenians had been saying all along that Mountainous Karabagh was a political problem. The Kremlin solution, though, was to be administered by the same Azerbaijani government that stood accused of calculated repression. The matter of funding was disturbing as well. Soviet budget woes were hardly a secret in 1988. Even those who believed that the Kremlin resolution was sincere questioned whether 400 million rubles ($676 million at the official exchange rate in 1988) would be available. Moreover, funding allocated by Moscow would first pass through the notoriously sticky fingers of Baku *apparatchik*s.

Apparently, Moscow anticipated that most Armenians would find the reform package unacceptable. Without waiting for the official announcement on March 24, the Soviet army had rolled into Yerevan two days earlier. Armored personnel carriers rumbled down Lenin Prospekt ahead of the evening rush hour while helicopters lumbered above central Yerevan. Residents awoke the next day to find Theater Square and the opera house ringed by fresh-faced soldiers, and the city's main streets under army control. As many observers had predicted, the hammer had come down.

With the arrival of the Soviet military on 22 March, the outlines of the Kremlin's still nebulous strategy became clearer. The first step had been to get the demonstrators off the streets in February. The meeting of Balayan and Kaputikyan with Gorbachev served that purpose in Yerevan. Of course, Armenians in Mountainous Karabagh proved more stubborn. On 29 February, Pyotr Demichev reported in Stepanakert that the Central Committee would investigate the oblast's problems. Karabagh Armenians, however, did not suspend their strike until 2 March. On 9 March, Gorbachev bought himself more time, disclosing that the Central Committee had established a special commission to study Mountainous Karabagh.[11]

In Yerevan, the Karabagh Committee was left baffled. A meeting at the Kino Tun cinema in Yerevan scheduled by Muradyan for 19 March served as an eight-hour forum on strategies and tactics. With nearly 1,000 activists representing work sites in the republic crammed inside and thousands more packed near the entrance listening to loudspeakers, speaker after speaker took the podium to debate the usefulness of further strikes and demonstrations. Most supported taking the movement back to Theater Square, but the group was divided on whether to wait until 26 March. Muradyan even warned that Moscow's failure to resolve the Karabagh issue would turn Armenia into a "non-party Soviet republic"—a remark that was converted into ammunition against him by the media.[12]

In terms of broadening the Karabagh movement's base, the Kino Tun meeting was more successful. Muradyan had wanted to join forces with Armenia's established intelligentsia. The executive committee of the Karabagh Committee that emerged from the 19 March session accomplished that. Balayan, Kaputikyan, and Viktor Hambartsumyan agreed to serve alongside younger activists, such as Hambartsum Galstyan. A network of subcommittees was also created to extend the reach of the movement.

The successes and failures of the Kino Tun meeting, of course, were quickly overshadowed by the military crackdown. Official measures were enacted to rein in the movement. Among the authorities in Armenia, many may have privately sympathized with the goals of the Karabagh movement but few were willing to defy the Kremlin and jeopardize their careers. When the time came to act, the Armenian Supreme Soviet outlawed the Karabagh Committee. In a televised address on 22 March, Karen Demirchyan reiterated the argument that the emotions generated by the February demonstrations were capable of spinning out of control. The Armenian first secretary asked:

> Do we have the right, the political, moral, or human right, to ignore the danger that exists, of losing in a moment the unstained reputation of our people, which has been built up over many centuries?[13]

Likewise, the Azerbaijani government dissolved the *Krunk* (Crane) Committee, which had spearheaded organizing efforts in Mountainous Karabagh.[14] Demonstrations in both republics were effectively banned under new regulations. In Armenia, public gatherings had to be officially approved at least ten days in advance.[15]

Rather than compliantly disappearing, however, the Karabagh Committee called on Yerevan residents to stay home Saturday, 26 March, to transform the republic capital into a "dead city." And 26 March was indeed quieter than most Saturdays, but government officials made sure that at least party members appeared on the sidewalks. Perhaps a more effective retort was the Armenian sense of hospitality and dark humor. No sooner had soldiers taken their positions around Theater Square than female college students showed up to hand them flowers. One local joke had a boy pleading with a Russian soldier: "Look," he says, "we'll forget about Mountainous Karabagh. Just give us back the opera house." Meanwhile, the rocket-equipped helicopters swooping low over Yerevan were quickly dubbed "the first swallows of *perestroika*." When Soviet Defense Minister Dmitri Yazov arrived in town to oversee the occupation, one resident stationed himself beside the VIP hotel where Yazov was staying and held up a sign instructing helicopter pilots to "Strike Here." [16]

By the end of March, though, Armenians were faced with the sobering reality that their movement had come up against a wall. The military presence in Yerevan receded, but the ban on meetings remained in place. University students answered with a one-week boycott of classes in early April. In Mountainous Karabagh, strikes resumed with full force in late March, only a few days after 40,000 Armenians in Stepanakert had celebrated the decision of the central committee of the oblast's Communist Party to support unification. Troops blocked off Stepanakert's Lenin Square. As Ashot Manucharyan put it, the events of March were like a punch in the stomach. They knocked the wind out of the Armenian people for a month, but the blow was not deadly.

 Without public meetings, rumors filled the information vacuum in April. More precisely, rumors regained their preeminence. Like most closed societies where power rests in the hands of an isolated few, the Soviet Union had always been a hothouse for conjecture. Instead of putting an end to the trade in rumor, *glasnost* provided additional raw material from which Soviets invented still more incredible tales. Armenians were particularly imaginative, and by April they had concocted a smorgasbord of outlandish fantasies.

 Among the most widespread: Alex Manoogian, an American-Armenian industrial magnate and philanthropist, would buy Mountainous Karabagh for $10 million; President Ronald Reagan would visit Armenia during his May 1988 summit meeting with Gorbachev and insist on a solution; the Armenian Revolutionary Federation, the strongest political party of the diaspora, had organized a 40,000-man army in the Middle East that would soon be dispatched to Armenia.[17]

 The Karabagh movement had been fueled by rumors from the outset. Hopes rose and fell with each round of insider reports from Moscow. Even as they digested each morsel of news, Armenians understood that the Soviet leadership was the master of the game. In the course of seventy years, the Kremlin had turned the manipulation of public opinion into a quintessentially Soviet science. Stalin and his successors fed the tendency with their own paranoid need to exercise total control over their people. From the show trials of "counterrevolutionaries" in the 1930s to the bogeyman of "international Zionism," there had been no shortage of villainous cabals lurking in the shadows. But whereas fear had once cast a long shadow over Soviet society, rumors in the *glasnost* era were often colored by rising expectations. At least that is how many Armenians chose to see things.

 Gorbachev was the main target of Armenians' prayers. On 4 March the Soviet leader told Austrian Communist Party head Franz Muhri that the unrest in Mountainous Karabagh had resulted from the harsh and insensitive nationalities policies of the past.[18] A week later in Yugoslavia, he broke with the stern official tone of the Kremlin and noted that the Karabagh movement was neither anti-Soviet nor secessionist.

"What it was about," he said, "was that there are issues of a cultural and ethnic character that have recently been overlooked. Problems have accumulated."[19]

Armenians had stoked their expectations with other equally minor news items. During the Reagan–Gorbachev summit of December 1987, for example, a group of wealthy American-Armenians had presented the general secretary's wife, Raisa, with a seventeenth-century Slavonic manuscript and a painting by the nineteenth-century Russian-Armenian seascape master, Ivan K. Aivazovsky. Aside from Mrs. Gorbachev's platitudes on the "long-standing friendship" among Soviet peoples, politics were not discussed. Footage of the meeting, however, was aired on Armenian television.[20] In early March 1988, a smuggled TASS news release similarly raised hopes in Armenia. Although stamped "For Foreign Broadcast Only," the report supported calls to unify Mountainous Karabagh with Armenia.[21] By the middle of the month, the rumor circulating among well-informed circles in Yerevan was that the oblast would be upgraded to the status of an autonomous republic. Whatever one's prognosis, few in Armenia imagined in mid-March that their movement would not meet with success in a month or two. More cautious voices were dismissed as naysayers for suggesting that six months would be required.[22]

By mid-April, though, a more pragmatic school of political analysis had begun to emerge. Armenia remained rife with rumor—including those spawned by a *Washington Post* story about a supposed Central Committee meeting on the Karabagh question that was slated for June—but activists were now more clearheaded regarding the possibilities for the oblast. Top-level meetings between Armenian officials and Politburo members suggested that the Kremlin would soon take action. Six alternatives were given credence:

1. Grant more political authority to Karabagh Armenians by making the oblast an autonomous republic. As such, Mountainous Karabagh would have remained within Azerbaijan but could have adopted its own constitution and designated Armenian as an official language.

2. Permit dual Armenian and Azerbaijani administration. Since four of Mountainous Karabagh's districts were overwhelmingly Armenian, while the fifth was overwhelmingly Azerbaijani, local committees could have aligned their districts with either Armenia or Azerbaijan without encountering much opposition.

3. Impose presidential rule on the oblast for five or ten years. Just as Washington directly governed states of the American South during Reconstruction, Moscow would have administered Mountainous Karabagh and ultimately conducted a referendum on the oblast's future.

4. Alter the Soviet constitution to clearly assert the right of peoples to self-determination. With such a path open, Armenians in Mountainous Karabagh would have been able to reunify with Armenia through democratic means.

5. Swap territory in southeastern Armenia, specifically a strip of land running through the town of Meghri that separated Azerbaijan from Nakhichevan, in exchange for Mountainous Karabagh.

6. Hold plebiscites in various zones of the disputed territory, allowing residents to choose between Armenia and Azerbaijan.[23]

While Armenians were surveying the possibilities, however, Moscow moved to further muddy the intent of the Karabagh movement. On 25 March, Soviet authorities arrested Paruir Hairikyan, a veteran of the Brezhnev GULAG (the network of Soviet prison camps) and leader of the Union for National Self-Determination. Along with a few dozen hard-core adherents, Hairikyan had long advocated immediate independence for Armenia. Bitterly anti-Soviet, Hairikyan was part of a small circle of Moscow-based dissidents who maintained close ties with the Western media. Sergei Grigoryants, the editor of *Glasnost* magazine and an associate of Hairikyan, was responsible for passing along the first videotape of the Yerevan demonstrations to Western journalists.[24] Hairikyan himself was mentioned in many of the stories on Armenia that appeared in the Western press during the first weeks of the Karabagh movement. In reality, though, Hairikyan had no connection with the demonstrations, a fact his supporters conceded.[25] In his only appearance in February before the microphone in Theater Square, Hairikyan had warned that MVD tanks were on their way to Yerevan. Many in the crowd jeered him as a provocateur, and a few even jostled him as he left the speaker's platform. Nonetheless, that did not stop the Soviet media from portraying Hairikyan as the behind-the-scenes mastermind of the Karabagh movement.[26]

With Theater Square blocked off and other channels of political expression closed, only Hairikyan's supporters were willing to take to the streets after the military occupation. Their demonstrations in late March and early April were noisy enough to attract the local police, but drew only forty or fifty protestors. In addition, Nobel Peace Prize winner Andrei Sakharov wrote Gorbachev on behalf of Armenian claims in Mountainous Karabagh, although his letter was ignored by the Soviet press.[27] Otherwise, Yerevan was fairly quiet. Spring gradually crept into Armenia, spilling over the Ararat plain before climbing into the highlands. In Yerevan, brisk winds scrubbed the hazy grime from the skies and cast the city in stark, bright sunlight. Life acquired more of a normal routine. All the while, though, the electricity of February continued to hum in the background. No one quite dared to reclaim Theater Square, and yet few were able to get on with their day-to-day affairs as if nothing had happened. Wildcat strikes shut down factories sporadically. College students walked out of class with little provocation. Raised fists sprang up at bus stops.

Sunday, 24 April, was warm and sunny—the height of Yerevan springtime—and more than one million people joined the annual procession to the genocide monument. Even the authorities in Armenia recognized that the commemoration would be no ordinary 24 April. For the most part, they stayed away from Tsitsernakaberd and made little effort to police the marchers. Framed portraits of Sumgait victims, black banners, and mourning wreaths found their way to the base of the monument. University students also carried a 1,000-pound *khachkar* (stone cross) up the hill and planted it like a tombstone beside the entrance to the eternal flame. Inscribed "Sumgait—1988," the ornately carved *khachkar* seemed all the more conspicuous flanking the sharp, modernistic lines of the genocide memorial. A few officials inspected the graceful etchings; some insisted it be hauled away. But at half a ton, the *khachkar* held its ground into the week. That left the massive slab of stonework to face a million pairs of eyes as the procession strode solemnly past. The question posed was obvious: Was this to mark the end of a surreal moment in history, or the beginning of a new era? Yerevan waited.

Chapter 5

Renewal

*A*rmenians were never the most enthusiastic of commu-
nists. From the start, official Soviet holidays in Armenia lacked the pride
and wide-eyed reverence found in the Russian Soviet Federated Socialist
Republic (SFSR). Even the authorities had few illusions. To compensate,
they turned up the volume an extra notch on the loudspeakers that pumped
out the prerecorded waves of muscular "hurrahs" at public events.

On 1 May 1988—International Labor Day—the loud-
speakers in Yerevan were pushing their limit. After a pleasant and sunny
April, the new month opened with a chilly rainstorm. Armenian First Secretary Karen Demirchyan should have taken the weather as an omen. Many
had expected him to cancel the rally to avoid reigniting the Karabagh
movement. But Demirchyan insisted on performing his role as leader of the
republic's working class. Doing his best to appear dignified, he stood at the
speaker's platform in Lenin Square and smiled under darkened skies.

The mood was hardly festive, however. The crowd in the
square was largely hostile. Even with the loudspeakers blaring, boos and
whistles nearly forced Demirchyan off the podium. More embarrassing to
the authorities were the several hundred marchers who showed up shouting
chants from the February demonstrations. Plainclothes policemen stepped
in to snatch away banners and placards, including one that read, "All Power
to the Soviets." Meanwhile, television cameramen filming for the evening
news kept their lenses focused above the fray. (Next time, protesters vowed,
they would put their placards on longer sticks.) After a few minutes of
commotion, the marchers left the square and the rally concluded unevent-
fully. Demirchyan, however, should have recognized that Armenia would
not stay quiet for much longer.

As with nature itself, early May was a time of renewal for the Karabagh movement in Armenia. Following the ban against demonstrations, two or three photocopy machines had largely served to keep the movement alive. Information sheets were distributed to activists in workplaces throughout Yerevan. Research institutes, large factories, and the university system were the most vital links in the chain. Before long, something of an alternative media had been fashioned. News focused on events in Mountainous Karabagh, but there were also reports on fund-raising efforts for Sumgait refugees and the movement's progress in gaining support outside of Armenia. Workplace leaders of the *samizdat* network also funneled charitable contributions and volunteers toward the Karabagh Committee.

Away from the public eye, Igor Muradyan had used the lull in March and April to strengthen his ties with the Demirchyan regime. Somewhere along the way, concluded insiders in the Karabagh movement, Muradyan and the Armenian first secretary cut a deal to permit a new round of demonstrations. For Demirchyan, the crowds represented his last hope to save an otherwise doomed political career. For Muradyan, the demonstrations would serve to renew the pressure on Moscow as the Communist Party conference scheduled for late June approached.

The seventh of May marked the first sign that something had indeed changed. Muradyan assembled nearly 1,000 people in front of the Armenian Academy of Sciences near the Communist Party Central Committee to protest the scheduled arrival of a "friendship train" carrying World War II veterans from Baku. The presence of Viktor Hambartsumyan, head of the Armenian Academy, afforded a guarantee that the police would not interfere. Hambartsumyan assured those gathered that the trip through Armenia had been canceled. Muradyan then turned the crowd's attention to the restrictions against public demonstrations and proposed a mass meeting be held on 12 May to challenge the ban.

On 12 May, the local police were again cooperative. Armenian militia forces surrounded Theater Square late in the afternoon, but there was no effort to stop people from gathering two blocks away in a public park named for Alexander Tamanyan. As the workday ended, 40,000 demonstrators streamed into the rectangle of greenery hemmed in by four- and five-story apartment blocks. Many climbed up the concrete stairway that extended nearly one-quarter of a mile up to Victory Park. Although hooking up the public announcement system to a source of electricity took nearly three hours, the police did not step in to disperse the gathering. Rather, everyone waited patiently until Muradyan had an opportunity to speak. His message had changed little since February, except that he concluded by proposing that no further demonstrations be held until after the party conference.

In the meantime, events were moving too fast for even the most agile of manipulators. On 11 May, Armenians in Stepanakert spilled into the central square to vent their displeasure with Baku's appointment of an Azerbaijani deputy prosecutor for the oblast. On 15 May, Soviet troops intervened to break up a clash between Armenians and Azerbaijanis in the Armenian town of Ararat.[1] The next day, the first trial stemming from the Sumgait massacre concluded with an Azerbaijani locksmith receiving fifteen years in a labor camp.[2]

News of the decision by the Sumgait court sparked gatherings in Armenia and Azerbaijan. In Mountainous Karabagh, Azerbaijani anger was vented toward the Armenian community in the fortress city of Shushi. Within a few days, nearly 2,000 Armenians had left Shushi in response to acts of harassment and intimidation. Most headed a few miles north to Stepanakert, where Azerbaijanis were similarly being made to feel unwelcome.

In Yerevan on 17 May, 50,000 people lined the steps of the Mesrop Mashtots Institute of Ancient Manuscripts (known as the Matenadaran) at the end of Lenin Prospekt. The police made no attempt to intervene. The reaction in Baku to the Sumgait trials was even more dramatic. As local authorities looked the other way, nearly 100,000 people assembled in the Azerbaijani capital on 18 May—the first large gathering in the republic since the start of the Armenian demonstrations. Armenian protesters felt that the sentence was too lenient, while those in Azerbaijan complained that the punishment was unduly severe.

The emotions of Sumgait notwithstanding, 17 May marked a key turning point in Armenia. Without warning, almost without thinking, the Karabagh movement had reemerged. Again, the outpouring had come spontaneously. Unlike February, however, curiosity had not brought the people out. Rather, the crowd of 17 May consisted of the newly politicized. They came with a sense of purpose, a conviction that unfinished business remained in Theater Square. But while politicization had given Armenians initiative, it did not supply them with a sense of direction. After Sumgait, the crackdown in March, and the uneasy respite in April, demonstrators recognized that the rules had changed. The themes sounded from the microphone on 17 May reflected the transition. Most of the speakers chose not to stray from the predictable: opening up the Sumgait trials to the public, the participation of Armenians as judges and prosecutors, the investigation of the Ararat clash. Igor Muradyan, however, did not show up until late in the evening, offering an opening for activists seeking to stretch out the parameters of the movement. For the first time, Ashot Manucharyan broached the issue of popular representation at the upcoming party conference. Levon Ter Petrosyan, Vano Siradeghyan, and others raised the question of democratization in Armenia as well. The Karabagh movement had arrived at a crossroads.

Meanwhile, Karen Demirchyan had come to a dead end. As spring turned to summer, Demirchyan's removal seemed virtually certain. With little to lose, the Armenian first secretary made one final effort to turn the movement to his advantage. For assistance, he drew on the relationship he had established with Igor Muradyan. Following the 17 May demonstration, the pair tried their skills at organizing another rally. Muradyan had no particular interest in salvaging Demirchyan's political career, but he considered the fate of the Armenian community of Shushi crucial. For hundreds of years, the commanding heights of Shushi had been seen as the strategic center of Mountainous Karabagh. Muradyan feared that the expulsion of the city's Armenians would doom efforts to unite the oblast with Armenia.[3]

From Armenian Central Committee headquarters, word spread that a government-sanctioned rally would be held on behalf of Mountainous Karabagh on 19 May. Party and KGB officials bussed in communist stalwarts. Most members of the Karabagh Committee, however, were in no mood to play along. They countered with their own communiqué via Yerevan's grapevine and called on people to stay away.

By evening, there were roughly 30,000 people in Theater Square—hardly the overwhelming show of support Demirchyan had desired. Moreover, a majority of them were not there to prop up Demirchyan. As those gathered milled about, a heated debate took place on the stage of the square. Muradyan wanted to go ahead with the meeting to alert the crowd about the situation in Shushi. Manukyan, however, argued that a rally would lend support to Demirchyan. Most of the other activists sided with Manukyan. Without resolving the dispute, Muradyan announced that he needed to confer with Armenia's KGB chief, Marius Yuzbashyan. Muradyan returned after a few minutes and insisted on speaking before the crowd. Most of his speech drew attention to the persecution of the Armenian community in Shushi, but Muradyan also made statements that undermined his standing within the Karabagh Committee. He maintained that the movement should cooperate with Demirchyan, and belittled those who saw the demonstrations as a vehicle for democratization. Muradyan then fired off a string of insults at the Azerbaijani people and called on Armenians to meet violence with violence in response to Azerbaijani attacks. He went so far as to urge crowd members to arm themselves with iron rods (the most widely used weapons during the Sumgait massacre) and Molotov cocktails to defend Armenian interests, and suggested that atrocities against Armenians in Shushi be countered with eye-for-an-eye revenge. A few in the audience raised clenched fists in support and joined Muradyan in holding a separate rally on Abovyan Street. The great majority in the square, however, answered with boos and whistles.[4]

The events of 19 May were an odd turn for a man of Muradyan's political skills. Since the beginning of the Karabagh movement, Muradyan had been the focus of attention in Armenia and beyond. He was singled out in the Soviet and Western media as a masterful organizer. Behind the scenes, he had lobbied for the economic integration of Mountainous Karabagh and Armenia as a strategic stepping stone toward unification. He had met with Politburo members, reportedly even threatened to seek support from foreign sources, and played political poker with the highest authorities in Armenia. He had dominated the Karabagh Committee with the swagger of a long-time party boss. And, above all, he had let it be known that the ends justified the means, as long as the sole end was Mountainous Karabagh.

Many of the activists around Muradyan had come to resent the approach and philosophy of the Karabagh Committee leader before May. Most unpalatable to Manukyan, Manucharyan, and others was Muradyan's chumminess toward Demirchyan and close association with Yuzbashyan.

The drama of 19 May provided the turning point many activists had been anticipating. Even as Muradyan was shaking his fist at imagined enemies, Manucharyan was on the steps of the opera house urging the crowd to voice their condemnation of Muradyan's message. After the demonstration on 19 May, the most prominent activists of the Karabagh movement assembled at Manukyan's apartment. Manukyan wasted no time in upbraiding Muradyan's leadership. His main point was that the Karabagh movement had evolved into a long-term political struggle, and that Muradyan was ill-suited to be at the helm. Manukyan proposed the formation of a broad-based committee to guide the movement in Armenia. There was no place for Muradyan in his plans.

Most of the others gathered in Manukyan's living room agreed with the assessment. Manvel Sargsyan and Gagik Safaryan, however, were upset by Manukyan's exclusion of Muradyan and the suggestion that the movement's agenda should extend beyond Mountainous Karabagh. Outvoted by their fellow activists, they left the apartment soon after Muradyan. Those who remained established an eleven-member committee.

For at least a few days, the new Karabagh Committee was absorbed primarily in overcoming Muradyan's dominance of the movement. On 28 May at a commemoration of the seventieth anniversary of the battle of Sardarabad twenty miles outside of Yerevan, a list of the committee's membership was circulated among those in attendance. Many in the crowd responded with chants of "Igor, Igor." Muradyan came forward to tersely say that the eleven-member Karabagh Committee would be responsible for organizing demonstrations in Armenia. At the same time, he announced that he intended to form a separate group, *Miatsum* (Unification), to concentrate exclusively on the unification of Mountainous Karabagh with Armenia.

The split between Muradyan and the Karabagh Committee was to remain an irritant for the Karabagh movement in the weeks that followed. Committee members were frequently challenged in Theater Square to justify their break with Muradyan. They often countered by lashing out at Muradyan's imperious style: "The Armenian people don't have a need for a Fuhrer," and "The Karabagh movement without democracy is like a child without his mother."[5] Another speaker unleashed a more chilling accusation:

> Can't you see that Igor Muradyan is a provocateur? For six weeks no one has spoken in the square. The militia were occupying it. Then, suddenly, they open the square. Don't you understand that the powers that be and the KGB are giving him an opportunity to lead you astray?[6]

Accurate or not, the charges punctured Muradyan's credibility. *Miatsum* attracted a small, committed following, but Muradyan did not regain his former stature.

The new Karabagh Committee was something of a misnomer. With the departure of Muradyan, Safaryan, and Sargsyan, not a single member of the group had roots in Mountainous Karabagh. That is not to say that committee members were not devoted to the oblast, but their outlook was fundamentally different from that of Muradyan. Muradyan's purpose had been to create a complement to the *Krunk* Committee of Mountainous Karabagh, uniting the leading sources of power in a single-issue pressure group. Indeed, *Krunk* was a very appropriate model. Within its ranks were seven members of the party committees at the oblast and municipal levels, four oblast and city soviet deputies, twenty-two enterprise and association leaders, and three secretaries of factory party committees. The group's sole purpose was the unification of Mountainous Karabagh with Armenia. Formed a few days before the resolution on unification was passed in Stepanakert, the *Krunk* Committee (or the Committee of Fifty-Five as it was also known) received official registration in Mountainous Karabagh on 5 March 1988.[7] A couple of weeks later, members pushed an endorsement of the 20 February resolution for unification through the oblast party committee.

In contrast to the *Krunk* Committee, the new Karabagh Committee was dominated by a unique breed of intellectual. Most of the eleven members were in their thirties and forties, idealistic, and to a large extent living in a self-imposed exile outside of the corrupt communist system.[8] The amorphous notion of *glasnost*-era democracy commanded the ultimate allegiance of members. They scrapped Muradyan's dictatorial model of organization and in its place adopted a collective approach to decision-making. Within committee meetings, issues were debated, voted on, and the majority view prevailed. Three members—Vazgen Manukyan, Levon Ter Petrosyan, and Ashot Manucharyan—took on leading roles in the committee. Manukyan, a professor of mathematics at Yerevan State University, occupied himself with managing the committee's day-to-day strategy, and at the same time fleshed out the movement's philosophical underpinnings. Syrian-born Ter Petrosyan, a senior scholar at the Matenadaran specializing in Armenian and Syriac philology, served to ground the committee's objectives within the framework of the Soviet constitution and sought to cultivate support for the movement among intellectuals in Armenia and beyond. Manucharyan, a vice-principal at an experimental school in Yerevan and the junior member of the troika, placed the movement at the vanguard of democratic forces in the Soviet Union and articulated the committee's expanded critique of Armenian society.[9]

Manukyan recalled the sense of duty that bound committee members to one another and to a common set of ideals:

> The Karabagh Committee was under great pressure from outside by the people. The pressure was so great that the Karabagh Committee could not break up. I am not talking about the inner atmosphere, which was truly very friendly and cooperative, but the fact that people had put a great responsibility on the committee made a great difference and to break that committee up and quit was tantamount to treachery. That kept us psychologically stuck together.[10]

Together, Manukyan, Ter Petrosyan, and Manucharyan brought with them many of the experiences and attitudes of Armenia's post-World War II generation. For Manukyan and Ter Petrosyan, born in 1946 and 1945 respectively, the crystallizing event of their youth had been the demonstration that took place on 24 April 1965, the fiftieth anniversary of the genocide. Both were university students in Yerevan at the time and were caught up in the flurry of political activity that surrounded the rally. They were part of the informal clusters of young people that came together within the Armenian Cultural Club to hear the personal histories of genocide survivors and to study the turn-of-the-century revolutionary movements.

They were also among the university students who skipped classes on 24 April 1965, marching instead toward Yerevan's Lenin Square and gathering supporters along the way. The student-led procession had swelled to nearly 150,000 by the time it spilled into Theater Square, where a subdued, official commemoration of the genocide was taking place inside the opera house. In addition to hoisting homemade posters calling for recognition of the genocide, members of the crowd raised the issue of Mountainous Karabagh and called for the return of historical Armenian lands in eastern Turkey. A few threw rocks at the windows of the opera house and were countered by fire hoses. Patriarch Vazgen I, catholicos of the Armenian Apostolic Church, was required to appear to quell the protest. The following year, Ter Petrosyan was arrested, along with a few dozen others, for his involvement in political activities. Meanwhile, Manukyan's studies as a graduate student at Moscow State University were cut short when he was expelled for his attempts to organize a commemoration of the genocide.

Although the Brezhnev regime quickly snuffed out the handful of student groups that coalesced in 1965 and 1966, Manukyan and Ter Petrosyan had been baptized into a small circle of young activist intellectuals. The experience marked Manukyan with a deep streak of anti-Soviet, even anti-Russian, sentiment. On the first day of the demonstrations in Yerevan in 1988, he made his views known. Manukyan was not much of an orator, however. A faint voice and his Russian education undercut his ability to sway the crowds in Theater Square. Rather, Manukyan was most effective in the strategy sessions of the committee. Beginning in February, most of them were held at his apartment near the Writers' Union in central Yerevan. There, his training as a mathematician was evidenced in his keen, calculating approach. Even before the formation of the Karabagh Committee in May, his fellow activists looked to him to draft a far-reaching manifesto for the Karabagh movement. Manukyan also brought two of his colleagues from the university, Babgen Ararktsyan and Davit Vardanyan, into the committee. Ararktsyan was a mathematician; Vardanyan taught in the biology department. The three men frequently spent their evenings playing cards together.

Ter Petrosyan drew a different lesson from his student days. As the son of a prominent communist, Ter Petrosyan had grown increasingly disillusioned with the party's program for his people. Instead, he delved deeper into history, developing a special interest in the period that culminated in the short-lived Armenian Republic of 1918–20. Ter Petrosyan's perspective was strongly colored by his family background. As children, his parents had survived the genocide and wound up in refugee camps in Syria. In 1924, Ter Petrosyan's father helped establish the United

Communist Party of Syria and Lebanon. He served in the politburo of the organization through World War II, facing persecution from the French authorities and heading an anti-Nazi guerrilla group. In 1946, a year after Levon was born in Aleppo, the senior Ter Petrosyan and his family repatriated to Armenia, where he was to work in a furniture factory until his retirement.

Ter Petrosyan's status as a repatriate branded him as something of an outsider in Armenian society. Ter Petrosyan was also a relative latecomer to the Karabagh Committee. His first involvement in organizational efforts came in early March 1988, when he helped coordinate efforts to collect signatures from Armenian Supreme Soviet deputies to hold an extraordinary session. (Vital to the assignment was Ter Petrosyan's access to one of Yerevan's few high-quality photocopy machines at the Matenadaran.) At the same time, Ter Petrosyan worked to distribute an open letter written by Rafael Ghazaryan, who had also been arrested in the mid-1960s. Those around Ter Petrosyan, however, realized that he could not have stayed away for long. Ter Petrosyan was a political thinker by nature, and viewed the Karabagh movement as an opportunity to redeem Armenian history. Like Vano Siradeghyan, his frequent companion at the café in the Writers' Union, Ter Petrosyan had a hunger for political conversation. Once he joined the Karabagh Committee, he quickly became a commanding presence.

A decade following the rebellious youth of Manukyan and Ter Petrosyan, Manucharyan similarly collided with state power during his student days at Yerevan State University. Manucharyan, however, channeled his disenchantment with the Soviet system into a renewed commitment to social activism, developing a worldview that extended well beyond Armenia. He was almost a throwback to the self-sacrificing revolutionaries of the nineteenth century—a practical-minded political thinker most in his element when speaking before a crowd of factory workers. Once the movement was underway, Manucharyan steered unswervingly toward confrontation with the authorities.

Other than their time at the university, Manukyan, Ter Petrosyan, and Manucharyan had little organizing experience. Within the original Karabagh Committee, Muradyan's activities in the mid-1980s had established Muradyan as the political tactician of the group. Without Muradyan to give orders, committee meetings took on the tone of a debating society. Manukyan and Ter Petrosyan were the chess masters of political discourse, but the others were quick with their opinions as well. Everything was up for discussion, from the long-term geopolitical position of the Armenian people to Gorbachev's latest economic reforms. Decisions were made by consensus, and only after each member had an opportunity to voice his point of view. The atmosphere was congenial, typically warmed by good humor, although not always productive.

Manucharyan conceded, "We're all children in terms of political experience. But at least we understand that our people can easily become a pawn." [11] The committee also understood how Karabagh had become a code word for everything that was wrong in Armenian life. Environmental pollution, corruption, Russification, mediocre educational standards, economic backwardness—committee members took a look at the range of problems that had come to the fore in February and recast them in the context of the struggle for democracy. Rafael Ghazaryan explained:

> This entire movement began with the desire for a just resolution of the problem of Mountainous Karabagh, but with the first stirrings of Soviet democracy, it immediately grew to encompass a much wider set of questions. This is not just an ethnic conflict between two Soviet republics over a small piece of land. Neither is this some sort of religious struggle between Christianity and Islam, as others have hinted at. We don't agree with the Politburo that our movement is nationalism. We think it is instead a struggle for democracy. We believe that it deepens, rather than undermines, the attempt at reform currently underway. We insist that only this kind of popular movement can really guarantee that the changes taking place now will last, that they won't disappear in the first reaction by those in power who are scared of real change. [12]

Of course, democracy was in vogue throughout the Soviet Union in May 1988. Everyone from Lithuanians advocating independence to communist factory directors pushing for increased production seemed to embrace the notion of democratization. Among the general population in Armenia, the concept was just as vague as elsewhere in the Soviet Union. Karabagh Committee members, however, did not lose their sense of perspective. They believed that the path to democratization in Armenia ran through Moscow. Developments in the Baltic republics were encouraging, but ultimately the fate of democratic reform in the entire Soviet Union depended on the direction of Russia. Thus, in the view of the Karabagh Committee, the movement in Armenia belonged to the broader current of change that was beginning to gather momentum throughout the USSR.

As long as Armenia was in the vanguard, the Karabagh movement had a crucial role to play in defining the meaning of democratization in the Soviet Union. The first step involved a different attitude toward government. Defying the very nature of the communist system, the Karabagh Committee sought to make the governing structure a vehicle for democratic expression. Never mind that every possible avenue toward democracy in the Soviet state apparatus had been systematically blocked off, the committee was prepared to shove the rhetoric of *perestroika* down the government's throat. Second, the Karabagh Committee insisted on conducting the movement as a working model of democracy. Decisions—to strike or not to strike, for example—were to be made in Theater Square. Competing strategies were to be debated before the people. News reports were to be presented at every gathering.

Theater Square, located in the center of Yerevan, was vital to the process of popular democracy. Indeed, the Armenian word for square, *hraparak*, serves as the root for the Armenian equivalent of *glasnost* (*hraparakainutiun*). Moving the mass meetings to Hrazdan Stadium on the outskirts of the city, as the authorities suggested, would have meant shunting the movement to the periphery of Armenian life, in the view of the committee. By late May, the rallies in Theater Square looked like a familiar, albeit distant, cousin of a New England town hall meeting. Democracy was still a new idea in Armenia, but the people at least believed they were putting it into practice.

At a few locations in the republic, democratic ideals had sunk deeper roots. One such place was an experimental grade school on the outskirts of Yerevan that became intimately associated with the Karabagh movement. School #183 was established in a neighborhood that was officially marked as Southwest Massif, but was more commonly referred to as Bangladesh because of its remoteness from the central city. Built during the 1970s and early 1980s to accommodate Yerevan's rapid growth, the area in 1988 was still healing from the bludgeoning scars of the bulldozer. Fourteen-story apartment buildings had been set on bare patches of land, surrounded by the standard allotment of shops, parks, and bus stops. School #183 fit the environment. The complex that opened in 1984 was a boxy, three-story structure, sharing the same exterior of pink tufa stone that characterized the rest of the neighborhood.

Whatever its aesthetic defects, educator Ashot Dabaghyan saw in School #183 a potential paradise. Dabaghyan had been lobbying officials at the Ministry of People's Education for an opportunity to try out some of his ideas in school reform. His chance came in 1984 when he was appointed principal of the "Bangladesh" school at the age of 29. Dabaghyan immediately plunged into a regimen of fourteen-hour days to create a new model for education in Armenia. The stakes were high. Dabaghyan believed that education was the surest route to a democratic and humane society. Within two years, he had persuaded ministry officials to grant the school experimental status, a designation shared by only forty other schools in the Soviet Union at the time. The decision meant Dabaghyan was able to throw open the doors to curricular reform and student democracy. He recruited nearly twenty of his personal acquaintances to serve as teachers and administrators. Most were disaffected doctoral candidates leaving behind prestigious positions at institutes and research centers. For science teacher Alexan Martirosyan, Dabaghyan's promise of freedom was most attractive:

> I had worked at the Physics Institute in Yerevan before but there was no challenge. It was bureaucracy, filling out forms, drinking tea. I got bored, so now I'm here. A different kind of student is growing up in this school. They mature quickly and are more likely to ponder life's big, existential questions. Our relationship is different too, more open, based more on mutual respect and trust.[13]

Dabaghyan had a consistent message for Martirosyan and his colleagues: create your own courses; write your own curricula; try out your own theories. Teachers were responsible for their own success. By 1987, there were 250 applicants for 30 teaching positions, and the school was attracting attention throughout the republic. At the same time, the cafeteria had become an intellectual hub. Over plates of rubbery hot dogs and mashed chickpeas, teachers, administrators, and high school students gathered to debate proposals for changing the course of the Soviet Union and Armenia. As events later proved, the jump from holding bull sessions at School #183 to jump-starting a national reawakening at Theater Square was a short one.

When demonstrations began on 20 February, dozens of teachers and administrators from the school were among the core group of activists who met in Theater Square. Their commitment to democratic reform had already been molded by their common experience at School #183. Until May, they were willing to work under Muradyan's direction. However, a collision was inevitable, and ultimately the philosophy of democratization fostered at the school was the dividing line. The reconstituted Karabagh Committee included four members connected to the school: Ashot Manucharyan, history teacher Samson Ghazaryan, and part-time lecturers Hambartsum Galstyan and Alexander Hakobyan. Dabaghyan, Martirosyan and others were also deeply involved in the movement.

Even before the reorganization of the committee, the staff of the school had already faced challenges presented by their own students. In April, dozens of high schools in Yerevan were hit by student boycotts. Administrators in many schools had forbidden discussion of the Karabagh movement and teachers had been forced to go along with the ban. At School #183, though, the movement was integrated into the daily schedule. Each morning began with a five- to ten-minute high school assembly to inform students of the latest developments. Social studies teachers in particular were encouraged to weave issues raised by the movement into their lesson plans. After the final bell, Karabagh Committee members held secret meetings in classrooms. Representatives from subcommittees based in other workplaces were often invited to analyze government statements, debate strategy, and share information. The seven or eight computers in the school's computer science laboratory served as word processors for many of the committee's broadsheets. Secretaries typed out, with triple carbon, copies of open letters that were circulating in Yerevan.[14]

The symbiosis between the school and the movement was perhaps best personified in Manucharyan. The same age as Dabaghyan, Manucharyan was officially the vice-principal responsible for the civic and moral upbringing of School #183's students. Physically, he had the look of a martyr: a clean-cut, almost boyish face; soft, brown eyes; a gentle smile; and a humble demeanor. Manucharyan had grown up in a well-connected family of teachers in Yerevan and had embraced communism with a sincerity almost unheard of in Armenia. As a student at Yerevan State University, he rose quickly through the ranks of Komsomol, the communist youth organization, and was elected bureau secretary of the university committee in the fall of 1977. Together with Galstyan, Hakobyan, and Dabaghyan (who also held leading positions at the time), Manucharyan planned to democratize the organization. He would later recall his university days as a time of innocence quickly lost. Manucharyan's election had seemed to herald a fresh spirit at the university, and his supporters reveled in revolutionary songs popularized under the Marxist government of Salvador Allende in Chile. Manucharyan pledged that all Komsomol posts at the university would be filled through student elections rather than Central Committee *diktat*.

Manucharyan's confrontation with the communist authorities lasted hardly two months. University Rector Sergei Hambartsumyan and Armenian Komsomol Central Committee First Secretary Haik Kotanjyan (individuals who would later figure prominently in the Karabagh movement) went after members of the forty-person plenum that had chosen Manucharyan, eventually pressuring a majority of them to reverse their decision. Manucharyan was removed from his post. He was allowed to graduate with a degree in physics, but he never reconciled himself with the Soviet system. As one friend recalled, "Ashot in fact believed those ideals and ideas which remained only as phrases within Komsomol."[15]

After failing to gain admittance to the university's graduate program in physics, Manucharyan studied philosophy, history, and sociology, then served in the army. He worked briefly as a researcher at the

Yerevan city soviet, but in 1984 turned to education. Dabaghyan's school was precisely what he had been looking for. To a large extent, Manucharyan was behind efforts to give older students a voice in the administration of the school and to promote a teacher–student relationship based on mutual respect. His weekends were frequently devoted to field trips to historic monuments, while afternoons often found Manucharyan shoulder-to-shoulder with students digging out the basement for a planned recreational facility. In February, he and Ghazaryan invited students from the upper grades to accompany them to Theater Square.

The sudden intrusion of the Karabagh movement was accepted dutifully by Manucharyan. By May 1988, however, the burden of responsibility was becoming heavy:

> There are some who are attracted to the sense of power, others who enjoy the turmoil, but most are just tired and tense. Most don't expect anything positive personally to come out of this movement.[16]

In Manucharyan's case, the Karabagh movement had also contributed to family discord. Manucharyan's uncle was a top official in Yerevan's municipal government and feared that his nephew's prominence in Theater Square would be held against him by his superiors in the party.

If the movement had left Manucharyan troubled and fatigued, Demirchyan could have been characterized as shell-shocked. After failing in May to use the people as a shield, the first secretary was left waiting for the ax to fall. On 21 May the final blow came. Politburo member and Gorbachev ally Alexander Yakovlev arrived in Yerevan to oversee Demirchyan's replacement. Suren Harutiunyan, who had built a career mostly outside of Armenia as a party functionary, was named as the new first secretary. At the same time in Baku, Abdul Rakhman Vezirov, formerly a top Komsomol official and Soviet ambassador to Pakistan, was taking the place of Kyamran Bagirov as Azerbaijani first secretary. Officially, both Demirchyan (age 56) and Bagirov (age 55) were retired for health reasons.

Most Armenians were glad to see Demirchyan go, but the Kremlin's handling of the political reshuffling created a new source of friction. Many were dismayed to see Demirchyan lumped with Bagirov, the official held responsible for the Sumgait massacre. More disturbing, though, were the remarks of Yegor Ligachev, who directed the promotion of Vezirov. During the course of the plenum session in Baku, Ligachev publicly scolded the five Armenian deputies from Mountainous Karabagh and declared the issue of the oblast's unification with Armenia to be closed.[17]

In contrast, Yakovlev had made a point of visiting the genocide monument at Tsitsernakaberd and the Matenadaran, and seemed genuinely sympathetic to the Armenian cause.[18]

With Demirchyan out, the Karabagh Committee had an opportunity to try a new approach in working with Armenia's government. Few expected Harutiunyan to rise above his *apparatchik* background, but, according to the consensus view, he could hardly be as antidemocratic as Demirchyan. On the evening of 25 May, the committee took part in a rally with the new government's blessing at Theater Square. The mood was conciliatory, even syrupy. Balayan, Kaputikyan, and others counseled patience and trust in Harutiunyan's leadership, asserting that the time for demonstrations had passed. The following day, however, a new strain of the movement emerged. A few dozen university students began a sit-in on the steps of the opera house overlooking Theater Square. Their purpose was to protest Ligachev's statement in Baku and to express solidarity with strikers in Stepanakert.

Along with School #183, the university and the Scientific Research Institute for Computing Machines of Yerevan (more commonly known as the Mergelyan Institute) had stood out as focal points of activity. The faculty had largely taken the lead at the university. Students had boycotted classes, but for the most part remained on the periphery of the movement. That changed quickly with the sit-in. By the end of the month, more than 1,000 students were camped day and night on the opera house steps. Volunteers ran a rope a couple of hundred feet to cordon them off from onlookers in the square. The camaraderie among the students was infectious. They wore straw hats or fashioned headgear from the latest issues of *Pravda* and *Izvestia*. Black headbands instantly came into fashion, many bearing the word "Artsakh"—the ancient name for Mountainous Karabagh—in white lettering. The clenched fist salute served as the accepted greeting. During the evenings, guitars accompanied mass sing-alongs. Many students were eager to learn the ballads written in homage to the *fedayeen* of the turn of the century. Some stayed only for the day shift. Others spent their nights on the opera house steps. The most zealous, both men and women, committed themselves to remaining in the square until the Armenian government took up their cause.

Armenian anthropologist Levon Abrahamyan noted that the Karabagh movement had opened a new window onto the world for Armenia's newly politicized youth:

A colleague of mine who was visiting from Moscow was astonished that Armenian teenagers in the [Theater] Square were speaking about human rights, international law, [and] points of the

Soviet constitution while youngsters elsewhere, in other parts of the USSR, were committing acts of hooliganism.[19]

Not since the 1960s had students come together with such esprit de corps. One joke circulating among the students had a mother chiding her son for not getting married. "Can't you find a suitable girl?" she frets. "And where should I find one?" the son replies. "For months now we have all been like brothers and sisters!" [20]

At the same time, the supercharged atmosphere produced another offshoot. On 28 May, a few thousand demonstrators gathered in Theater Square to commemorate the seventieth anniversary of the establishment of the 1918–20 Armenian Republic. The outlawed tricolor of the republic was unfurled by a supporter of Paruir Hairikyan, and a few speakers called for Armenia's independence. Although Vazgen Manukyan had made sure to include an associate of Hairikyan, Samvel Gevorgyan, in the Karabagh Committee, raising the issue of independence clearly conflicted with the group's overall goals.

The following day, Sunday, 29 May, the Karabagh Committee sounded its own themes in Theater Square to usher in a new phase of the movement. The campaign was aimed at the government—specifically at the Armenian Supreme Soviet. Speakers called on the heretofore rubber-stamp legislature to hold a special session on Mountainous Karabagh and endorse the 20 February resolution on unification passed by the oblast's legislature. Without prompting, the crowd of more than 50,000 in Theater Square indicated its choice of weapons, chanting *Gortsadul! Gortsadul! Gortsadul!* (Strike! Strike! Strike!). Kaputikyan appealed once again for patience but was flustered by an outburst of jeering. Manucharyan tried a more innovative approach, suggesting that Theater Square serve as a courtroom for a mock trial to probe official villainy in Moscow, Armenia, and Azerbaijan. Perhaps most hard-hitting, though, was an unpolished worker who said, "Armenians are not bad. It's the system that destroys the people and turns them into animals." [21]

Yerevan was again mobilized. By noon each day, a field of umbrellas had sprouted on the steps of the opera house to shield sit-in participants from the strong Yerevan sun. The ranks of the students increased to 4,000. A contingent of thirteen students decided to take their case closer to the seat of power. They occupied the grounds in front of the Supreme Soviet building for a few hours until police forced them out. "You have Theater Square. Go demonstrate there," the students were told by the deputy chairman of the Supreme Soviet. Instead, they regrouped across the street around the Marshal Bagramyan subway stop, and soon attracted more students to join their sit-in. Their banners made plain their contempt for the authorities: "The Hunger Strike in Theater Square Is the Shame of the Fat Government," and "Wanted: Deputies of the Supreme Soviet." The following day, the mothers of the students who had been evicted from the grounds of the Supreme Soviet rallied a few hundred women for a protest in front of the Central Committee.

On 4 June, five students began fasting under an English-language banner announcing, "We Go On A Hunger-Strike." They were soon joined by two heroes of socialist labor. The group, including one woman, was an apt symbol for the hard-edged determination of the movement. The seven hunger-strikers camped under a canopy tied to the pedestal of the Alexander Spendiaryan monument in the square. They slept on a few grubby blankets, wore bright orange shirts, and tossed aside indifferently the roses and carnations that were offered them. Teary-eyed Armenian matrons, who pleaded with them to end their fast, received the same brusque treatment. In fact, the hunger-strikers imposed their regime of self-sacrifice over the general populace. For as long as their fast continued, eating and smoking in Theater Square were forbidden. Some families even cut back on their meals at home as an expression of moral support.[22]

In the streets, there was a youthful exuberance bordering on the explosive. Crowds of up to 10,000 showed up unannounced at the residences of Supreme Soviet deputies to gain their signatures on a declaration endorsing the unification of Mountainous Karabagh. The names, addresses, and telephone numbers of the deputies were posted on bulletin boards around Theater Square in early June, convincing some of the legislators to seek temporary sanctuary outside of Yerevan. One deputy, well known for accepting bribes, stopped coming home when protestors stationed themselves outside his apartment. Eventually, they found him in his car and confronted him with a declaration. He still refused to sign. Someone in the crowd suggested that he be paid for his signature, and those present responded by showering the deputy with coins and ruble notes. In the end, he signed.[23]

Meanwhile, the numbers at the rallies in the square steadily swelled, surpassing the 100,000 mark by early June. Banners and poster art, often dwelling on the themes of genocide and Sumgait, adorned the walls of the opera house. Theater Square settled into a frenetic routine. The call of a trumpet signaled the beginning of each meeting, followed by one of the theme songs spawned by the movement. Most popular was the plaintive *Who Are They?*, which elicited responses of "Ehh!" from the crowd as the singer played out the answer to the song's title. Another anthem of the movement was *Why Does the River Speak?*—a song from the musical score of an Armenian film based on William Saroyan's play, *My Heart Is in the Highlands*. The performance ended with a series of chants, and then a salute of upraised fists.[24] The Karabagh Committee was forced to serve as a restraining force. Speakers kept their comments subdued so as not to distract attention from the Reagan–Gorbachev summit that took place in Moscow in early June. Rallies began around 6 or 7 P.M. to minimize interference with work schedules. Vazgen Manukyan prepared the crowd for what he foresaw as the inevitable disappointments to come: "When we began this movement, we were all aware that there was little hope." To the insistent chants of *Gortsadul!*, Hambartsum Galstyan reminded demonstrators that a strike was the movement's ultimate weapon and must be thoroughly organized.[25] Many of the students who took the microphone, though, were in no mood for caution. Some tried their hand at theatrical demagoguery. Others sang protest songs they had written. A few voiced the politics of rage, directing their anger at the Soviet state. In a society that had traditionally valued age, the spring of 1988 was a chance for youth to experience the rebellion their counterparts in the West had known twenty years earlier. Something of a generation gap opened up, with young people at the forefront of the boldest and most radical path to change. The Karabagh Committee could barely keep up.

Suren Harutiunyan was also forced to move swiftly. To please Moscow, he made a public appearance with Abdul Rakhman Vezirov on 29 May, first stopping in the Azerbaijani city of Kazakh and then traveling to Ichevan in Armenia. (Vezirov was born in Mountainous Karabagh and spoke some Armenian.) The meeting marked the first time Armenian and Azerbaijani leaders had gotten together in fifteen years. Three days later, in a bow to the popular will, the first secretary addressed the crowd in Theater Square. "I am with you," he assured the gathering, then added, "but I can't work under these conditions." Instead, Harutiunyan called for restoring order in the republic and faith in the central government. The crowd responded with *Gortsadul!*[26]

Harutiunyan had been brought in as a conciliator. And for a few weeks at least he would not be forced to choose between Moscow or Yerevan. For the time being, the Karabagh Committee was more than willing to cooperate with the new first secretary. Unlike Muradyan, committee members pledged to deal with the authorities in the open. The first sign of the new relationship came from the media. Scenes from Theater Square were broadcast nightly along with unfiltered comments from demonstration participants. Newspapers published analyses about the Sumgait massacre, corruption in Armenia, cultural repression in Mountainous Karabagh, and other formerly taboo subjects. Most important was the nightly news of 7 June, when *Lraber* (Messenger) announced that the Armenian Supreme Soviet would consider the Mountainous Karabagh question in an extraordinary session on 15 June.

Although the Karabagh movement remained a struggle between the authorities and the people, developments in June raised hopes that Harutiunyan would listen more closely to Theater Square than to the Kremlin. The reorientation would have marked a historic change of direction. Relative to other non-Russian Soviet republics, Armenia had always been a trusted servant of Moscow. Whereas Russians had dominated the party ranks of many non-Russian republics in the early decades of the Soviet Union, Armenian communists had held sway in their republic from the outset. In return, Armenian communist leaders seldom resisted Moscow's dictates. Indeed, the fate of Armenian First Secretary Aghasi Khanjyan served as a strong argument for loyal obedience.

Mountainous Karabagh, as might be expected, was a different story. Oblast party leaders often took the lead in drawing attention to the plight of Armenians. A number were purged, exiled, or worse. Boris Kevorkov, the oblast's first secretary from 1973 until his dismissal in February 1988, was a striking exception. Kevorkov not only protected Baku's interests in the oblast, but often bent over backwards to suppress the claims of his own people. He banned party functionaries from traveling to Yerevan and stifled cultural and academic exchanges between the oblast and Armenia.[27] In 1977, he told visiting journalists that Karabagh Armenians happily accepted their separation from the Armenian republic.

The history of *Nagorny* (Mountainous) Karabakh is closely interwoven with Azerbaijan's. The region has economic bonds with Azerbaijan, and is especially closely linked with *Nizmenny* (Lowland) Karabakh, a neighboring district inhabited by Azerbaijanians. By contrast, the region is close to Armenia geographically but is separated by high mountains, which were an insuperable barrier [sic] in the past for any extensive contacts.[28]

Kevorkov also went along with Baku's economic neglect of Mountainous Karabagh. Reports were consistently falsified to conceal stagnant production, while scant attention was given to complaints that running water was available to apartment dwellers for only one to two hours daily. When Kevorkov was sacked in 1988, even his party colleagues charged that he relied on "toadies and flatterers."[29] Soon after, he was expelled from the party as well, and moved on to serve as a department chief in the Azerbaijani Ministry of Justice. Kevorkov's replacement as Mountainous Karabagh's first secretary, Henrik Poghosyan, also had his detractors. After all, he had built his career by rising through the Azerbaijani Communist Party. Poghosyan's patriotism, however, could not be questioned, and even his critics within the *Krunk* Committee held him in respect.

Compared to Kevorkov and some of his predecessors in Armenia, Demirchyan had the appearance of a defender of the national heritage when he came to power in 1974. He had a flair for gushing oratory at cultural events and solemnly led 24 April commemorations. But like Kevorkov, Demirchyan well understood that outspokenness on nationalities issues was a sure road to political oblivion. Instead, Demirchyan followed orders from his superiors in Moscow and was given free rein in pillaging the republic's economy. Although not particularly noteworthy by the standards of Transcaucasia, Demirchyan's system of cronyism was singled out for criticism in more than forty articles by the Soviet press during 1987 and 1988.[30]

In June 1987, the Armenian first secretary was mentioned by Gorbachev himself at a Central Committee plenum. A fuller account of Demirchyan's corruption came from one of Armenia's communist insiders, Haik Kotanjyan, at a July 1987 plenum of the Armenian Central Committee. Kotanjyan, first secretary of the Hrazdan district, attacked Demirchyan's role in promoting a "shadow economy," falsifying government reports, and fostering systemic bribery. Describing Armenia's course as "counter-*perestroika*," he called for Demirchyan's resignation.

In December, Kotanjyan again slammed into Demirchyan at a meeting of the Armenian Central Committee. This time he was joined by Sargis Khachatryan, chairman of the party's Commission for Political Control. Khachatryan detailed ties between Armenian law enforcement and the underground economy. Kotanjyan followed by claiming that the situation had worsened since July, and blamed the republic's first secretary for whitewashing or ignoring serious problems. After Kotanjyan left the podium, twenty-four Demirchyan appointees took the rostrum to accuse Kotanjyan of careerism, pseudopatriotism, political adventurism, and schizophrenia.[31] The next month, many of Kotanjyan's charges were repeated in articles that appeared in *Pravda* and *Izvestia*. As for Khachatryan, he was relieved of his duties after rejecting Demirchyan's recommendation that he retire.[32]

Corruption aside, many Armenians would have granted Demirchyan a respectable niche in history if only he had backed the Karabagh movement. Instead, as a statement of the Institute of Philosophy and Law noted, Armenian government officials provided a sharp contrast to their Azerbaijani counterparts. According to the 11 March 1988 statement:

It is interesting that from the very beginning of the demonstrations, the leaders of the [Armenian] republic fell prostrate or were overtaken by a lethargy which grips them up to the present time. Meanwhile, the leaders of the neighboring republic of Azerbaijan made themselves ever more visible by constantly reviling "Armenian extremists" in the local press and on television. [33]

Demirchyan, of course, set the tone—refusing to recognize the concerns of the movement, addressing the demonstrators with patronizing language, declining to express sorrow after the Sumgait massacre. Most other officials, from jaded ministers to career-minded young cadres, cautiously sided with their superiors. Observers outside of government were disappointed but hardly surprised. After the first secretary's removal, Zori Balayan said:

> February 20, Demirchyan could have accepted Karabagh's proposal and become a national hero. Instead he proved himself to be a coward. The fact that our own Armenian government rejected the appeal of their fellow Armenians was a disgrace. We were embarrassed before all the peoples of the Soviet Union, the entire world for that matter.[34]

Demirchyan's performance served to illustrate the gap between the people and the leadership, and strengthened the case for democracy that members of the Karabagh Committee had been making all along. In the words of committee member Rafael Ghazaryan, the movement:

> is all about the right of any people to control their own affairs. Our government is not elected by our people today. It is instead filled with corrupt scoundrels who consistently violate the public trust with illegal methods of rule.[35]

A share of that same revulsion was aimed at the most prominent members of Armenia's intelligentsia. With the exception of Viktor Hambartsumyan, few well-known cultural figures or scientists clearly stood with the crowds in Theater Square during the first months of the Karabagh movement. Even those who were conspicuously present—such as Balayan, Kaputikyan, and actor Sos Sargsyan—were suspect because of their association with the communist system. Others were reproved for not coming forward more promptly. Poet Gevorg Emin, himself censured by Moscow in the 1950s for standing up to overbearing central authority, was subjected to a minute-long gale of piercing whistles when he tried to speak to the crowds for the first time in June.

In an open letter to fellow members of the Soviet intelligentsia, Kaputikyan conceded that Armenian writers had long shunned involvement in the problems of Mountainous Karabagh:

This occurred, first of all, in order to preserve at least the "outer shell" when the friendship of the two peoples was being celebrated in the years of stagnation, and second, because we were meekly fearful that suddenly we would be presented with the above-mentioned accusations [of nationalist agitation].[36]

From the perspective of most Karabagh Committee members, the lukewarm response of the established intelligentsia was yet another example of Armenia's leadership abdicating its proper role. Ashot Manucharyan observed:

In the Baltic republics, for example, it's the professors, the writers, who are out in front on important issues. Here it's the youth in the streets. Our established intellectuals for the most part have not been very outspoken. They praise the leadership, avoid controversy. Look at the Karabagh movement. Again it's the young, people without important positions.[37]

Hambartsum Galstyan's analysis of the generation gap in political attitudes was similar, with the addition of a historical insight:

We don't have a [Hovannes] Tumanyan, a [Paruir] Sevak today to lead our people. Consider how much we've lost: genocide in 1915, purges during Stalin's time, mediocrity, docility and self-serving hypocrisy under Brezhnev. Our older generation still has that Stalinist fear deep within them. Now we have to start over again with a new generation. You see the little kids, five, six years old, chanting "Karabagh, Karabagh." That's something.[38]

For a few days in June 1988, Galstyan and his fellow Yerevanis watched a new generation seemingly grow up before their eyes. The announcement that the Armenian Supreme Soviet would hold an extraordinary session on the Karabagh question opened the most exhilarating week of the movement since February. As never before, there was a belief that the people and the leadership of the republic were moving toward a common purpose.

Evidence came on 11 June when Suren Harutiunyan reported to the crowd at Theater Square on a meeting held in Moscow two days earlier featuring the first secretaries of Armenia, Azerbaijan, and Mountainous Karabagh. On the table was a proposal put forth by Yegor

Ligachev to upgrade Mountainous Karabagh to the status of an autonomous republic. Harutiunyan and Henrik Poghosyan, however, rejected the plan after learning that Mountainous Karabagh's borders would be expanded to include areas populated largely by Azerbaijanis. Harutiunyan also rebuffed an Azerbaijani effort to dismiss Poghosyan as first secretary of the oblast.[39]

Harutiunyan's apparent defense of Armenian interests, as well as his concern over resettling refugees from Sumgait and even a pledge to fast for Mountainous Karabagh, won him the tentative approval of the nearly 100,000 people gathered at Theater Square. Three of the seven hunger-strikers called off their protest in response to the government's new policy. The following evening, they led a column of torch-bearers into the square to dramatize public interest in the 15 June Supreme Soviet session. More than 250,000 demonstrators turned out to back the call for a one-day general strike scheduled for 13 June.

Many of the demonstrators took to the streets of Yerevan Monday morning, 13 June, to make sure the work week did not begin. They concentrated principally on shutting down the public transportation system. Groups of politically minded vigilantes stationed at the subway entrances persuaded passengers to turn back, and then convinced transportation workers inside to quit their posts for the day. University students boarded buses, cable cars, and trolleys to urge drivers to abandon their routes. Others staged sit-ins at Armenia's main airport and blocked the tracks leading out of Yerevan's central railroad station. By mid-morning, Yerevan's factories and stores were almost completely idle. Cities outside the Armenian capital also reported that the strike had succeeded.

Theater Square was once again the focal point of the republic. By noon, 700,000 people had gathered. Marchers from outlying towns entered the square, including one group from Leninakan accompanied by a police escort.[40] A solo trumpet sounded a familiar theme song. At 1:30 P.M., Harutiunyan appeared before the crowd to read a draft resolution endorsing Mountainous Karabagh's unification with Armenia. He assured demonstrators that the Supreme Soviet would also address the Sumgait massacre. His message was more personal than official: "If you can't trust the Central Committee, at least trust me."[41]

Facing Harutiunyan at the rear of the plaza was a huge banner reminding the first secretary of what the crowd in Theater Square expected to see on his political agenda. Five issues were featured: (1) Acceptance of the 20 February decision of the Mountainous Karabagh oblast soviet; (2) Condemnation of Stalin's role in determining the status of Mountainous Karabagh in 1921; (3) Recognition of the Sumgait massacre as an act of genocide; (4) Fair trials by the USSR Supreme Court of those involved in the crimes of Sumgait; and (5) A just decision by the USSR Supreme Soviet on the future of Mountainous Karabagh.[42]

Harutiunyan was followed by popular representatives from dozens of idle factories. Later in the afternoon, five newly discharged veterans of the Afghanistan war mounted the stage and told the crowd that they had chosen to come to Theater Square before returning home. "For killing Afghanis we were hailed as internationalists," one of them remarked. "Now for wishing to defend our homeland we are labeled as nationalists." As evening fell, rumors passed from mouth to mouth that mobs in Baku were threatening Armenian neighborhoods. A report by the Voice of America, later proven false, that eighteen Armenians had been killed rippled ominously through the gathering.

The atmosphere of 14 June was more relaxed. A few work stoppages continued. Crowds milled around Theater Square dissecting the latest news. The following day, the city was quieter still during the morning hours. Nearly the entire population stayed home to watch the televised proceedings of the Armenian Supreme Soviet. Although the prepared speeches were uneventful, debate arose on three issues: the condemnation of the Sumgait massacre; recognition of the 1915 genocide; and an amendment to direct the Mountainous Karabagh question exclusively to the USSR Supreme Soviet, rather than to both Moscow and Baku. As discussion strayed further from the agenda, the broadcast was unexpectedly interrupted at 12:30 P.M. Within minutes, 50,000 people converged on the legislative building. MVD soldiers bearing plastic shields and truncheons formed a human wall in front of the building. A two-hour confrontation ensued, punctuated by shouts of "Take away the soldiers!" and "Fascists!" Deputies periodically emerged from the legislative chamber to calm the crowd. Finally, the troops were replaced, trotting as they left, by a few dozen Armenian policemen. An hour later, the mood turned festive as people learned that the session had largely accepted the popular agenda. One hundred thousand people joined in an impromptu celebration in Theater Square. One speaker declared, "We will mark this date in the future as a victory for the Armenian people." Others urged that the movement seek to pressure the government on such issues as ecological problems, the danger of nuclear energy, and corruption.[43]

That evening, *Lraber* reported the session's official decisions. As expected, the Armenian Supreme Soviet endorsed the 20 February decision of the Mountainous Karabagh oblast soviet, citing article 70 of the USSR constitution as guaranteeing the right of self-determination for all nations. The legislature addressed its appeal exclusively to the USSR Supreme Soviet and, in a separate resolution, condemned the crimes that took place against Armenians in Sumgait.[44]

Ultimately, the impact of the Armenian Supreme Soviet's resolutions was hardly felt outside the republic. For the moment, though, the people reveled in the fact that they had forced the government to act in their name. In the process, many had convinced themselves that they could play a role in charting the course of events. Yerevan went back to work on 16 June with rare enthusiasm. Many factory workers volunteered for weekend shifts to meet production quotas. In Theater Square, the four remaining hunger strikers had cleared away their makeshift campsite, while participants in the student sit-in picked up scraps of paper, cigarette butts, and other litter. Activist Hrair Ulubabyan looked back over the first four months of the movement and saw the beginning of a national metamorphosis: "This movement has cleansed our people. Tomorrow they may extend this new consciousness to Sumgait refugees, next to all Armenians, and eventually the entire world."[45]

Even as Armenians rejoiced, however, there was reason for concern. The action of the Armenian Supreme Soviet had in fact only formalized the republic's impasse with Azerbaijan. Two days before the Armenian decision, the presidium of the Azerbaijani Supreme Soviet had declared Mountainous Karabagh's resolution on unification "unacceptable." On 17 June, the Azerbaijani legislature officially rejected Armenia's resolution. The report by the chairman of the Azerbaijani Supreme Soviet, S. B. Tatliyev, was adamant:

> In the course of discussion in the [Azerbaijani Supreme Soviet] Presidium, the opinion was expressed unanimously that the question of Nagorno Karabakh has been raised without justification, contrary to the preservation of the historically existing unity of the whole of Karabakh, an age-old Azerbaijani land, without consideration of the interests of citizens of all nationalities living in the oblast, and contrary to the wishes of the majority of the republic's population.[46]

The conflict was now within the domain of the USSR Supreme Soviet, and there was little to indicate that the issue would be resolved in favor of the Armenians.

Meanwhile, Armenian–Azerbaijani tensions boiled over in Masis, a town of 10,000 residents with a substantial Azerbaijani population located ten miles south of Yerevan. Clashes between the two groups on 18 June left eight Armenians and eight Azerbaijanis injured.[47] A week later, forty-five Armenian women in the area were hospitalized as a result of a gas leak in a textile factory. Local Armenians immediately placed the blame on Azerbaijani saboteurs.[48]

In Mountainous Karabagh, the 15 June decision of the Armenian Supreme Soviet was cause for pressing ahead with the campaign for unification. The demonstrations and strikes continued until 26 June, when party leaders and factory directors persuaded the crowds in Stepanakert to temporarily halt their protests in anticipation of the Nineteenth Party Conference. Moreover, the oblast's soviet on 21 June called on the USSR Supreme Soviet to administer Mountainous Karabagh until the resolution of its status.[49]

  As attention shifted toward the opening of the party conference on 28 June, Armenian hopes rested on an unlikely collection of prospective national heroes. The republic's representatives to the conference had been chosen in typical pre-*perestroika* fashion a month earlier— fifty-one delegates nominated for fifty-one positions. Most were cronies of Karen Demirchyan. As they left Yerevan for Moscow, at least a few wry observers could not help but note that Armenia's former first secretary had left his people with a fitting going-away present.

Chapter 6

Collision

*S*ummers in Yerevan are hot and dry, with temperatures often topping 100 degrees and afternoon breezes kicking up sheets of powdery dust. During the Soviet era, many Yerevan residents took advantage of the summer lull to escape the grit and pollution of the city and renew their bonds to village life in the republic.

Most Yerevanis were no more than a generation or two removed from peasant roots, and almost all had relatives happy to share with them the pleasures of the countryside. Shish kebab (known as *khorovadz* in Armenia and typically made from pork rather than the traditional lamb) would be roasted over open fires fueled by the stumps of grape vines. Young children learned the secrets of baking the thin unleavened bread called *lavash* against the sides of cylindrical ovens built into the earth. Summers also gave city folk a chance to lend a helping hand on individual plots of farmland. Gardens of up to two or three acres were meticulously tended. Weeds were plucked, pebbles sifted out, the soil kneaded with composted leaves and barnyard manure. In the lowlands, the first cucumbers were ready for picking by June. Tomatoes, peppers, eggplants, Jerusalem artichokes, red onions, and okra were not far behind. Fresh vegetables were pickled and canned for the coming winter. Fruits were stewed to make compote or simmered to a thick paste and spread flat to dry into sweet, gooey sheets.

The summer of 1988 found much of Yerevan retreating as usual to the countryside. The indolence of past seasons, however, was slow in coming. Even after the 15 June session of the Armenian Supreme Soviet, swarms of aspiring kremlinologists buzzed around Theater Square with the latest open letters and *samizdat* broadsheets. Khachik Stambolt-

95

syan, a tireless activist distinguished by a tangle of unruly, salt-and-pepper hair that barely left room for a pair of dark, penetrating eyes collected signatures after work each afternoon for popular nominations to the upcoming party conference. Calls for an investigation into the alleged poisoning of forty-five women in Masis were tacked onto the snowballing list of Armenian demands. Rumors about the conference's anticipated pronouncements on Mountainous Karabagh jolted the city with the energy of the afternoon thunderstorms that occurred with uncommon regularity into early July 1988.

Thus, when the Nineteenth All-Union Conference of the Communist Party came and went with hardly a mention of Mountainous Karabagh, Armenians were left feeling neglected. Never mind that senior party officials had already made it known that the constitutional impasse put the Karabagh question within the domain of the Supreme Soviet, Armenians were expecting at least a few sympathetic words for their troubles. What they received was Gorbachev's most damning rebuke of the movement to date. In his opening speech on 28 June, the general secretary accused Armenians of taking advantage of "democratic rights for anti-democratic purposes." Gorbachev went on to rule out demands for "the recarving of frontiers." "The Central Committee of the party," he added, "believes that such abuses of democratization radically contradict the tasks of *perestroika* and go against the interests of the people." [1]

Gorbachev's remarks on the Karabagh movement hurt all the more because they were largely forgotten in the course of the free-wheeling debate that continued for more than four days. In the end, the conference was viewed as a watershed event for non-Russian peoples. Not since the 1920s had non-Russian party leaders spoken so frankly on the abuses of central planning and pressed so openly for greater autonomy in the republics. The resolution on the national question adopted by the conference pushed decentralization along faster than Gorbachev had likely intended. [2]

Amid the tumult, Suren Harutiunyan's speech on 29 June hardly stood out. The Armenian first secretary characterized the "extremist" label often pinned to the Karabagh movement as "painfully offensive to national feelings," but otherwise analyzed the oblast's problems largely in the context of *perestroika*:

It was precisely the anti-democratic practice of suppressing information and showing indifference, the desire to brush aside the acute and complex problems that actually exist, and attempts to drive them underground or to resolve them by authoritarian methods, that have led to such an explosive manifestation of them today. [3]

Both Harutiunyan and Azerbaijani First Secretary Abdul Rakhman Vezirov agreed that Moscow should play a greater role in resolving the conflict. Two Armenian delegates, Yerevan State University Rector Sergei Hambartsumyan and Literature Institute Director Edward Jrbashyan, offered more specific proposals at a separate press conference. As a step toward resolving the dispute, they suggested linking Mountainous Karabagh either to the Supreme Soviet, the Russian SFSR, or the Stavropol region in the North Caucasus.[4]

The sting of the party conference did not last long in Armenia. Expectations quickly shifted toward the upcoming session of the Presidium of the USSR Supreme Soviet. The meeting was originally scheduled to take place on 5 July—sixty-seven years to the day after the Caucasian Bureau had placed Mountainous Karabagh under the jurisdiction of Azerbaijan—but was postponed to 18 July.

Back in Yerevan, many of the young people who were veterans of the sit-ins and marches of a month earlier were too impatient to bother viewing the televised proceedings of the party conference. The day following Gorbachev's opening speech, groups of 200 to 300 protesters roamed the streets of the city chanting *Hai-er Mi-a-tsek!* (Armenians Unite!). On the evening of Sunday, 3 July, 100,000 people assembled in Theater Square largely to vent their displeasure with the party conference. *Gortsadul!* (Strike!) was the immediate rallying cry. The rationale of the Karabagh Committee for backing a strike was more refined than the logic of the young demonstrators. With the Presidium of the Supreme Soviet initially scheduled to consider the Mountainous Karabagh question on 5 July, Karabagh Committee members hoped that a general strike would send a message to Moscow that Armenia was united. Student demonstrators needed little prompting. If anything, they favored still more dramatic tactics to make Armenia's voice heard.

Although a few of the speakers suggested that a strike be postponed until more concrete objectives were defined, in the end the decision was put to the crowd in Theater Square. The clenched fists shot up in near unanimity.

The youth in the streets had come of age in an era of rising expectations. Economically, the Soviet Union had peaked out in the mid-1970s, but the creeping stagnation had not dampened the desire for better material conditions. On the contrary, the first Soviet generation to grow up without hunger increasingly used the prosperous consumer societies of the West as a yardstick. In Armenia, the mid-1970s saw emigrants leaving on a large scale to the United States for the first time. Of the more than 37,000 who emigrated from 1975 to 1981, enough came back as visitors bearing samples of the good life to fuel impatience for change.

Besides being spared from hunger, the younger generation was also not haunted by memories of Stalinism. Survivors of Stalin could hardly help but be psychologically scarred from living under one of history's most repressive regimes. For many of them, speaking out against the communist system was unimaginable. Moreover, the paranoia and warped sense of human nature that permeated Stalin's Soviet Union were passed down to the children of the 1950s and 1960s. Armenia's political fault lines corresponded closely with Stalin's legacy, and in turn colored perceptions of Gorbachev's reform efforts. Among the older generation, the choice was between moderate *perestroika* or a return to the 1930s. Fear was too deeply embedded to conceive of asking for more than what the government was willing to give. For the youth, though, the choice was between Gorbachev and Andrei Sakharov. In their minds, the Stalinist past was dead and the path was open toward a future of liberal, Western-style democracy.

The Karabagh Committee straddled the generation gap. Of the eleven members, six were born before 1950. Even those in their mid-thirties could not entirely escape the influence of Stalin. Most expected that the government would eventually lash out against them. Some considered prison a likely destination. Nonetheless, most committee members believed that there were limits to state repression in the Soviet Union of the late 1980s. In May, Ashot Manucharyan claimed:

> Five years ago this would have been impossible. Now broad repression is not possible. The world is watching. A standard has been established. Of course, there's still a danger of persecution and arrest, but as things got underway [in February], the fear diminished. I really don't worry about it anymore.[5]

For many of the protesters ten to fifteen years Manucharyan's junior, fear was even less of a concern. On 4 July, they made sure that the work week began without public transportation, forcing many of Yerevan's major factories to shut down their production lines early in the morning. As the strike spread, Yerevanis poured into Theater Square.

The tone of the meeting that afternoon picked up not far from where the crowd had left off three weeks before. A few of the party conference delegates reported on the decisions of the gathering, hoping to convince the crowd that a settlement was in the works. Their emphasis on patience, however, was spurned by many. Instead, the sentiment in Theater

Square seemed to favor broadening the strike. Already, news had arrived that one of fifteen departments at Armenia's Zvartnots Airport had stopped work. A few voices in the crowd called on protesters in the square to join in closing down the airport.

Karabagh Committee members had hoped that a strike at the airport would break through what they viewed as a Kremlin-orchestrated information blockade against the movement, but they recognized the danger of a mass convergence on Zvartnots. Rumors of an impending crackdown in Armenia had again been circulating, and many feared that a disturbance would be contrived at a site of union-wide military and economic significance. Committee members called for order from the microphone. The appeal to head for the airport was labeled a "provocation." Nonetheless, six buses suddenly appeared to transport a few hundred demonstrators for the eight-mile trip to Zvartnots. By evening, the airport had in fact been shut down. Karabagh Committee members and Armenian officials negotiated with protesters and striking airport workers through much of the night but failed to establish an atmosphere of trust. Meanwhile, volunteers showed up to house the women and children who were among the stranded passengers for the night.[6]

When talks resumed the next morning, protesters offered to end their strike after six hours if the Soviet newscast *Vremya* agreed to cover the story in Armenia. While discussions were still underway, a squad of MVD troops trained in riot control suddenly entered the departure lobby armed with truncheons and shields. An *Izvestia* correspondent later recalled that the protesters were hardly prepared for a confrontation. Instead, they responded with mock applause and continued their sit-in.[7] The helmeted troops were under orders to clear the building. Their commander demanded that the crowd disperse within thirty seconds. The troops charged even before the deadline elapsed, swinging their truncheons at protesters and passengers alike. Within minutes, they had accomplished their mission and were flown out on a waiting plane.

With the MVD unit gone, cadets from the Ordzhonikidze Militia Academy were left to contend with the rapidly overheating crowd that had assembled outside the airport building. Hundreds had come by foot from the city that morning. As the cadets tried to force the new arrivals back to the main road, a few in the crowd reacted by throwing rocks and bottles. At the same time, a military guard truck driving along Echmiadzin Road found itself trapped by the retreating mob. The driver of the truck found sanctuary in a nearby house, but a corporal shot into the crowd and killed a 22-year-old veterinary student, Khachik Zakaryan. Ironically, Zakaryan had brought along his camera to document MVD abuses.[8]

Yerevan was by now a city nearing hysteria. News of the troop actions at the airport terminal reached the city within minutes. Calls for a mass march to the airport drowned out a rally in Theater Square by the Union for National Self-Determination. In response to the rising anger, the organizers of the demonstration advised the crowd to wait for the return of Karabagh Committee members from the airport. They also temporarily unplugged the microphone at the speaker's platform.

The first committee member to appear in the square was Rafael Ghazaryan. Although visibly shaken, he reported that nothing serious had taken place at the airport, only a few bloody noses. He urged people to go home.[9] Much of the crowd did indeed disperse, but calm could not be so quickly restored. The injured from the airport confrontation, many bearing streaks of dried blood from scalp wounds, soon began arriving at the square on their way to the hospital. Cars racing back down Echmiadzin Road brought news about the shooting of Zakaryan. Some protesters warned that the army was readying to march on the city. Without the Karabagh Committee to offer guidance, a few Yerevanis took matters in their own hands. Bus drivers parked their vehicles across Lenin Prospekt to block the expected advance of armored personnel carriers. On Echmiadzin Road, Armenian police stood shoulder-to-shoulder with demonstrators for the first time and formed a human barricade. Meanwhile, cars sped through the central city with horns blaring.[10]

The attack on Yerevan never took place. Rather, troops quietly moved into the city during the early morning hours of 6 July and surrounded Theater Square. In contrast to the army occupation in March, the MVD forces took a decisively menacing stance. Stationed a few feet apart around the perimeter of the square, the soldiers stood three deep. The first row was unarmed; the second row carried truncheons and shields; and the third held automatic rifles. In the square itself, a few tanks were visible. Yerevan showed a different face as well. Instead of young women offering carnations, the soldiers faced a human wall of angry protesters. Hundreds of cars circled the square—black flags of mourning tied to radio antennas and headlights faintly glowing under the July sun. Horns sounded until late in the evening, forcing many of the troops to stuff cotton into their ears. Homemade placards were written in Russian for the benefit of the MVD forces: "Army, Go Home!" and "Get Out of Yerevan!" Opposite the square, roses dangled from black streamers that had been hung from tree branches. Women wore black kerchiefs. A half dozen students circled aimlessly within the walls of a makeshift prison they had fashioned by stacking up the standard works of Marxism–Leninism.[11]

The MVD troops around Theater Square gave way to Armenian police on 7 July, but the airport incident remained at the center of Yerevan's thoughts. The funeral of Khachik Zakaryan, the student who had been shot on Echmiadzin Road, was scheduled as a public event. Torch-bearers led a silent procession from the city center to the Zakaryan residence in the Shahumyan district. Armenian police permitted the marchers to enter Theater Square with the open casket before continuing down Lenin Prospekt. Thousands of onlookers lined the sidewalks, raising clenched fists as the procession passed. In delivering the eulogy, Khachik Stamboltsyan tried to draw those present away from their immediate rage. "I do not ask you to have peace in your hearts," he said, "although maybe peace is what we most need. I ask you to keep faith that we will find peace in another world. We will not despair and we will not let bitterness enter our hearts." [12]

Stamboltsyan's message, however, could not reverse the sudden swing toward anger. The student sing-alongs on the steps of the opera house and the republic-wide celebration on 15 June were all but forgotten. Zori Balayan remarked on the tidal shift in Armenian attitudes: "Five thousand people buried one person. Some say our people are used to spilling much blood. Now they won't forgive a drop of blood." [13] Adding to the popular wrath were the Soviet media's efforts to brand the airport incident as an example of the violence generated by the Karabagh movement. Officially, 5 July had produced injuries among three cadets and thirty-six civilians, including twelve women. Newspaper reports, however, led readers to believe that protesters inside the airport terminal had put up fierce resistance to MVD troops and jeopardized public safety. [14] Interviews with passengers left stranded by the protest took a different angle toward swaying mass opinion. One tour leader complained on Soviet television that her group of thirty children had been sleeping on the floor and going without hot meals for two days. [15]

Most damning, though, was an unscheduled twenty-five minute documentary that followed the *Vremya* newscast on 14 and 15 July. The broadcast consisted entirely of interviews with soldiers involved in the airport incident. Again, the protesters were blamed for sparking the clash inside the airport by throwing rocks and bottles at troops. One cadet commented on the bitter attitude of Yerevanis, noting, "Now we cannot talk to people, little children throw stones at us." The documentary also featured a mountain of knives, axes, and chains that had been confiscated at roadblocks set up around Yerevan since 4 July. [16] While an officer cadet claimed that some of the weapons were found at the airport itself, no mention was made of the fact that almost all the items were farm tools and kitchen utensils. Indeed, the roadside inspection teams had taken shish kebab skewers and meat cleavers from Yerevanis en route to weekend picnics in the countryside.

Although Armenians did not have an opportunity to set the record straight before an all-union audience, local television at least provided an incontrovertible illustration of the central media's distorted coverage. *Vremya* had aired an interview with a passenger from Tallinn who had been a witness to events at Zvartnots on 5 July. Queried about his reaction, he replied that he had "never dreamed of witnessing such scenes in the Soviet Union." Later, the complete interview was replayed on Armenian television, revealing that the passenger had finished his sentence by adding, "that Soviet soldiers could beat up completely defenseless people like that." [17]

Even without viewing the unauthorized footage, the vast majority of Armenians had accepted the airport incident as another morality play. Among the Karabagh movement's most ardent participants, 5 July became known as "Bloody Tuesday." Khachik Zakaryan joined the victims of the Sumgait massacres as a martyr of the cause. In cities across Armenia, black flags of mourning were hoisted by pairs of standard bearers keeping vigil over his memory. At the conclusion of Zakaryan's funeral, more than 200,000 mourners swept into Theater Square to review a new genre of placards: "*Perestroika* through Fascism," "Murderers Out of Armenia!" and a hammer and sickle transmogrified into a swastika.[18]

For the next ten days, the Karabagh movement was gripped by rage. The crowds heard references to "fascist S.S.," the "army of occupation," and simply the "generals."

The truth was that the Karabagh Committee had been backed into a corner after the airport incident. Politically, the issue of Mountainous Karabagh had run up against opposition in the Kremlin. Psychologically, the movement had been sapped by the one-two punch of the party conference and Zvartnots. Many in Theater Square assumed that a broader crackdown would follow and that popular leaders would soon be arrested.

With their faith in *perestroika* shaken, even members of the Karabagh Committee were caught up in the emotions of the moment. A committee communiqué went so far as to charge Suren Harutiunyan with implementing Moscow's orders to crush the movement. In Theater Square, Hambartsum Galstyan promised to reveal the names of the two MVD generals responsible for the Zvartnots clash. "This is the same army that has been committing genocide in Afghanistan," he added.

Committee member Vano Siradeghyan informed the crowd on 8 July that officials from the Yerevan Communist Party committee and the prosecutor's office had insisted on presenting their views in Theater Square. Siradeghyan contended that their intent was to provoke panic within the gathering by announcing that soldiers were approaching. That evening, the Armenian Ministry of Internal Affairs reported that a city official, H. Grigoryan, had been beaten in the square after Siradeghyan's accusations. The statement went on to say that Theater Square would be closed, and, sure enough, MVD troops were back in their positions surrounding the square the next morning.[19]

The shutdown of Theater Square marked a shift for the demonstrations, both physically and attitudinally. With respect to location, the meetings moved to the Matenadaran on 10 July and began attracting nightly turnouts that stretched four or five blocks down Lenin Prospekt. As for the message, Ashot Manucharyan came forward to place the goal of a democratic revolution at the top of movement's agenda. Although at odds with those who framed the Armenian cause as a national liberation struggle, Manucharyan's assault on the Soviet system and his critique of the forces arrayed against the movement in Moscow, Baku, and in particular Yerevan, nonetheless won popular approval. As for style, Manucharyan's approach was oddly dispassionate: a soft, controlled voice that seldom rose above the level of a living-room conversation; language meant to elucidate rather than inflame; fast-paced and engaging analysis not unlike the classroom lectures given by Manucharyan at School #183.

"How many of you," he asked one gathering, "have heard that ministers' positions are up for sale in our republic?" Manucharyan's query was met by a mass of upraised hands that extended nearly a quarter of a mile. Rather than stop at condemnation, though, Manucharyan implanted the notion of an alternative.

> [Boris] Yeltsin asked the party conference where our party dues go. They go to salaries for party officials, for special hospitals and special stores for them and their families and for vacations abroad. Party workers should be working out of concern and dedication to their society, not for personal benefit. Let us be the first republic to eliminate salaries and privileges for party workers. We will be willing to pay many times the present dues from our monthly salaries if we know the money is being used for social welfare programs.[20]

With the same plain-spoken understanding of the Soviet Union's fundamental flaws, Manucharyan extinguished a surge of anti-Russian feeling that emerged after the airport incident. From the microphone, he implored, "Don't allow this to kindle a hatred of Russians. This wasn't done by the Russians. This was done by the powers that be. Power doesn't have nationality."[21] Manucharyan also made sure that a Russian eyewitness to events at Zvartnots, S. Frolov, was given an opportunity to speak on behalf of his people on 8 July. Frolov, an engineer from Leningrad, confirmed reports that MVD troops had attacked the protesters inside the airport without warning and then noted the shame he felt as a Russian in light of the violence.[22] The comments of Frolov and Manucharyan went a long way toward defusing tensions in Armenia. In Frolov's case, however, reports soon appeared in the Soviet press that the engineer was being charged with economic crimes. Manucharyan also paid a price for his outspokenness. In mid-July, he was expelled from the Communist Party.

For anyone who asked, Manucharyan had always described himself as "a real communist," meaning that he was attracted to the ideology's promise of a better world rather than the party's monopoly of the Soviet career ladder. From his position in the Karabagh Committee, he was bound to butt heads with the Yerevan *apparat.* When the party moved to revoke his membership, Manucharyan was prepared to strike back. At a gathering of nearly 300,000 on 16 July, he laid out in detail his program for democratizing Armenia's political life:

> I have no place in a party that shares the ideas of this leadership. If the majority of the party is honest and good, let's work together to kick out the scum. . . . Armenia should be the first republic with fifteen or so Central Committee members, and with the rest of the party workers being unpaid volunteers. . . . The question here is not only about Karabagh, we must take note of the great power of our enemies.[23]

Manucharyan then went on to suggest mechanisms for building democracy in the republic from the bottom up. He urged worker collectives to elect responsive representatives, who in turn would be able to remove corrupt directors from their positions. Unity within the labor force would deprive officials of their usual methods of intimidation: job dismissal, denial of housing rights, and arrest. Manucharyan also believed that the popular pressure directed against the Armenian Supreme Soviet in June could be applied to other governmental bodies as well. He proposed that local collectives call on the Yerevan city soviet to press for the withdrawal of troops from the city. Inaction on the part of the authorities, Manucharyan recommended, should be met with recall movements aimed at individual deputies and a demand for new elections. Manucharyan noted the case of Armenian Supreme Soviet Deputy Vazgen Harutiunyan, who had been recalled by a vote of the Physics Institute in early June but had yet to be removed from office. The legislature's unwillingness to confirm the recall decision, Manucharyan said, was reason for insisting on an extraordinary session. Looking ahead to fall elections for the Armenian Supreme Soviet, Manucharyan saw an opportunity to enlist the ballot box in

the cause of democratic change. "No scum" became shorthand for rejecting self-serving *apparatchik*s.[24]

Electoral democracy in Armenia, however, remained a
tool for tomorrow. For the moment, the labor strike that began 4 July was
the weapon of popular choice to spur change. Originally, the strike had
been conceived as a signal to Moscow in anticipation of the Presidium
session on Mountainous Karabagh. After the airport incident and the
army's occupation of Theater Square, Armenians felt they had something to
protest that went beyond symbolism. During the ten days that followed
Zvartnots, many of the largest factories in the republic were shut down. The
strike was far from total—food processing and health care operated nor-
mally, and the Karabagh Committee funneled donations to those hurt by
the work stoppages—but aimed at plants plugged into the Soviet military-
industrial complex. Just as the Kremlin portrayed the problem of Mountainous Karabagh as an economic issue, so the movement would pull
economic levers to make its point.

The Karabagh Committee had learned from its experi-
ence in June that the solidarity of the public transport workers was crucial
to the strike's effectiveness. On 7 July, the support of bus, cable car, and
trolley drivers was almost unanimous. In addition, workers in the subway
system refused to collect tolls. The authorities, of course, were also quick
to recognize that the main battleground of the strike was public transportation. Within a few days, they had posted MVD soldiers aboard the most
heavily traveled bus lines in Yerevan. Transport workers reported that they
were being threatened with the loss of their jobs and apartments unless
they returned to work.[25]

Television also served the government's cause. On the
evening of 7 July, Silva Kaputikyan and Patriarch Vazgen I, catholicos of
the Armenian Apostolic Church, spoke on behalf of restoring public order.
The catholicos, who had disappointed many Armenians by his reticence
during the early weeks of the Karabagh movement, raised the specter of
massacre in urging allegiance to the Soviet state:

> I have heard during recent days some have resorted to extreme
> antistate and anti-Soviet expressions, the consequences of which
> could—God forbid—offer Armenia on a platter to our centuries-old
> enemy. I do not want to believe that such persons exist. . . . If you do
> not listen to me—your patriarch—I will curse my destiny and remain
> silent until eternity.[26]

Suren Harutiunyan and Viktor Hambartsumyan later is-
sued their own televised appeals to end the strike. Noting the upcoming

session of the Presidium of the Supreme Soviet on the Mountainous Karabagh question, Harutiunyan reported on a meeting he held with Gorbachev
following the party conference and lauded the "warmth and good will on
the part of Mikhail Sergeyevich [Gorbachev] toward the Armenian people." [27] Following Harutiunyan's lead, the Armenian Supreme Soviet Presidium called on the USSR Supreme Soviet to resolve the Karabagh
question.

The government's position aside, there were grounds for
debating the wisdom of the strike. To justify their tactics, strike organizers
had held up Armenia as a model for demonstrating the power of the people.
Manucharyan presented the rationale at an 11 July rally:

> The significance of our strike is not economic. The Soviet
> Union is used to losing billions of rubles due to waste and corrup-
> tion. Our strike is of political significance for all peoples of the
> Soviet Union and the socialist bloc in general. Our people has served
> as an example for other peoples in the Soviet Union and Eastern
> Europe. If you've followed the news, following our movement there
> has been a great surge of democratic movements in the Baltic repub-
> lics, Poland, East Germany, and Hungary.[28]

In rebutting Manucharyan, many argued that Armenians
had stuck out their necks too far. First Secretary Harutiunyan calculated
that the strike cost 93 million rubles ($157 million at the official exchange
rate in 1988) in lost production.[29] Not since the bloody first years of
agricultural collectivization in the early 1930s had the Soviet command
economy faced such widespread defiance. And yet, the strikers expected
that the same central authorities ordering Armenians back to work would
eventually accede to their demands on Mountainous Karabagh. Even Karabagh movement activists questioned the logic. Rafael Ghazaryan, for example, considered the work stoppages a mistake.

Law school professor Vladimir Nazaryan feared that the
strike flew in the face of the movement's efforts to place the Karabagh
issue on solid legal ground. Nazaryan, who in early June had framed the
question of the oblast in the context of the constitutionally guaranteed right
to self-determination, told a journalist from *Argumenty i fakty* a month
later that the strike was counterproductive:

> The organizers of these measures seem to see some connection
> between their actions and the normal work which is underway on this
> question at various levels of state power. It is true that strikes have
> coincided with the adoption of specific decisions at times. From this

the conclusion was drawn that it was all thanks to the strikers. However, in reality such a cause-and-effect relation does not exist.[30]

Nazaryan was perhaps overplaying the likelihood of the Karabagh movement's success. Simply put, Moscow was not about to back the cause of the Karabagh Committee under any circumstances. On 8 July, ten days before the session of the Supreme Soviet Presidium was set to convene, Politburo member Alexander Yakovlev told an Italian newspaper that at best Mountainous Karabagh might receive greater autonomy.[31] Even before Yakovlev's statement, the Karabagh Committee had expected little in the way of good news to come from Moscow. Committee members had in fact been regularly briefed by Suren Harutiunyan's office since June and were given advance notice of the Presidium's decision. They moved to defuse another potential confrontation. On Sunday, 17 July, committee members won agreement from a crowd of 300,000 to call off the strike and schedule the next rally for 19 July. Vazgen Manukyan predicted that the Presidium session would not do more than "make promises to set up committees." Forecasting another let-down, he explained that the Karabagh Committee sought to "avoid taking decisions under the sway of emotions." That same evening, MVD reinforcements arrived at Zvartnots airport.[32]

Although an end to the strike represented a truce offer on the part of the Karabagh Committee, the Soviet press was in no mood for peace. As Armenians were going back to work, the central newspapers were running articles condemning their strike as selfishly insensitive to the well-being of other Soviet workers. In Belorussia (present-day Belarus), a trade union official at a factory making heat generators complained that the plant's production had been stalled by the failure of a factory in Armenia to deliver motors:

> Do people there, in Yerevan, really not realize that we have no other source of earnings? The impression is created that Yerevan workers are not suffering as we do. Otherwise how can we explain this frivolity—strikes in plants?

Other articles pointed out what the strike organizers considered their primary source of leverage, namely that the interconnected nature of the Soviet economy meant that hundreds of factories throughout the country were dependent on components made in Armenia.[33] Indeed, Yerevan was a center for chemicals, machine tools, electronics, precision instruments, computers, and construction materials.

The Soviet press also left no doubt about the true villains behind the strikes. *Izvestia* branded the Karabagh Committee as "national philistines, intellectuals without convictions, political adventurers hoping to make a career of provocations and blackmail." The assessment of the overall goals of committee members was equally harsh: "Their main task is to seize power through the destabilization of Armenia's economy and public life." TASS not only accused committee members of attempting "to cover up for 'shadow economy' dealers, for clans of careerists and bribe-takers," but also published the monthly salaries of Rafael Ghazaryan (800 rubles—nearly quadruple the Soviet average at the time), Babgen Ararktsyan (400 rubles), Levon Ter Petrosyan (400 rubles), and Ashot Manucharyan (340 rubles).[34] Still more reminiscent of the pre-*glasnost* era was the claim of the news agency that Armenian activists were distributing leaflets that read, "Let the Russian–Jewish–Turkish–Tatar bloc drown in our blood." [35]

The Soviet media's smear campaign only deepened a rift that had begun at the party conference and then split wide open during the angry days of July. In less than a month, the Karabagh movement had taken on an anti-Soviet tone. Of all the non-Russian republics of the Soviet Union, Armenia was the last place expected to provide a home for such sentiments. Not that Armenians were without grievances against the center, but along with the complaints about the boundary arrangements of the early 1920s, Armenians recognized that they enjoyed a few valued privileges in the Soviet context. For example, only in Armenia, Azerbaijan, and Georgia were the respective languages of the republics protected as official state languages by the republican constitutions of 1938 and 1978.[36] Other republics, especially Azerbaijan, were also envious of the relatively open ties between Soviet Armenians and their compatriots in the diaspora. After Stalin's death, the catholicosate of the Armenian Apostolic Church in Echmiadzin was allowed to publish religious materials and raise funds abroad for the restoration of ancient churches. The Armenian Church, which by 1977 was limited to forty active parishes and six monasteries, was also not a target of the persecution aimed at the Catholic Church of Lithuania and the Uniate Church of Ukraine.

Geography was the most convincing argument for Armenian allegiance to the Soviet state. With memories of the 1915 genocide by Turkey still fresh, the authorities in both Yerevan and Moscow were quick to draw the connection between Soviet loyalty and Armenian patriotism. Soviet soldiers stationed in Armenia often remarked on the hospitable attitude of the local population. In the eyes of most Armenians, the troops were there as protectors rather than occupiers. The military record of Armenians during World War II also illustrated how the defense of Armenia was intertwined with fidelity to the Soviet Union. Armenians at the time of the Nazi invasion feared that Turkey would enter the war on the side of Germany if the Soviet Union were defeated. The possibility of a Turkish attack on the defenseless republic had much to do with the taste for martyrdom that distinguished Armenian units on the southern front. Their most decisive stand came in September and October of 1942, when the German First Panzer Army thrust south in a drive to capture the oilfields near Grozny and seize the Rostov–Tbilisi highway through the Caucasus Mountains in an attempt to reach the oil riches of Baku. The Nazis, however, were turned back in the foothills of the Caucasus. Armenian soldiers played a key role in thwarting the advance. Hundreds dove beneath German tanks with grenades and land mines clutched to their chests. All told, Armenians suffered one of the highest casualty rates among the peoples of the USSR. In the post-war era, Armenians were the only non-Slavic nationality (other than the Jews) to be overrepresented relative to their population within the officer corps of the Soviet armed forces.[37]

With the Soviet army occupying Theater Square, however, Armenians abruptly awoke to the fact that they were part of an empire. The strike provided Armenians with a hands-on economics lesson about their role within the overall Soviet economy. Many began to openly question the benefits of Soviet rule. At mass rallies, speakers increasingly put the blame on central planners in Moscow for polluting Armenia's environment and fostering economic dependence. Others claimed that the republic's mineral resources, particularly molybdenum and copper, were being recklessly depleted under the Soviet system. From their viewpoint, the shutdown of the molybdenum plant at Alaverdi was a national service. As for the troops, Ashot Manucharyan captured the feelings of many when he warned: "Those who sent in the army should know that the Armenian people consider this army to be a colonial force."[38]

Closer scrutiny of Armenia's position within the Soviet empire inevitably led to a broader critique of the Soviet experience, beginning with the entry of Bolshevik power into Armenia. Officially, the communist takeover that occurred late in November 1920 had been a local affair, with the Red Army being invited into the republic only to block the advance of Turkish forces. The reality, though, was that communists in Armenia constituted a minor party at the time and played a small role in the sovietization of the republic. The economic modernization of Armenia that began in the 1930s was another inviting subject for revisionists. Again, Moscow's line had emphasized the huge investments undertaken by the central government to make Armenia one of the most highly industrialized republics of the Soviet Union. On paper at least, Armenia looked to be in a privileged position.

From 1928 to 1935, industrial production in Armenia

increased from 21.7 percent of the republic's economic output to 62.1 percent.[39] According to 1985 statistics, Armenia had the second largest industrial work force per capita among the fifteen republics and the fourth highest level of urbanization. In terms of educational attainment, Armenians had long ranked at the top, along with the Georgians, among Soviet nationalities. From 1961 to 1985, national income in Armenia grew at a faster clip—7.8 percent annually—than in any other republic.[40] The flip side of development—first articulated by environmental activists in the mid-1980s—revealed that many of the industries located in Armenia were predicated on the availability of cheap electricity and abundant fresh water. Although the republic was not particularly well endowed with either resource, Moscow planners had factored the depletion of Lake Sevan into their calculations for the construction of chemical and cement factories.

Soviet internationalism was also an easy target for critics. For seven decades, conflicts among national groups had been glossed over while the Soviet system promoted sanitized displays of folk culture and limited national self-expression to a standardized set of celebrations, monuments, and artistic performances. Each republic had its own writers' union and state publishing house to make sure that literature did not stray far from Soviet norms. Even the gargantuan Mother Armenia statue that stood vigil over Yerevan from its pedestal above Lenin Prospekt had counterparts in the other republics. (The same pedestal had originally supported the biggest Stalin statue in the USSR.) In the end, observers noted, Soviet internationalism was just another product of Moscow's central planners. Again, Manucharyan:

> Internationalism today represents dance festivals, ethnic food, etc., not real brotherhood. All Soviets more or less know Russian history and culture, not deeply, but at least the official version. But they don't know anything about other peoples [of the USSR]. I, for instance, know much more about India or France than about Estonia.[41]

Taking the issue a step further led to the more troubling subject of Russification—a topic that gained sudden relevance in July 1988. In the first heated days after the airport incident, anti-Russian feeling boiled to the surface in Yerevan. The episodes amounted to no more than a few curse-filled outbursts, but their occurrence was shocking nonetheless. Under their breath, Armenians might have referred derogatorily to Russians as "onion heads" (an allusion to the onion-shaped domes of Russian churches), while Russians would have countered with the pejorative "black asses" (a term that applied to everyone from the Caucasus), but by and large relations between the two peoples had been amicable. Once passions had cooled, there were more serious discussions about the relationship between Armenians and Russians.

Russification had deep roots in Armenia, and the process accelerated during the Soviet period, particularly after Stalin began to stress in the mid-1930s the importance of Russian as the lingua franca of the USSR. The sovietized elite that emerged after World War II zealously embraced Russia's language and culture. As elsewhere in the USSR, Russian was the language of academic research in Armenia. Notwithstanding the provision within the republic's constitution recognizing Armenian as the official language, doctoral students were required to submit their dissertations in Russian. Moreover, the top layer of officialdom was filled with graduates from Moscow State University. Over half of Armenia's highly educated specialists left the republic, the great majority relocating to Russia.[42] Many leading officials in the republic had done their bureaucratic apprenticeships in the Russian republic. Not surprisingly, by the 1980s over 90 percent of Armenia's administrative paperwork was conducted in Russian. More ominously for the future, members of the Armenian intelligentsia were increasingly sending their children to schools where the basic language of instruction was Russian. In 1988, nearly 100,000 Armenian students within the republic were enrolled in Russian-language schools.[43]

Of the fourteen non-Russian republics, Armenia most readily accepted the tutelage of the USSR's elder brother. Karen Demirchyan put his people's Russophilia on public display at the Twenty-Fifth Party Congress in 1976, declaring his nation's motto to be: "Blessed be the sacred hour when Russians set foot on our soil!"[44] (Demirchyan's words echoed those of Khachatur Abovyan's pioneering nineteenth-century novel, *Verk Haiastani* (Wounds of Armenia).) From the pronouncements of the political leadership, the sense of cultural inferiority inevitably trickled down to permeate every level of society. On the streets of Yerevan, old women spoke to their grandchildren in unpolished Russian. Armenian-language periodicals and newspapers were largely snubbed by educated Russian speakers.

Historian and linguist Rafael Ishkhanyan was one of a handful of intellectuals before 1988 to voice concern over the pace of Russification in Armenia. For him, the Karabagh movement took place not a moment too soon. Without a national revival, Armenia would be headed for complete Russification within a few decades, he believed.

Ishkhanyan's prognosis struck many as alarmist. In the Soviet context, Armenian culture hardly seemed under threat. When proponents of Russification, for example, had tried in 1978 to rescind the article in the Armenian constitution that recognized Armenian's status as the official language of the republic, a barrage of letters and speeches from respected members of the Armenian intelligentsia persuaded them to back down. Indeed, the 1979 census reported that 99.4 percent of Armenians in Armenia considered Armenian to be their native language.[45] Traditionally, Ukraine and Belorussia had been the favored targets of intense Russification. During the Brezhnev era, for example, hundreds of Ukrainian-language schools were closed and a number of Ukrainian-language scholarly journals were converted to Russian. As a result of Moscow's efforts, one in five Ukrainians came to consider Russian as their native language.[46]

As a more appropriate standard of comparison, though, Ishkhanyan looked toward the Georgians and the Estonians, who vigorously resisted the encroachment of Russian.[47] According to Ishkhanyan, the process of Russification that he saw in Armenia was in many respects a natural byproduct of Armenia's political misfortune.

Ishkhanyan, who in 1988 helped establish Mashtots (named in honor of the creator of the Armenian alphabet), a group dedicated to revitalizing the Armenian language, said:

> Our historians and both communist and non-communist political leaders have always inspired the thought that [Armenia] cannot survive without Russia, that Russia is the savior of Armenia, etc. In other words, they have always argued that we cannot live without the third force. This line of argument reinforced the slavishness that has developed among stateless Armenians since 600 A.D., at least for the last 900 years since the fall of Ani. The extent of russification among Armenians is due to the reinforcement of this slavishness.[48]

Ishkhanyan's views were channeled into the Karabagh Committee through Vazgen Manukyan, Ishkhanyan's son-in-law.

As Ishkhanyan would have argued, Armenians in Mountainous Karabagh had not been as vulnerable to the forces of Russification. Historically, the region had been one of the few bastions of cultural security for the nation. During the summer of 1988, the assertive past of Karabagh Armenians undoubtedly sustained the dogged determination of their movement.

Other than for a few weeks of overtime production in the weeks between Gorbachev's birthday on 2 March and the announcement of the Kremlin's reform package on 24 March, and again around the party conference, the strike in the oblast dating from February had never been completely abandoned. As in Armenia, the work stoppages were part of a larger strategy to shut down industries deemed vital by central planners in

Baku and Moscow. Schools, essential services, and agriculture continued to operate. Unlike their countrymen in Armenia, though, Karabagh Armenians had grounds to suspect that Baku would retaliate by withholding supplies during the coming winter. An intermittent blockade had been imposed by Azerbaijani authorities since the passage of the resolution on unification, with Karabagh Armenians in turn occasionally cutting off access to Azerbaijani-populated areas. In anticipation of a difficult winter, *Krunk* activists had devised plans to keep the harvest within the oblast's boundaries. With idle factory workers providing extra help in the countryside, 1988 was a bountiful year for Mountainous Karabagh's farmers.

On the legislative front, the most important news of the summer was the 12 July resolution approved unanimously by 101 deputies in the Mountainous Karabagh oblast soviet to secede from Azerbaijan and to rename the oblast the Artsakh Armenian Autonomous Region.[49] The move represented a further escalation of the ongoing political battle. Less than a month earlier, the Mountainous Karabagh legislature had failed to persuade the Supreme Soviet to place the oblast temporarily under Moscow's rule. The decision of 12 July provoked a much sharper reaction. That evening, the Azerbaijani Supreme Soviet Presidium declared the resolution "null and void" under the constitutions of the USSR and the Azerbaijani republic. The following evening, a report on *Vremya* not only branded the resolution on secession as illegal, but claimed that police had confiscated 52 grenades, 800 rounds of ammunition, 12 rifles, 5 pistols, 2 revolvers, and 2 sawed-off shotguns in the oblast during the previous month.[50]

The 18 July session of the Presidium of the USSR Supreme Soviet served as the culmination of the constitutional tug-of-war over Mountainous Karabagh's status. As Armenians had long desired, the question of Mountainous Karabagh received the undivided attention of the Soviet government's highest body. For eight hours, the thirty-nine members of the Presidium considered nothing else, hearing speakers from Armenia, Azerbaijan, and Mountainous Karabagh, as well as from their own ranks. But, as had been feared, the Armenians came out the clear losers.

The resolution that was passed at the end of the session ruled out any change in borders. The decision cited article 78 of the Soviet constitution, which prohibited territorial changes without the consent of the republic involved. As a token gesture to Armenian concerns, the resolution went on to approve sending representatives to Mountainous Karabagh to guarantee the implementation of its ruling. A special commission under the Soviet of Nationalities was also formed to further examine the situation in the oblast.[51]

Perhaps more significant than the outcome of the Presidium session was the drama of the proceedings. The two and one-half hours of television coverage shown on 19 and 20 July laid out the anatomy of the controversy for the first time to the Soviet public. And while the footage was edited to cast Gorbachev as the balanced mediator, viewers were nonetheless treated to a string of lively exchanges. In Armenia, virtually the entire republic stayed up until the early hours of 20 July to watch the broadcast that began after *Vremya*.

Reputations were made or broken overnight, as Armenia's representatives jousted with the Soviet leader. One hero to emerge was Sergei Hambartsumyan, rector of Yerevan State University. Hambartsumyan won points from the outset of his presentation by dismissing the formulaic rhetoric of previous speakers: "I would describe as naive the hope that the people's movement can be stilled and nullified by appeals to strengthen internationalism and the friendship of the peoples." Gorbachev shot back by contending that Hambartsumyan's speech was the first to contain "not even a hint of self-criticism or compromise." [52] "Maybe you're trying to make a cheap reputation for yourself?" the Soviet leader interjected, and then questioned Hambartsumyan's popular mandate. "You keep on citing the public, saying the public thinks this, the public does this, the public does not see a way out," Gorbachev observed. "Are you sure that you are speaking on behalf of the public?" [53] But rather than retreat, Hambartsumyan seized Gorbachev's admonition on hurdling obstacles to restructuring and argued for new thinking on the nationalities question. He also suggested that Mountainous Karabagh be placed temporarily under Moscow's jurisdiction. [54]

In a more mundane fashion, Mountainous Karabagh First Secretary Henrik Poghosyan bolstered his stature as one of the oblast's most able advocates. His report on Baku's abuses incorporated figures showing that the oblast turned over 91 million rubles annually to the Azerbaijani government while operating on a budget of 42 million rubles. Lopsided funding was indicative of a pervasive policy of discrimination, according to Poghosyan. "Please understand me," he urged:

> The Armenian population cannot be satisfied solely with material benefits to the detriment of national cultural and spiritual development. The unjust resolution of the Nagorno Karabakh problem, as experience shows, will lead inevitably to the Armenian population being driven out of their homeland.

Pointing to the fate of Armenians in Nakhichevan as a precedent, Poghosyan asserted that Mountainous Karabagh had to be removed from Azerbaijani control. [55]

Ultimately, the most memorable retort of the session belonged to Viktor Hambartsumyan. After being interrupted by Gorbachev, the chairman of the Armenian Academy of Sciences snapped back with such bracing effect that Soviet editors removed his words from the television broadcast:

> Young man, I am eighty years old, and a member of sixty scientific and technical organizations throughout the world. I am not here to discuss petty nationalism, as you have charged. As an astrophysicist who studies cosmology, the broadest possible issue in the universe, I can hardly be accused of having a narrow perspective. Neither am I accustomed to being interrupted when I try to speak. Whatever I have come here to say, you will be so kind as to be silent until I have finished it![56]

There were others, however, who came back to Yerevan humbled by their encounter with the general secretary. Writer Vardges A. Petrosyan, for example, tried to compensate for remaining largely on the sidelines of the Karabagh movement by boldly demanding that Mountainous Karabagh be removed from Azerbaijan and that the Sumgait massacres be classified as an act of genocide. Gorbachev pounced immediately on the latter assertion:

> How can you talk about genocide? You know what kind of word it is and the weight it carries. You are flinging around accusations that you will regret for the rest of your life.

After warning of the consequences of an unjust decision on Mountainous Karabagh, the diminutive Petrosyan found himself on the defensive for the remainder of his face-off with Gorbachev:

Gorbachev: But are you thinking about other peoples too?
Petrosyan: Of course we do.
Gorbachev: Therefore you ought to be urging us to think about the peoples' common fate, what their lives must be like. Right?
Petrosyan: Yes.
Gorbachev: This comes first. This is a very important clarification, because this is the only way we can think—about everyone. We cannot disregard either the Armenian people, or the Azerbaijani or any other people.
Petrosyan: Absolutely correct. [57]

Gorbachev then gave the head of the Armenian Writers' Union a guided tour of the policymaking minefield bound up in the nationalities question, contending that the transfer of Mountainous Karabagh to Armenia would logically necessitate the same treatment for Armenians in Georgia, Tajiks in Uzbekistan, Uzbeks in Tajikistan, and Azerbaijanis in Georgia. "If the transfer of the NKAO [Nagorno Karabakh Autonomous Oblast] is the only way, then we must recarve our entire country," Gorbachev claimed. With the hapless Armenian representative vanquished, the general secretary offered a final suggestion: "But put yourself in our shoes, we, being responsible for the fate of the people, must weigh everything most thoroughly." Petrosyan replied sheepishly before turning over the rostrum: "I realize that this is complex and difficult." [58]

The other Armenian spokesmen, while not especially eloquent, also made an effort to present the position of their republic. Hrant M. Voskanyan, chairman of the Armenian Supreme Soviet Presidium, began the session by tracing the roots of the Mountainous Karabagh dispute back to the early 1920s. Later, First Secretary Suren Harutiunyan offered a number of compromise proposals to break the deadlock on the oblast. Over the course of the eight-hour session, however, the Armenian viewpoint was largely overwhelmed by the collective voice of top Soviet officials. Speaker after speaker condemned labor strikes, upheld the primacy of constitutional article 78 (ruling out territorial change without a republic's consent), and endorsed Kremlin decisions on the oblast made in March and June of 1988.[59]

In the end, it was Gorbachev himself who set the tone of the Presidium's resolution. In his lengthy address, the Soviet leader depicted the dispute as hopelessly deadlocked thanks to the intransigence of both Armenians and Azerbaijanis. "I will tell you that today's Presidium meeting," he said, interjecting his personal appraisal, "saw more self-criticism on the part of the Azerbaijanis and less on the part of Armenia's representatives."

Gorbachev then hammered away at the tactics and motives of the Karabagh movement:

Restructuring requires extremely great cohesion among the people, but what is offered is strife and national distrust. Restructuring requires democratization and *glasnost*, but under the flag of *glasnost* we see here shameless pressure upon labor collectives, upon the populations of the towns of republics on the part of irresponsible persons, and even pressure upon the organs of the authorities, including even upon the USSR Supreme Soviet Presidium. Look at the methods being used—constant mass demonstrations and meetings and, finally, strikes.

In other words, we can see that the democratic rights and the new conditions that were opened up and created by restructuring are clearly being used for undemocratic aims. Comrades, I think that this is unacceptable.[60]

Actually, the gist of Gorbachev's words had reached Armenia before the general secretary's televised address. TASS released the Presidium's resolution to the foreign press shortly after the session's conclusion, and listeners of the Voice of America and the British Broadcasting Corporation quickly spread the news throughout Yerevan. Officially, however, the task of breaking the story to the public in Yerevan was left to members of Armenia's delegation to the Presidium session. On the evening of 19 July, well before the broadcast of the session proceedings, Suren Harutiunyan tried to cast the Presidium's decision in a positive light. The crowd facing the Matenadaran never gave him a chance. Instead, the throng of nearly 500,000 turned its collective back on the Armenian first secretary, then whistled, jeered, and clapped for forty minutes until Harutiunyan and other government officials left the speaker's platform.[61]

In contrast, Karabagh Committee members later praised the performance of Armenia's representatives at the Presidium session. Levon Ter Petrosyan, basing his interpretation on copies of speeches given by the Armenian spokesmen, hailed the session as the first occasion where Armenian officials had backed the people on the Karabagh issue. "Our victory," he said, "is dependent upon the solidarity of the people and our leadership." [62]

In addition to rebuffing the demands of the Karabagh movement, the Presidium also made known its intent to restore order, and put Armenia's government on notice that further strikes and demonstrations were not acceptable. At a press conference on 19 July, Soviet Prosecutor General Alexander Sukharev warned that additional troops would be sent to Armenia and a curfew imposed if demonstrations continued. Pyotr Demichev, the deputy chairman of the Presidium, added that striking workers in Mountainous Karabagh might find their factories shut down if they did not return to their jobs.[63] In turn, the Armenian government adopted a sterner stance toward the Karabagh Committee. Yerevan's party chief, Levon Sahakyan, took the first step by painting committee members as political opportunists. At a broader level, the Armenian Central Committee adopted a resolution calling on local authorities to "take necessary measures to guarantee public order and . . . suppress any activities by instigatory elements directed at destabilizing the situation in the republic." A number of officials charged with failure to curb protest rallies were reprimanded and demoted. At the same time, forty-four protesters were arrested for crimes connected with the Zvartnots airport incident.[64]

On 28 July, the Supreme Soviet gave its warning sharper teeth. Without open debate, legislation was passed to empower MVD troops to suppress unauthorized political meetings and demonstrations, search the homes of suspected lawbreakers without a warrant, and conduct spot identity checks. Another decree required that organizers of public meetings apply to the government for permission ten days in advance of planned rallies. In early August, the authorities drew on the Supreme Soviet resolutions to break up demonstrations in Leningrad and Lvov.[65]

The message to Armenia was clear: the Soviet government was calling the Karabagh movement's bluff. Among the young, there were at least a few willing to defy the authorities, but the Karabagh Committee wanted no part of a potentially violent confrontation with Soviet power. At a brief rally after the Presidium, committee members urged restraint and limited their calls for labor strikes to sponsorship of a symbolic fifteen-minute work stoppage. Otherwise, most activists supported efforts to make up for lost production as Armenia went back to work. Rallies were scheduled after working hours, with a gathering of 250,000 on Friday evening, 29 July, passing without new calls for strikes. TASS reported that workers at more than 130 Yerevan enterprises put in extra shifts.[66]

Outside of Yerevan, the movement shifted gears as well. Attitudes in Leninakan had mirrored those of Yerevan. Activists had framed their cause around promoting democracy and campaigned against local corruption with the same intensity as their counterparts in Yerevan. They orchestrated an elaborate mock funeral of *Pravda* (Truth) to protest against the central media. The movement in Zangezur was also driven by calls for democratization, with Armenians and Kurds joining together in hunger strikes. Kirovakan, however, had a reputation for lagging behind. According to one anecdote, a group of protesters from Kirovakan (present-day Vanadzor) came to Yerevan to join the movement but could not find Theater Square. Throughout the republic, however, Armenians concluded that continuing the strike after the Presidium session would be counterproductive.

Even in Mountainous Karabagh, Armenians eased their strike in late July. Residents of the oblast remained as steadfast as ever— weddings continued to be consecrated without celebration and the festive sound of the piccolo-like *duduk* remained silent—but for the moment at least they returned to work to unload backlogged freight cars at Stepanakert's rail depot and to man neglected factory assembly lines. Although Karabagh Armenians were disappointed by the outcome of the Presidium session, oblast first secretary Henrik Poghosyan had made a good impression among his people and offered hope that something positive would come out of the decision to appoint a special commission to study the Karabagh issue. A pragmatist first, Poghosyan had discounted the possibility of territorial changes even before the meeting. He told an Armenian journalist in mid-July:

> Our people are maximalists. Of course, it would be very good if the question were to be solved in the way that the people proposed. However, at the same time, we should understand that the NKAO problem can be solved only within the framework of the USSR Constitution.[67]

The Presidium session also ushered in a new attitude toward Gorbachev. The televised broadcast of the session gave Armenians their first good look at the Soviet leader's bad side—arrogant, impatient, condescending, and imperious. Many were furious. At one late July rally, novelist Sero Khanzatyan went so far as to compare Gorbachev's style to that of Stalin.[68] The portraits of the general secretary, so emblematic of the earlier demonstrations, were now seen only in tatters. Gorbachev's wife Raisa became the butt of disparaging jokes.

The dissatisfaction with Gorbachev was far more than a disagreement over policy. In the eyes of many Armenians, 18 July was a betrayal of a personal sort. The wellspring of such emotional intensity can be found in the faith that many of these same Armenians had placed in Gorbachev and *perestroika*. As American-Armenian historian Gerard J. Libaridian noted in June 1988, *perestroika* had been embraced in the republic as Armenia's salvation:

> Soviet Armenians are looking at *perestroika* the same way as some traditional societies looked at westernization and modernization. It is an opportunity to be seized, as well as a challenge that must be faced. If Armenia sidesteps it or fails in the challenge, it is condemned to oblivion and irrelevance. But Armenia wants to help define it, not just accept the definition from above.

And, as Libaridian added, Armenians placed the Karabagh issue "squarely at the heart of the struggle for *perestroika*." [69]

From Yerevan, the matter indeed appeared clear-cut. "After all, what is *perestroika*?" Karabagh Committee member Levon Ter Petrosyan asked rhetorically in an interview with a *Wall Street Journal* reporter. "It is the state carrying out the will of the people." [70] In Mountainous Karabagh, that meant reuniting the oblast with Armenia. The Karabagh Committee put that goal in a broader context, viewing *perestroika* as an all-purpose effort to de-Stalinize the Soviet Union. Gorbachev himself had already begun rectifying many of Stalin's policies in economics and political life. The injustice imposed on the Armenians of Mountainous Karabagh seemed to logically fit the same agenda. In an open letter to the Soviet leader on 21 March 1988, Andrei Sakharov captured the Armenian viewpoint on Stalin's nationalities policies:

> The issues that I have raised in this letter—the fates of the Crimean Tatars and of Nagorno Karabakh—have become a touchstone of *perestroika* and of its ability to overcome the resistance and the undertow of the past. [71]

The cold reality, though, was that the perspective of Sakharov and the Karabagh Committee on *perestroika* was never shared by Gorbachev. Outside of the Soviet ruling class, *perestroika* had been embraced as a means for addressing the problems of the people, whether they be underpaid coal miners, the relatives of GULAG victims, or Armenians in Mountainous Karabagh. The expectation was that reform would respond to individual concerns. Within the circle of power, the overriding objective was to preserve the Soviet state. Popular disenchantment was inevitable. In the case of the Karabagh movement, the contrasting interpretations of *perestroika* created an unbridgeable chasm. As Armenians discovered in the summer of 1988, *perestroika* not only failed to offer a solution to their national grievances, but the Kremlin architects of reform did not deem their cause worthy of consideration.

In terms of his own background, Gorbachev was perhaps the most parochially Russian of any Soviet leader. Before becoming general secretary, he had spent his entire career either in the southern Russian city of Stavropol or in Moscow. [72] Gorbachev's childhood in a village in the Stavropol region was filled with non-Russian friends and neighbors, including many Armenians, and Gorbachev grew up believing that the Soviet Union had eliminated ethnic friction among its peoples. At Moscow State University and within the Soviet bureaucracy, Gorbachev's faith in "internationalism" was reinforced by the omnipresent values of *homo sovieticus* (Soviet man). Deeply felt ethnic identity was alien to his experience.

When Gorbachev assumed the reins of power, he saw nationalities problems as largely peripheral nuisances in the way of his broader goals. A Soviet analyst in the U.S. State Department observed that "while [Gorbachev] clearly is a master of bureaucratic politics, he not only does not understand ethnic feelings but acts in a way guaranteed to exacerbate them even if he does not intend to." [73] At the Twenty-Seventh Party Congress in February 1986, Gorbachev unveiled both his aim to embark on a program of serious economic reform and his disdain for the republican autonomy that had been tolerated under Brezhnev. Union interests in the Gorbachev era would take priority over local concerns, he stressed. The Soviet leader made plain that his intent was to get the USSR back on track without destabilizing Soviet society.

Gorbachev's Politburo became almost entirely Russian. A new generation of mostly Slavic technocrats was dispatched from the center with a mandate for economic reform. In Gorbachev's meritocracy, there was little room for attention to ethnic sensitivities. The first major backlash came in Kazakhstan, when Gorbachev replaced First Secretary Dinmuhammad Kunayev with a Russian in December 1986. As disgruntled nationalities became more restive under *glasnost*, Gorbachev began to realize that he had greatly underestimated the fervor underlying national identity. At a Central Committee plenum in February 1988, just as the Karabagh movement was getting underway, he conceded that national issues were of "vital importance." [74]

In fairness to Gorbachev, the record shows that the general secretary sought to dispel popular faith in the omnipotence of Moscow. He recognized that the innocent trust many Armenians placed in him contradicted his efforts to alter the relationship between the central government and the Soviet public. "It is necessary to expunge from the people's minds a belief in the 'good czar,' in the all-powerful center, in the assumption that someone at the top will impose order and organize change." [75] Tackling thorny nationalities disputes offered little return for a leader trying to salvage the Soviet system.

If Armenians were reading between the lines of Gorbachev's statements before July 1988, they gave no indication. On the contrary, most Armenians bought into the notion that the Karabagh issue was caught up in the battle between Gorbachev and the Politburo hard-liners led by Yegor Ligachev. According to this line of reasoning, Gorbachev first needed to vanquish his reactionary foes before Armenian concerns could be addressed. The black-and-white morality of this worldview was generally accepted by the crowds in Theater Square, although by May a number of intellectuals were beginning to question how far apart Gorbachev and Ligachev stood on the Karabagh issue. Hambartsum Galstyan, for example, believed that in regard to nationalities matters the two Politburo rivals were flip sides of the same coin. The outcome of the power struggle in the Kremlin, according to Galstyan, would make little difference in Transcaucasia. The interests of Moscow and Armenia simply did not coincide.

After 18 July, most Armenians shared Galstyan's conclusion, and were prepared to direct their outrage at Gorbachev and *perestroika* rather than at hard-line communists. As one post-Presidium session joke put it, an "extremist" (the Soviet media's favorite epithet for Armenian protesters) was an Armenian who had believed in *perestroika*. In the case of Gorbachev, there was more anger than black humor. Ter Petrosyan was particularly incensed by Gorbachev's browbeating oratorical tactics at the Presidium session, suggesting that, "Perhaps he was upset at raping the Armenian people." A 25-year-old engineer also put his feelings about the Soviet leader in personal terms while speaking to an American reporter: "Gorbachev just closed his eyes to all our problems," said Grigor Manukyan. "We are a people in a state of shock."

Once the shock was over, Armenian activists began reassessing the nature of the general secretary's agenda and the limits of *perestroika*. Merujan Ter Gulanyan, editor of *Garun* magazine, noted:

> Gorbachev has promised to have a Central Committee plenum on the nationalities question. But those plenums are much too short to solve anything. Usually Gorbachev has spoken in the language of humanity. But on Nagorno Karabakh he spoke like a bureaucrat.[76]

With distrust of the Kremlin running deep in Armenia, at least for the moment, there were few expectations attached to the decision of the Presidium to send Kremlin representatives to Mountainous Karabagh. Most locals saw it as a public relations smokescreen intended to salve wounded Armenian feelings.

The Presidium's mandate contained two components. First, Central Committee member Arkady Volsky was posted in the oblast to mediate disputes between Stepanakert and Baku, and to oversee the implementation of the 24 March economic development plan adopted by Moscow. Second, Avgust Voss, chairman of the Soviet of Nationalities of the Supreme Soviet, was to arrive in October to put together a report on Mountainous Karabagh for the Presidium, with an eye toward the long-anticipated Supreme Soviet conference on nationalities issues. Although the Voss Commission was the first ever formed within the Supreme Soviet of Nationalities, Volsky's work left a much greater impact on the Karabagh issue.[77]

Volsky himself was a practical-minded engineer who had risen to prominence during the 1980s, first under Yuri Andropov and then under Gorbachev.[78] After arriving in Stepanakert in late July, Volsky soon came to the conclusion that the Baku government was doing its best to make life miserable for the Armenian population.

"There is no excuse for the individuals who brought this mountainous area, where good, hard-working people live, to such a state," he reported in December 1988.[79] "In my trips around the country, I have never encountered the kind of neglect and disregard for people's future I saw in Nagorno Karabakh," Volsky wrote in *Pravda* the following month.[80] Under the authority vested in him by the Presidium, Volsky had the power to overrule decisions made in Baku and to expedite the construction projects called for in the 24 March reform package. And in fact, he attempted to restore a semblance of order to the battered economy and to hammer together at least a rudimentary consensus. On 2 August, for example, he brought together the party heads of Armenia and Azerbaijan to meet with him and Henrik Poghosyan in Stepanakert. When communal violence erupted the following month, he imposed martial law on the districts of Stepanakert and Aghdam, brushing aside Azerbaijan's contention that he was overstepping his authority. He also pushed forward plans to repair the nearly impassable road from Stepanakert to Goris in southeastern Armenia.

Volsky made an honest effort to carry out his mission. Economically, Mountainous Karabagh received more investment than ever before. Requests from local officials and collective farm directors were often met on the spot, with Volsky picking up the phone and ordering Moscow to send supplies. Volsky also facilitated the creation of economic ties between the oblast and Armenia. At the same time, however, Volsky could not buy off the movement.

Many Karabagh Armenians had believed that the Central Committee representative, himself a Jew, was on their side, and were embittered when events proved otherwise. Volsky had been charged with ending the strike and defusing the campaign for unification. To accomplish that, he seized the reins of power in the oblast and bulldozed over anyone who got in his way. Inevitably, his tactics brought him into conflict with the *Krunk* Committee. Likewise, Volsky was not prepared to deal with the bitter enmity that had settled over the region. Addressing the Supreme Soviet in November, he castigated Armenian and Azerbaijani officials, along with *Krunk* activists, claiming they had "supported the demagogues and increased tensions by their appeals to fight to the end, an eye for an eye, a tooth for a tooth, without thinking that the result would be the blood of the people."[81]

The Voss Commission, which whisked through Transcaucasia for a few days in early October with considerable fanfare, likewise rekindled hopes that the policy line presented at the Presidium session would be reversed. Rumors in Yerevan and Stepanakert predicted pro-Armenian recommendations. A Karabagh Committee member forecast that Mountainous Karabagh would be removed from Azerbaijan by December.

Henrik Poghosyan looked forward to a favorable report: "The conclusions drawn by this authoritative commission will make a large contribution to finding the right solution to the Karabagh problem." [82] As before, however, Armenians were to be disappointed by Moscow. Other commissions came and went. More meetings were held, villages inspected, and statistics recorded. Reports from political insiders in Moscow indicated that most findings justified the cause of the Karabagh Armenians. The release of the recommendations of the Voss Commission and its various successors, however, was repeatedly postponed. When the crucial juncture finally arrived in November 1989 during a meeting of the USSR Supreme Soviet, the commission was not given an opportunity to deliver its report. Other fact-finding missions met a similar fate. Many activists were left to conclude that the official indifference was all part of a larger plan.

Chapter 7

Respite

*T*he Armenian expression *yelk ch'ka* underwent a change in meaning during the first five months of the Karabagh movement. During the heady days of spring, *yelk ch'ka* was a confident, full-throated assertion: "There's no turning back!" By late July, however, the words had taken on a more ominous connotation. Accompanied by a fatalistic sigh, *yelk ch'ka* had come to signify, "There's no way out."

Among Yerevan's activists, *yelk ch'ka* rang with a particular foreboding. Back in February, no one had bothered to think in terms of contingency plans. Pessimists were those who believed that the unification of Mountainous Karabagh with Armenia would take up to half a year. The task at hand was simply to raise the issue, mobilize popular support, and then turn the question of resolving legal technicalities over to Moscow. In the new age of democratization, it all seemed very straightforward.

By mid-summer, however, the Karabagh movement had run out of maneuvering room. The Presidium session of 18 July had snuffed out hopes that had been directed toward Moscow, leaving the oft-promised Supreme Soviet conference on nationalities issues as the only other event on the horizon. Armenians wondered what had gone wrong. The Karabagh question had gained unprecedented attention; the people had turned out in unimaginable numbers; and yet Moscow had not played its assigned role. Karabagh Committee members had all they could do to avert a collision between the relentless popular force they had guided and the immovable power structure they had provoked. *Yelk ch'ka* indeed captured the irony.

With nowhere to go, the Karabagh movement reinvented itself after 18 July. Karabagh Committee members recognized that they had taken the issue of unification as far they could go under the Soviet constitution. Pressing their goals further would have meant abandoning the movement's commitment to legality and non-violence. What remained, though, was a newly politicized population. Somehow, this energy had to be directed away from confrontation and channeled toward a broader set of political objectives.

The challenge at hand appealed especially to the more politically minded members of the Karabagh Committee. For them, the Karabagh movement had always represented much more than Mountainous Karabagh. Theirs was a struggle in which the means—working within the framework of the constitution to secure civil rights—counted for at least as much as the ends. As a result, terms such as "national renaissance" and "new identity" were increasingly infused into the public face of the movement. As for Mountainous Karabagh, the committee members sought to project a long-term strategy by emphasizing the creation of economic and cultural ties between the oblast and Armenia.

There was also a less idealistic dimension to the committee's role in Armenian society. As with other national movements in the Soviet Union, a political opposition had coalesced around the Karabagh movement. The committee represented almost a shadow government. The mid-summer lull that followed the Presidium session afforded committee members an opportunity to consolidate their political stature and redefine Armenia's cause in their own terms.

The growing prominence of the Karabagh Committee was accompanied by heightened suspicion regarding the motives of its individual members. Yerevan was a city in which bonds of friendship and family wove through practically the entire educated elite. Committee members, as part of that select circle, possessed an insider's understanding of Armenian politics, even if they had spurned the inside track to power. What the Karabagh movement did was to thrust committee members into the center of the political process. They were still on the outside, but suddenly they were participants. From the speaker's platform in Theater Square, committee members were seen as an untainted alternative to the government. By the middle of the summer, though, even activists within the movement were beginning to question how long committee members would be able to resist the corruptive influence of power.

On the surface, the committee made an effort to present an image that meshed with its emphasis on popular democracy. One of the most succinct symbols of the movement's new outlook was an unimposing wooden table. At the end of July, demonstrators in Yerevan were told that volunteers would man the table, positioned on the steps of the Matenadaran, to collect suggestions on the future direction of the Karabagh movement. At the same time, daily rallies were replaced with weekly Friday evening meetings. A more systematic approach to ensuring access to information and public discussion was to characterize the movement's second phase. Levon Ter Petrosyan gave the crowds a foretaste of where the Karabagh Committee was heading by declaring:

> If there's a people now in the Soviet Union which runs its affairs democratically, it's the Armenians. The Soviet Union should look to Armenia as an example of people's democracy which originates from below and not from above as in Moscow.[1]

Within the Karabagh Committee, Vazgen Manukyan took the lead in shaping a framework for people's democracy. Since his student days—both in Moscow and Yerevan—Manukyan had held onto the dream of creating a broad-based popular organization. During the meetings of the Karabagh Committee, he had emerged as the most forceful strategist of the group. Elsewhere in the Soviet Union of the late 1980s, writers and artists were often at the forefront of reform movements. In Armenia, the mindset of the Karabagh Committee was molded to a large extent by mathematicians and physical scientists. The emphasis was less on the epic and romantic, and more on the structures and systems of Gorbachev-era politics. Manukyan was most at home in conceptualizing the Karabagh movement's position within the context of *perestroika*.

It was no surprise then that Manukyan would take the lead in formalizing the Karabagh movement's goals following the Presidium session of 18 July. The suggestions deposited in front of the Matenadaran were looked at, but for the most part Manukyan knew what he wanted to say. In addition, Manukyan was able to borrow language from democratic groups that had already formed in the Baltic republics. On 8 August, he released a draft platform. True to the committee's ideals, nothing would be finalized without popular approval. The document itself also conformed to the committee's image: four typewritten pages duplicated on an overworked photocopy machine.

The birth of the *Haiots Hamazgayin Sharzhum* (Armenian National Movement), or ANM, in fact attracted little fanfare. August was viewed as a respite after two whirlwind months. Other popular fronts had already formed in Estonia, Latvia, Lithuania, and Moldavia (present-day Moldova), each announcing programs that advocated reform beyond the limits set by *perestroika*. The ANM's platform fit the same mold. The essential principles of the movement had long since been presented to the crowds in Yerevan. Most significantly, the platform served to crystallize the nature of the Armenian democratic movement, especially among like-minded intellectuals in the Soviet Union and the political parties of the Armenian diaspora.

The manifesto issued in final form on 19 August contained four sections, outlining key principles, short-term goals, approach, and organization. The nine principles affirmed the movement's democratic convictions and reiterated its rejection of national chauvinism. Most revealing was the exposition of the movement's distinct worldview. In a sharp break with the mainstream of Armenian political thought since the late 1800s, the platform asserted that Armenia must not rely on other states for protection. Instead, the ANM envisioned an Armenia capable of living in peace and harmony with its neighbors. In line with that view, the document maintained that ideologies based on religion and race (i.e., pan-Turkism) played a declining role in international relations.

The short-term objectives were not nearly so controversial. Rather, the thirteen points followed the course charted by existing popular fronts in the Soviet Union, calling on Armenians to reclaim national rights and symbols repressed under Soviet rule. Included on the agenda were the establishment of ties with the Armenian diaspora, the promotion of the Armenian language, the bolstering of Armenian-language education, official Armenian and Soviet support for gaining recognition of the 1915 genocide by the United Nations, the declaration of 24 April and 28 May as national holidays, greater attention to the issue of historical Armenian lands, the acceptance of the tricolor of the 1918–20 Armenian Republic as a national symbol, expanded freedom for the Armenian Church, and the restoration of Armenian place names. The fifth point raised environmental concerns and pressed for closing the nuclear power plant at Medzamor and the Nairit chemical factory.[2]

As for approach and organization, the platform pointed the way to a formalized political role for the ANM. In addition to organizing rallies and strikes, the ANM would participate in elections and campaign for changes in Armenia's constitution and legal structure. The ANM also expressed its willingness to cooperate with the Armenian government and informal organizations throughout the Soviet Union to pursue common goals and interests. As with the Karabagh Committee, the ANM pledged to work within the framework of the constitution. Finally, the document set the stage for the creation of a representative council to flesh out the details of the movement's structure and organization.[3]

Like the democratic movements in the Baltics, the ANM staked its viability on further decentralization of Soviet power. The manifesto was one more bet that Gorbachev would have to move forward rather than backward to preserve the union. "In the old days, the Soviet Union's republics had to promise loyalty to the central government," a Karabagh

Committee member explained to a London *Daily Telegraph* reporter. "But now it's the central authority which has to prove loyalty to the republics." [4]

The creation of the ANM did not mean that the Karabagh question had gone away. Committee members realized that downplaying the oblast's importance would stir up resentment. Instead, the Karabagh question was given credit for illuminating a broad range of concerns. As the introduction to the ANM platform noted:

> It is not every problem that is capable of awakening the people, of uniting the nation around a collective idea, as is the issue of Artsakh's [Mountainous Karabagh's] unification. The awakened, living [Armenian] nation already is starting to also more sharply feel the pain of its other unresolved problems, to understand that all of these problems form a single chain. [5]

At Friday meetings as well, the Karabagh question remained at the center of the movement. During August and September, volunteers collected hundreds of thousands of signatures on a petition calling for the Armenian Supreme Soviet to declare Mountainous Karabagh part of Armenia. The familiar symbols of earlier months held firm: clenched fists, the trumpeted theme songs, the rhythmic chants, the handwritten questions passed from the crowd to the podium. Only the growing prominence of the tricolor was new.

The tone of most orators had likewise not changed. If anything, Karabagh Committee members wanted to assure the people that the original struggle had not been abandoned, but was merely entering a different stage.

"We will continue to speak our minds," Levon Ter Petrosyan told a gathering in late summer. "And if anyone thinks the struggle in this part of the world has ended, or thinks Moscow has had the last word, they are wrong."

In explaining the tactical shift to a British journalist, Ter Petrosyan contended that time was on the side of the Armenian cause:

> Our strategy now is to put maximum and continual pressure on Moscow with a mass demonstration every Friday. When we meet senior Soviet officials—as we regularly do—we tell them that they have only two alternatives: either to give us back Karabagh or to send in the tanks. We do not think Gorbachev is in a position to do the second, because of the political realities of life in the Soviet Union today. He also knows that a large movement like ours has no fear of new laws against demonstrations. The more that time passes, the

deeper the political roots of our movement become, which is why it is in Moscow's best interests to solve the Karabagh problem quickly.[6]

To a large extent, the formation of the ANM signaled an acceleration of the process that had begun in February. Even at that time, the expansion of the Karabagh movement's agenda seemed inexorable. Subcommittees on environmental matters and refugee problems came together almost spontaneously. Attempts to hold elected Armenian officials accountable grew out of the campaign to pressure the Armenian Supreme Soviet in June. By August, many activists were ready to mount a direct challenge to communist domination of the legislative system. "If we can elect even a few dozen deputies out of the 340 in the Armenian legislature," said committee member Babgen Ararktsyan, "that will be enough to force authorities to take up our issues." The plan was to test the limits of democratization, or as Hambartsum Galstyan remarked, "They gave us a little bit of liberalization, but we are now well beyond that." [7]

Also rooted in the early days of the Karabagh movement was the ANM's emphasis on strengthening ties with other national groups. Levon Ter Petrosyan (dubbed "Lenin" Ter Petrosyan for his universalist outlook) and Ashot Manucharyan were among the strongest foes of ethnocentricism. They also fiercely resisted the attempts of Zori Balayan and Igor Muradyan to stamp the movement as anti-Azerbaijani.

In February, the movement's internationalism focused primarily on the Kurds. During rallies in Yerevan, Kurdish speakers had expressed solidarity with the Karabagh movement. A group of Kurdish women had been in the forefront of the march to the genocide memorial on International Women's Day.

Relations between the two groups had traditionally been amicable in the Soviet era. The republic's more than 60,000 Kurds, most of whom practiced the syncretic Yezidi faith, could claim a Kurdish-language daily newspaper, a section in the republic's Writers' Union, daily radio programs, and the Institute for Kurdish Studies in Yerevan.[8] Equally important, though, were the tens of thousands of Kurds who lived in Azerbaijan near the Armenian border. Under the rule of Baku, they had experienced much of the same cultural repression felt by Armenians in Mountainous Karabagh. Moreover, Stalin had decimated their community in 1941, abolishing an autonomous Kurdish district within Azerbaijan and deporting thousands of Kurds to Central Asia.[9] Nonetheless, the Kurds in Azerbaijan did not openly support the Karabagh movement. Particularly among Shi'ite Kurds, thousands of whom had migrated from Armenia to Azerbaijan during the Soviet era, the religious bond with the Azerbaijanis outweighed desires for greater autonomy.

The Karabagh movement also raised new questions for Armenian–Georgian relations. Although geography and religion had thrown Armenians and Georgians together in a common history of struggle against Muslim invaders, interaction between the two peoples had not always been fraternal, especially in the late nineteenth and early twentieth centuries. For its part, the Karabagh movement was perceived as an indirect threat by many Georgian nationalists. Some felt that the Karabagh Armenian cause spurred the separatist demands of the Abkhazians in northwest Georgia. Another concern was the Armenian community in southern Georgia that lived near the border of the two republics.

Outside of Transcaucasia, the Karabagh movement found allies among the Baltic peoples. By May, Hambartsum Galstyan was traveling regularly to Moscow to meet his counterparts from Estonia, Latvia, and Lithuania. Representatives from the Baltics also began showing up at Yerevan rallies, never failing to receive an exuberant greeting. The unfurling of the red, green, and yellow Lithuanian flag at Theater Square, for example, prompted chants of "Lithuania, Lithuania." [10] A few words in Armenian from Lithuanian activists triggered another round of cheers. The affinity was mutual. In July, a rally of 100,000 in Vilnius voiced its approval for a telegram to Gorbachev supporting a referendum or plebiscite on self-determination in Mountainous Karabagh. The following month, six Armenians briefly joined two hunger strikers in Vilnius under a banner proclaiming "Armenia Is with You." [11] The bonds between Armenians and Estonians were especially strong, as both peoples saw themselves yanking at the constraints of the Soviet empire. "The route between Estonia and Armenia," went the joke shared by the two peoples, "passed through the Soviet Union."

The connection between Armenia and the Baltic republics challenged prevailing ethnic stereotypes in the Soviet Union. On the crude hierarchy of national groups within the USSR, the Baltic peoples had been ranked at the top. Unmistakably European, prosperous, closely linked to the cultures of Scandinavia and Germany—the Balts possessed the traits envied by a great majority of Soviets. Armenians fell somewhere in the middle of the scale, above the Muslims of Central Asia but usually below the Slavic peoples. Although Armenians fared relatively well in terms of education, per capita income, and professional accomplishment, they also had to contend with the popular image they shared with Georgians and Azerbaijanis. The peoples of Transcaucasia were typecast as hot-blooded and conniving, given to petty feuds and blustery bravado. For most Russians in Moscow and Leningrad, the Armenians and their Caucasian neighbors were best known as vendors at farmers' markets who brought truck-loads of fruits and vegetables from the Soviet Union's southern tier.

Then came the Karabagh movement, and Armenians suddenly leapfrogged into the front ranks of Soviet peoples. Armenia's national democratic movement became a yardstick for mass participation. Photographs of awe-inspiring rallies in Armenia passed from hand to hand in Riga, Tallinn, and Vilnius. Baltic activists took notes on the discipline of the demonstrations and the organization of the republic-wide strikes. Kara-bagh Committee members imagined that they would eventually be called upon to introduce the lessons of the Karabagh movement to informal or-ganizations in other republics and even Eastern Europe.

Beyond the camaraderie that came with being pioneers in popular democracy, however, there was a wide gulf separating the interests of the Baltic republics from those of Armenia. Baltic activists sought inde-pendence from Moscow; Armenians were appealing for Kremlin interven-tion. History taught the Baltic peoples to fear Russia, whereas Armenians typically looked north with hope and admiration. There were also deep differences in the evolution of the Karabagh movement and the national movements among the Balts. Armenians often made the point that they were fighting three battles—against the authorities in Baku, in Moscow, and in Yerevan. In contrast, the movements in the Baltics began with a much broader base of support within the established intelligentsia and Communist Party hierarchy. Writers and artists in each of the Baltic republics took the lead in pressing Moscow to loosen its grip. Government officials in the three republics had long pursued greater cultural and economic autonomy, and had raised concerns about environmental pollution for decades. Reform-minded communists in fact spearheaded the formation of a popular front in Estonia in April 1988.[12] The popular fronts that emerged elsewhere in the Soviet Union during 1988 had similar membership rosters and agendas. Gorbachev himself, at least for a time, encouraged their development as a counterweight to party hard-liners.

The ANM had grown out of different stock. By August 1988, the Armenian movement had broken ranks with the mainstream back-ers of *perestroika*. In Armenia, the natural allies of Gorbachev's reform efforts were the relatively progressive members of the republic's cultural elite, many of whom belonged to the Association in Support of *Perestroika*. They had long been tightroping between the popular will and the interests of the Kremlin. In late September, Gorbachev loyalists—led by Silva Kaputik-yan, Sos Sargsyan, Petros Khurshudyan, and Grigor Guyumjyan—formed a popular front in Armenia. Officially, the front sought to offer another per-spective on the Armenian–Azerbaijani dispute. More important, the group hoped to undercut the appeal of the Karabagh Committee.[13]

The Transcaucasus under Soviet Rule

Soviet Armenia and Mountainous Karabagh

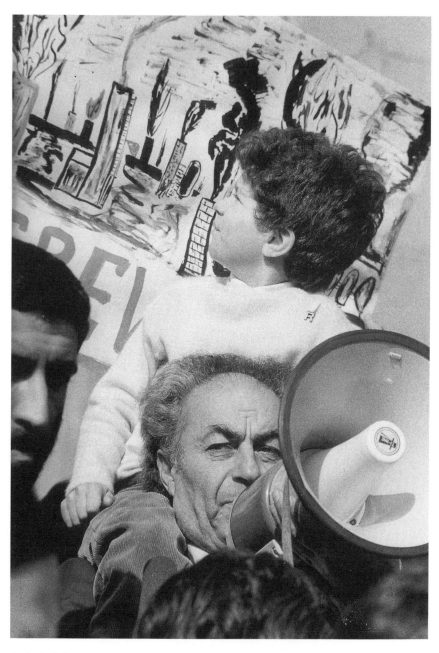

1. Rafael Ghazaryan voices concern about Armenia's environmental problems at a rally in Yerevan in October 1987. (photo by Zaven Khachikian)

2. Igor Muradyan addresses a crowd in Theater Square in February 1988. (photo by Rouben Mangasarian)

3. Yerevanis in Theater Square focus their attention on the speaker's platform at the rear of the opera house in February 1988. (photo by Mark Malkasian)

4. Soviet MVD troops and Armenian police enforce the closure of Theater Square in March 1988. (photo by Matthew Der Manuelian)

5. Photos of Sumgait massacre victims flank a *khachkar* [stone cross] beside Yerevan's genocide memorial on 24 April 1988. (photo by Mark Malkasian)

6. University students launch an around-the-clock vigil on the steps of the opera house in May 1988. (photo by Mark Malkasian)

7. Hunger-strikers maintain a fast in Theater Square, June 1988. (photo by Mark Malkasian)

8. Activists stage a sit-down protest in front of Armenia's Central Committee building in June 1988. (photo by Rouben Mangasarian)

9. The funeral procession for Khackik Zakaryan crosses Yerevan's Hrazdan River in July 1988. (photo by Rouben Mangasarian)

10. Political activists (from left) Vano Siradeghyan, Shahen Petrosyan, Vazgen Manukyan, and Levon Ter Petrosyan gather for a strategy session. (photo by Zaven Khachikian)

11. Ashot Manucharyan rallies a group of workers. (photo by Zaven Khachikian)

12. Khachik Stamboltsyan gives an interview during his hunger strike in Theater Square in October 1988. (photo by Rouben Mangasarian)

13. Survivors mourn the victims of the earthquake in northern Armenia in December 1988. (photo by Rouben Mangasarian)

14. Karabagh Committee members (from left): Samson Ghazaryan, Samvel Gevorgyan, Davit Vardanyan, Babgen Ararktsyan, Hambartsum Galstyan, Levon Ter Petrosyan, Khachik Stamboltsyan, Alexander Hakobyan, and Vano Siradeghyan greet the public on 2 June 1989—two days after being released from prison. (photo by Zaven Khachikian)

As an umbrella organization for diverse political forces, the popular front never had much chance for success. To create a coalition to rival the Karabagh Committee, the popular front invited the participation of an assortment of fringe groups, including the Union for National Self-Determination and the Association for the Defense of the Armenian Cause. The juxtaposition of upper-echelon communists and newly released political prisoners advocating immediate independence was enough to sink the front after a few meetings at the Armenian Academy of Sciences. Writer Karen Simonyan's attempt to form another popular front attracted even less support. Moreover, efforts in October to bring the two popular fronts together with the ANM quickly fizzled.

The environmental movement in Armenia should have afforded the popular front propitious ground for recruiting, except that the Karabagh movement had already won over the allegiance of most activists. Throughout much of the Soviet bloc, environmental causes had substituted for political action. Estonian activists, for example, risked imprisonment if they openly challenged Moscow's colonization of their republic. Under the guise of protecting the environment, however, they could campaign for the closure of newly built factories that employed mostly Russians. In 1987, Karabagh Armenians had couched their movement in the same terms.

The Armenian environmental movement that sprang up in the mid-1980s likewise foreshadowed the political activism of the Karabagh movement. The leading actors were often the same. The issue was framed in terms of a national life-or-death struggle. Even the battle lines were similar: liberal-minded scientists, educators, and writers vs. government officials and factory directors. Loosely organized soon after Brezhnev's death, Armenia's environmentalists flowered under Gorbachev. In March 1986, 350 prominent intellectuals of the republic directed an open letter to the Soviet leader detailing the consequences of industrial pollution in Armenia. According to the letter, Armenia's cancer rate had quadrupled between 1965 and 1985, while cases of abnormal births, leukemia, and mental retardation had likewise soared.[14] The letter marked the beginning of a genuine popular movement in Armenia at a time when similar efforts were getting underway in Lithuania, Estonia, Belorussia, and Ukraine.

In Armenia, as in other republics, concern over the ecology was confined largely to the educated class. Nonetheless, it galvanized a broad array of forces opposed to the Demirchyan way of doing business. Open meetings were held on a regular basis at the Writers' Union building, providing well-known artists and reform-oriented officials with an overflow audience to hear their criticisms of government policy. At the same time, *samizdat* writers and maverick filmmakers increasingly turned their attention to environmental themes.

Even by Soviet standards, the environmental conditions in Yerevan had reached crisis proportions by the mid-1980s. The city was the most polluted republic capital and ranked among the ten most polluted cities in the USSR. Framed by mountains to the north, Yerevan's geographic setting formed a natural amphitheater that opened up toward Mount Ararat. It also acted as a basin that trapped the air pollution of the Ararat plain. Smog was present more than 165 days of the year.[15]

In many respects, Yerevan was a victim of its own success. The Armenian capital contained over 35 percent of the republic's population, 40 percent of its motor vehicles, and over 60 percent of its industrial capacity. The number of privately owned cars shot up twenty-five times from 1960 to 1985, despite the opening of a subway line in 1981. The city's population growth also spurred an expansion of the construction materials industry. Factories producing cement, gypsum, prefabricated concrete, sand, gravel, and asphalt contributed 35 percent of Yerevan's air pollution.[16]

For most participants, the environmental movement had two very concrete targets. First was the nuclear power plant at Medzamor, twenty-five miles from Yerevan, which generated approximately 23 percent of Armenia's energy. Built in 1976 despite protests from seismic engineers, the dual reactors were blamed for causing an alarming rise in birth defects near the plant. Fears that an earthquake would strike the power station were also strong, especially after the consequences of the Chernobyl accident became known. Second, and even more prominent in the daily lives of most Yerevanis, was the mammoth Nairit chemical factory that sprawled over 500 acres along the subway line leading to Yerevan's Yerrord Mas district. The complex was an industrial-age nightmare of smokestacks, rusty pipes, foul-smelling toxic pools, and labyrinthine warehouses.

Construction of Nairit had begun in 1933 after an Armenian chemist, Stepan Hambaryan, developed a method for producing low-cost synthetic rubber. In what later became a dubious milestone of progress, Armenia was chosen as the site of the Soviet Union's first rubber plant because of the availability of limestone, hydroelectric energy from Lake Sevan, and pure water from mountain springs.[17] Originally, the facility was located on vacant marshlands two and a half miles from the center of Yerevan, but by the 1950s newly built neighborhoods had already engulfed the complex. Other huge industrial complexes were constructed nearby, including a polyvinylacetate manufacturing plant, a tire factory, and an aluminum factory in Kanaker.[18] As early as 1956, the USSR Council of Ministers decreed that Nairit and seventy-five other industrial enterprises be moved out of Yerevan to protect the health of the city's population. The planned relocation of industry never took place. Rather, new smokestacks were added to Yerevan's skyline over the next three decades. By the time the environmental movement emerged in Armenia, Nairit was the leading source of pollution in one of the Soviet Union's most poisoned cities. Official statistics in 1986 reported that the plant annually discharged 23,900 tons of toxic chemical pollutants into Armenia's air and water. Prodded by the republic's intelligentsia, the chief government public health officer of the USSR called in 1987 for the older of Nairit's two production lines to be shut down.[19] In September, the Armenian Council of Ministers agreed to close the older facility.

But Nairit also had its defenders. The plant was the Soviet Union's only producer of high-grade chloroprene rubber—a vital component for the country's military-industrial complex. (Chloroprene rubber stands up to extreme heat and chemical corrosion, and in 1987 was made by only eleven factories in the world.) Officially, the Soviet Ministry of Chemistry and Nairit's Yerevan director led the campaign to keep the plant open, delaying implementation of the Council of Ministers' decree until April 1988. In the meantime, Zori Balayan turned up the heat by publishing an emotional article in the widely read *Literaturnaya gazeta* (Literary Newspaper) that lamented the pollution of Nairit and the depletion of Lake Sevan.[20] On 17 October, the day after the article appeared in Yerevan's *Grakan tert* (Literary Newspaper), Balayan led a rally of 4,000 protesters in Theater Square decrying Armenia's environmental situation.[21] However fiery his oratory, Balayan and other representatives of the *nomenklatura* knew their limits. Balayan, for instance, conceded that Nairit's newer facility could not be shut down until Moscow had built a similar factory elsewhere in the Soviet Union. Likewise, he criticized the location of the Medzamor nuclear reactor, while defending the need for nuclear power in the republic.[22]

By early 1988, Armenia's environmental movement was beginning to register successes. Along with the closure of Nairit's older facility, an aluminum factory in Yerevan and a chemical plant in Kirovakan were forced to change their methods of operation, and a facility producing asphalt was relocated outside the republic's capital. Perhaps most important, though, were the movement's steady inroads into the general Armenian population. Indeed, many of the first participants in the Karabagh movement in Armenia on 20 February had also taken part in an environmentalist march.

The growing environmental consciousness had the effect of undercutting the appeal of Armenia's most well-established dissident group—the National Unification Party (NUP)—at a critical juncture in

Armenian history. Just as Armenians in 1987 were beginning to weigh the ecological price of industrialization, Gorbachev was releasing thousands of political prisoners from the Soviet GULAG. The most prominent Armenian among them was Paruir Hairikyan, the charismatic leader of the NUP.

Hairikyan was 16 years old when the first genocide commemoration took place in Armenia on 24 April 1965. Although too young to play an active role, Hairikyan found a purpose for his life in the mass demonstration. He also condemned himself to years of official persecution. Hairikyan and a handful of others from his generation were among the few who were not intimidated by the crackdown that followed the 1965 commemoration. On 24 April 1966, they held a small rally on the grave of composer Komitas Vardapet.[23] Three activists were jailed for fifteen days as a result of the commemoration. While in prison, they formed the National Unification Party. When the founders of the group were arrested and sentenced to lengthy terms in 1968, Hairikyan became the leader of the NUP. The next year, Hairikyan also was arrested while still a student at the Yerevan Polytechnic Institute.[24]

For Hairikyan, his conviction in 1969 began a seventeen-year odyssey in Soviet prison camps that transformed him from a boyish author of patriotic songs to a relentless champion of Armenian independence. With his black goatee, widow's peak, and smoldering dark eyes, Hairikyan was every bit the opposite of the bland, baggy-suited communist officials he detested. In 1974, Hairikyan reshaped the program of the NUP, removing the anti-communist ideology and the emphasis on reclaiming historical Armenian lands in eastern Turkey. Instead, Hairikyan made Armenian independence the NUP's all-encompassing goal and adopted the popular referendum as a tool compatible with the Soviet constitution. A *samizdat* leaflet begun in 1966, *Paros* (Beacon), was issued sporadically in Armenia to publicize the organization's views. Hairikyan and five other imprisoned NUP members staged a three-day hunger strike to dramatize their appeal to UN Secretary General Kurt Waldheim to investigate the Soviet record in Armenia.[25] Imprisonment also introduced Hairikyan to a who's who of Soviet political dissidents. Hairikyan entered the GULAG at the height of the Brezhnev-era crackdown against the dozens of *samizdat* publications and protest movements that had mushroomed in the mid-1960s. His prison-made connections and unbreakable will earned him a prominent place within the circle of Moscow-based human rights activists that rose to prominence in the Gorbachev era.

In one way or another, Hairikyan and the NUP were tied to political dissidence in Armenia throughout the 1970s and early 1980s. When a group was established in Armenia in 1977 to monitor the human rights provisions of the Helsinki accords, one of its original members was

Shahen Harutiunyan, a founder of the NUP. (Before the year was over, the group had been broken up and Harutiunyan sentenced to three years imprisonment. Monitoring groups in Russia, Ukraine, Georgia, and Lithuania were likewise suppressed.) That same year, Stepan Zatikyan, Hairikyan's brother-in-law and another of the NUP's founders, was charged with setting off an explosion in a Moscow subway station that reportedly killed seven people. Although the arrest of Zatikyan and two alleged accomplices drew protests from international human rights organizations, the trio was executed in 1979 after a secret trial.[26] Officially, they were the only dissidents condemned to death during the Brezhnev regime. In 1981, five members of an NUP off-shoot—the Union of Armenian Youth (UAY)—were sentenced to prison terms. The indictment named Marzpet Harutiunyan, brother of Shahen Harutiunyan, as the guiding spirit behind the UAY. On the last day of their trial, the UAY members asked to send a letter to President Ronald Reagan, who at the time was recovering from an assassination attempt, to extend their best wishes and express their hopes that the staunchly anti-communist president "would be true to his promises."[27]

Meanwhile, Hairikyan built his reputation on unwavering dedication. After being released from prison in 1973 and 1981, he immediately resumed his political activity and, each time, wound up back in the GULAG within a few months. Following his release in 1987, he again picked up where he left off, recasting the NUP as the Union for National Self-Determination, putting out a new publication called *Ankakhutiun* (Independence), and demanding the legalization of his organization.[28] Hairikyan was also instrumental in organizing a gathering of Armenian, Ukrainian, and Georgian dissidents in Yerevan in January 1988. The meeting resulted in the establishment of the International Committee in Defense of Political Prisoners. By summer, the group included representatives from the three Baltic republics and had evolved into the Coordinating Committee of Patriotic Movements of the Peoples of the Soviet Union.[29]

Hairikyan's record earned him the respect of political activists throughout Armenia. Some even agreed with his philosophy on independence. But once the Karabagh movement developed, few saw him as a potential national leader. Hairikyan had spent almost his entire adult life in prison. He had missed out on the formative events of a whole generation. He had never held a job.

During most of February and March, Hairikyan watched the Karabagh movement from the sidelines. His familiarity to Moscow dissidents, such as Sergei Grigoryants, and Western reporters allowed him to serve as a conduit of information between Yerevan and the outside world, but even he acknowledged that the demonstrations in Armenia were not of his making. When the KGB arrested him on 25 March, many Armenian activists detected a ploy designed to muddy the purpose of the movement. As one Karabagh Committee member argued during a May rally:

> How else can one explain the jailing of a man who had little to do with us, who has tried to speak here but has been asked to leave, as demonstrators do not share his position, and who has in fact left the podium, a man who in no way could be construed to represent a danger to the security of the state, who is less threatening to the government in the streets than in jail.[30]

The thesis of the Karabagh Committee member was seemingly confirmed by media efforts to keep Hairikyan's name in close proximity to the movement. In early April, Hairikyan was officially charged with slandering the Soviet state. Several Soviet press reports identified him as a behind-the-scenes manipulator of the demonstrations. At the same time, Hairikyan's hard-core supporters could be counted on to turn out a few thousand protesters on behalf of their leader. They challenged the ban on demonstrations in April by congregating in Lenin Square and supplied the loudest calls for independence on 28 May. Hairikyan's arrest also prompted a more broad-based rally for political freedom in front of Yerevan's KGB headquarters on 22 June, blocking one of the city's main streets.

The Hairikyan case culminated in July. Shortly after considering the status of Mountainous Karabagh, the Supreme Soviet Presidium stripped the Armenian dissident of his citizenship and expelled him from the country—the only such case under Gorbachev. Within a few weeks, Hairikyan had moved his base of operations to the Armenian community in Los Angeles. Hairikyan's connections in the West gave him at least modest celebrity. A State Department spokeswoman went so far as to deplore the expulsion and to laud Hairikyan as "a leading figure in the human rights movement in the Soviet Union."[31]

In the United States, however, Hairikyan faced well-entrenched competition for the right to speak on behalf of the Armenian people. The three main political parties of the far-flung Armenian diaspora had long ago defined the parameters of the Armenian cause. As the political party behind the establishment of the short-lived Armenian Republic, the Armenian Revolutionary Federation (ARF) had opposed Soviet rule in Armenia and had borne the standard of Armenian independence. Meanwhile, the Ramkavar Liberal Party and the Hunchakian Social Democratic Party had defended Soviet Armenia, both to buttress the Armenian homeland and as a means to set themselves apart from the ARF.

The pursuit of the Armenian cause after Stalin's death followed a fairly neat arrangement. Soviet Armenian officials, at least behind the scenes, conceded that they could do little in the international arena to gain recognition of the 1915 genocide or to press claims for historical Armenian lands. Rather, the tasks of lobbying foreign governments, appealing to international organizations, and raising awareness were left to the diaspora political parties. Over the years, the gulf gradually widened between nationalistic rhetoric and geopolitical realities, but leaders of the diaspora and Soviet Armenia generally went along with their longstanding relationship. Occasional symbolic victories in the U.S. Congress, European Parliament, and United Nations were parlayed into a source of legitimacy for the struggling political parties of the diaspora.

The Karabagh movement, however, ended the modus vivendi between Soviet Armenia and the diaspora. For one thing, members of the Karabagh Committee had little concept of the concerns of the diaspora. Levon Ter Petrosyan had been born in Syria, but the other members all traced their origins to Armenia.[32] Initially, they made no effort to establish ties with organizations outside the Soviet bloc. Meanwhile, the diaspora parties were slow to grasp the magnitude and breadth of the popular movement in Armenia. News reached the diaspora only haltingly, largely through the mainstream Western media. The ARF responded by organizing solidarity demonstrations in dozens of Armenian communities, but at the same time portrayed the movement as focusing entirely on territorial issues. ARF leaders were much more comfortable with the irredentist language of the *Krunk* Committee and Igor Muradyan's *Miatsum* than with the Karabagh Committee's sweeping critique of Soviet Armenian society. The Ramkavar and Hunchakian parties, jolted by the stinging attacks on Soviet Armenia's officialdom, reacted even more warily.

The first public sign of tension between the diaspora and the Karabagh movement emerged 4 October 1988, when a joint communiqué was issued by the three political parties. The statement reiterated earlier expressions of support for Armenians in the homeland, but the penultimate paragraph struck many in Armenia as almost a betrayal of the movement:

> We also call upon our valiant brethren in Armenia and Karabagh to forego such extreme acts as work stoppages, student strikes, and some radical calls and expressions which unsettle the law and order of the public life in the homeland and subject to heavy losses the economic, productive, educational and cultural life as well as the good standing of our nation in its relations with the higher Soviet bodies and also with the other Soviet republics. These zealous atti-

tudes also provide the fodder for the ulterior motives of the enemies of our people.[33]

As one Armenian activist quipped, the diaspora parties seemed to have borrowed a page from the Kremlin's propaganda manual.

Chapter 8

Khojalu

*F*our miles separated Stepanakert from Shushi, the center of the Azerbaijani community in Mountainous Karabagh in 1988. On a clear day, residents of Shushi could look down from the plateau on which their town rested and practically follow the traffic on the streets of Stepanakert. There was a road that connected Stepanakert with Shushi and then continued on to Zangezur, but even in the best of times travel had never been easy. Inaccessibility had always been the curse, or the blessing, of the land.

Armenia was also mountainous. But whereas Armenia was mostly barren and open, Mountainous Karabagh was impenetrable. Topography and vegetation had conspired to throw obstacles up in front of every vista. Hillsides were rutted with deep ravines. Valleys were sheltered by gnarled oaks. Huge boulders marked the banks of winding creeks. Forts guarded almost every mountaintop. Karabagh had always been a good place to hide. In earlier times, outlaws and exiles sought refuge in the mountains. Armenians went there in the eighth century to escape Arab invaders. Princes resisting the Ottomans and the Safavids retreated into the fortress sanctuaries of the highlands. The faithful built monasteries on craggy hillsides. In the nineteenth century, revolutionaries fled into the wilderness to elude tsarist police.

Geography had shaped the temperament of Karabagh Armenians. They were hospitable, like all peoples of the Caucasus, but they were not particularly fond of outsiders. And they did not take orders from anyone. By September 1988, Karabagh pride had been roiled, if not bent toward outright resentment, by the political movement in the Armenian capital. Yerevan had been relatively calm since the end of July. The impatience of earlier months had given way to talk of a broad, long-term struggle. With the emergence of the ANM came the charge that Karabagh Committee members had used the cause of the oblast as a stepping stone to their own bid for power.

Among those pointing fingers of accusation were Zori Balayan and Igor Muradyan. Both traced their family roots to Mountainous Karabagh, and had insisted that the focus of the Karabagh movement not stray beyond the oblast. The thrust of Muradyan's own group, *Miatsum*, contrasted sharply with the goals of the ANM. After his expulsion from the Karabagh Committee in May, Muradyan facilitated the *Krunk* Committee's work to build institutional ties at the economic, administrative, and academic level between Mountainous Karabagh and Armenia. At the same time, the Sumgait massacre impelled him to take steps toward bolstering the self-defense capabilities of the oblast's Armenian community, mainly by stocking up on hunting rifles and shotguns.

As he had made clear in the spring, Muradyan had no great interest in political reform, fighting corruption, or cleaning up the environment. On the contrary, Mountainous Karabagh stood alone on the agenda of *Miatsum*—framed in the context of an irreconcilable battle against pan-Turkism. Muradyan's stance gained credence from the court proceedings against seventy-nine Azerbaijani defendants arrested in connection with the Sumgait massacre. Throughout much of 1988, accounts of the trials blew through Armenia and Azerbaijan like a sandstorm. Most of those arrested were charged with "hooliganism" and received relatively light sentences, ranging from six to thirty months.[1] On 8 July, however, the USSR Supreme Court and prosecutor general's office transferred the jurisdiction of the trials involving three Azerbaijanis accused of murder from Azerbaijani courts to those of the Russian republic. Earlier, the party leader and mayor of Sumgait had been removed from their posts. Armenians, though, were disturbed that the suspects were to be tried as individuals, rather than as members of a single group, and that the court refused to investigate the possible role of Soviet officials in the massacre. Moreover, Armenians continued to chafe at the Kremlin's unwillingness to officially express condolences to the families of Sumgait victims.[2]

Even without the backwash of the Sumgait trials, residents of Stepanakert had endured a tense summer with their Azerbaijani neighbors. Increasingly, sheep were being stolen, passing cars pelted with stones, and factories and schools divided along national lines. Refugees from Sumgait brought with them horrific stories of massacre. Soon, volunteers began manning nighttime self-defense posts in the streets of the oblast center. In addition, forty local Armenians were arrested and charged with manufacturing weapons.[3] Behind its fortress walls, Shushi was filling with Azerbaijani refugees from Armenia. From a population of 20,000, 13 percent of which was Armenian, Shushi grew rapidly during the summer of 1988. Stepanakert Armenians had taken in hundreds of their own country-men from Sumgait, but in the case of Shushi they suspected the govern-ment in Baku of attempting to tip the demographic balance of the oblast in favor of the Azerbaijanis in time for the ongoing national census. They also believed that Baku was increasingly channeling money from the 24 March reform package to fund construction projects for the oblast's Azerbaijani community. With the arrival of more than 1,000 Azerbaijanis from the Masis area in August and September, Karabagh Armenians decided to protest the influx. On 12 September, they intensified the general strike in Stepanakert.[4]

The potential for serious violence in Mountainous Kara-bagh had risen steadily during the *glasnost* era. Many were surprised that the oblast had not blown up prior to 1988. By September, expectations on both sides of the conflict were understandably edgy. All it took to ignite the flame was a convoy of relief trucks driven by university students.

The students were among the many volunteers from the Armenian republic who had been delivering supplies and bolstering morale in Mountainous Karabagh since the early weeks of the Karabagh move-ment. The overland route from Armenia to Mountainous Karabagh had become more treacherous over the course of the summer, but with the intensification of the strike traffic picked up along the road from Vardenis. The travelers who touched off September's strife were transporting little other than their symbolic presence and a load of mattresses. They had come from Yerevan to help with the grape harvest in the oblast. Painted on the side of their bus was the word "Armenia" in Russian lettering.

Khojalu, an Azerbaijani-populated village about six miles north of Stepanakert, had long been known among Armenians as a place to avoid. Teenagers often threw rocks at passing cars and shouted curses. The incident that took place on the evening of 18 September was more serious. As the convoy was heading south to a nearby vineyard, attackers stoned the trucks and then opened fire with hunting rifles and shotguns, wounding eighteen of the students.[5] Travelers passing on the road quickly relayed news of the ambush to a crowd gathered in Stepanak-ert's main square. In response, hundreds of Armenians boarded buses and trucks, and headed for Khojalu. Others set off on foot. Many were stopped by MVD troops before reaching the village, but others broke through and traded gunfire with the Azerbaijanis well into the night.[6]

Over the next three days, the conflict spilled into the oblast's two largest towns. In Stepanakert, Armenians burned Azerbaijani houses, while in Shushi Azerbaijanis burned Armenian houses. Before the violence ended, 49 people had been wounded—33 Armenians and 16 Azer-baijanis—and more than 30 houses and buildings had been set on fire, according to Arkady Volsky.[7] In addition, a 61-year-old Armenian carpenter had been killed. On 21 September, Volsky banned demonstrations, introduced a 9 P.M. to 6 A.M. curfew, and imposed a special status on Stepanakert and the adjoining Aghdam district.[8]

News of the Khojalu clash was transmitted to Yerevan soon after it reached Stepanakert, setting in motion a predictable chain of events. First, crowds gathered at Theater Square and in front of the Armenian Supreme Soviet building. As the work week opened on 19 September, strikes paralyzed the public transportation system of the Armenian capital and idled factories. University students boycotted classes. Protesters demanded that the Armenian Supreme Soviet hold an extraordinary session on Mountainous Karabagh. After the crowds in Theater Square topped 500,000 at mid-week, Moscow once again made its presence felt, dispatching MVD troops and armored personnel carriers to guard key government and party buildings. Lenin Square was completely cordoned off by soldiers. A few dozen yards in front of the armored personnel carriers facing Theater Square, students erected a symbolic barricade. Forming a human wall across one of central Yerevan's main streets, the young people sat with their backs to the MVD troops. Between themselves and the armored personnel carriers, they had stacked the works of Lenin in neat columns.[9] On the evening of 22 September, troops were posted around Theater Square while a rally took place. Students staged an all-night vigil in hopes of preventing the occupation of the square. And again, the senior representatives of the republic's intelligentsia—including Silva Kaputikyan and Viktor Hambartsumyan—appealed for calm on local television.[10]

Theater Square itself recalled earlier days as well. Hunger-strikers were back, camping out beside the Tumanyan and Spendiaryan statues. Students staged a sit-in on the steps of the opera house and fashioned paper hats out of the latest issues of *Pravda*. Loudspeakers carried speeches both at noon and again in the early evening. Reports on events in Mountainous Karabagh were issued regularly to combat the official media's seeming news blockade of the oblast. Posters and billboards competed for attention along the fringes of the square. One of the most popular featured a cartooned lineup of the republic's most notorious officials and invited passers-by to pin one ruble notes onto the outstretched palms.

Behind the scenes, though, the events of September marked a departure from the past. For one thing, once the strike was underway the government turned to the Karabagh Committee to intercede on its behalf. Armenian Presidium Chairman Hrant Voskanyan met with committee members twice in late September, and Gorbachev issued his own personal appeal to urge the activists to maintain order.[11] There was little give-and-take, however, on the committee's demand that the Armenian Supreme Soviet convene an extraordinary session. On 19 September, Voskanyan tried to placate the crowds by suggesting that the legislature would meet in the coming days, but the government's real intent was to deflect the increasingly effective efforts of the Karabagh movement to apply political pressure.

The experience of June had given activists a good idea of whom in the legislature sided with their cause. At the same time, students were more than ready to present their case directly to office-holders at government buildings, despite the presence of MVD troops. The lobbying efforts brought results. Within days of the Khojalu clash, the Karabagh Committee could claim that 150 of the Armenian Supreme Soviet's 340 deputies—well above the one-third required by the Armenian constitution to convene the legislature—supported a special session.[12] But the authorities had also learned from recent events. For Armenian officials, the lesson of the 15 June resolution and the 18 July Presidium was that the Armenian government could push the Kremlin no further. On 24 September, the Armenian Supreme Soviet Presidium officially rejected appeals for an extraordinary session. Instead, the Presidium called on Moscow to expedite preparation of the Voss Commission's report, to push for the implementation of other decisions taken on 18 July, and to guarantee the security of Azerbaijan's Armenian residents. Complaints of Karabagh Committee members that the Armenian Presidium had violated the constitution were countered by charges that activists had intimidated the deputies.[13]

By the end of September, the tempo of political activity in Armenia had slowed. The Karabagh Committee called for an end to strikes. According to Ashot Manucharyan, a top KGB official had told committee members "that we were personally responsible for organizing the protests and that it was our responsibility to calm the people down." [14] Flaunting the committee's influence, Vano Siradeghyan claimed, "We announced the strike and we ended the strike." [15] The 15,000 extra troops that had been sent to Armenia stopped patrolling the main streets. Students returned to class.

The situation in Armenia, however, could hardly be described as normal. Armenians were trapped in a confrontation with no apparent end. Novelist Hrant Matevosyan remarked:

> I don't really want to be a nationalist, and a lot of people feel the same. I would rather be international in my outlook and just be a normal man, a normal artist. But this is not possible, especially for a people like ours. For a small nation, the threat of disappearance hangs over us every day.[16]

Moscow's impatience with the Karabagh movement was mounting, as was evidenced by television news broadcasts that featured interviews with workers incensed by the strikes and demonstrations in Armenia. In addition, Karabagh Committee members were threatened with prison terms of up to six months and fines equal to a year's salary if they continued organizing mass meetings. Manucharyan, who was hit with a fine of 500 rubles, refused to appear in court to respond to the charges.[17]

In Mountainous Karabagh, the impact of the Khojalu clash also lingered, reinforcing the siege mentality that was part of the consciousness of Armenians in the oblast. Karabagh Armenians were not given to fear; if anything, they reveled in the mountaineer's reckless bravado. But Khojalu drove home the acute sense of isolation and vulnerability that haunted the people.

The Khojalu clash offered a preview of what civil war would be like in Mountainous Karabagh. Azerbaijanis from nearby Aghdam and beyond could be expected to join the battle; mob violence would tear apart towns with mixed populations; roadside ambushes would cut off transportation; and hunting equipment would provide a ready supply of arms. The three-day outburst of communal strife was also a blow to the political goals of the Karabagh movement. From the outset, Karabagh Armenians had been resolute in framing their campaign in constitutional terms. Khojalu, much like the Sumgait massacre six months earlier, turned it into an ethnic feud. The appeal of the oblast party bureau adopted the language of Old Testament enmity to sound a warning: "The notorious 'an eye for an eye, a tooth for a tooth' formula will lead us into an impasse from which there is no way out."[18]

More immediate were the new demographic realities emerging within Mountainous Karabagh. Khojalu dramatized the ethnic polarization that had begun to pull Mountainous Karabagh apart after the Sumgait massacre. The conflict had been simmering for months, with job dismissals of Armenians in Shushi and Azerbaijanis in Stepanakert. High school students were boycotting teachers because of their nationality. Even collective farms were being divided so as to separate Armenians from Azerbaijanis.[19] Armenians smelled conspiracy at every turn. When Education Ministry officials from Moscow arrived in Stepanakert to close a teachers' college in October, more than 200 Armenian students and professors staged a sit-in to resist plans to transfer them to Armenia. "They are trying to send our intellectuals outside the province," an Armenian trade union official at the college said.[20]

As a result of Khojalu, a sweeping exchange of populations took place in the span of a few days. By the end of September, Stepanakert and Shushi had ceased to be towns with sizable minority communities. For Armenians, abruptly abandoning Shushi with its three four-teenth-century churches and monastic complex left a deep wound. In addition, the creation of thousands of refugees brought a new set of problems. Mountainous Karabagh First Secretary Henrik Poghosyan blamed Azerbaijanis who had left Armenia for driving Armenians out of Shushi. And with 5,000 Armenian refugees crowding into Stepanakert, Poghosyan was especially upset by what he saw as an illegal effort to build housing and factories for the Azerbaijanis arriving in the oblast.[21]

Like most of his fellow Karabagh Armenians, Poghosyan put little stock in the claims of progress in the oblast played up by communist officials in Armenia. In theory at least, Moscow's 24 March reform package enabled Armenia and Mountainous Karabagh to develop ties in every sphere of activity. After visiting the oblast in October, Suren Harutiunyan said that Armenian state ministries and institutes involved in transportation, construction, industry, and food processing were already hard at work in helping Mountainous Karabagh.[22] Educationally, Armenia was to provide greater opportunities for the oblast's college-age students, and by the fall, 270 Karabagh Armenians were enrolled in Armenia's institutions of higher learning.[23] The Armenian first secretary and his Azerbaijani counterpart, Abdul Rakhman Vezirov, were in daily telephone contact to coordinate their efforts. Harutiunyan was able to cite other benefits as well: a new transmitter to broadcast Armenian television; improved postal, telephone, and radio links between the oblast and Armenia; and the shipment of almost 40,000 Armenian-language publications to Mountainous Karabagh.

Poghosyan, however, applied another set of calculations. He complained that plans for cooperation between Yerevan and Stepanakert largely remained on paper, although he had repeatedly made the point that the new construction called for in the 24 March reform package could not be carried out without assistance from Armenia. Still more worrisome for the oblast first secretary was the role of Baku. Back in March, many Karabagh Armenians had dismissed Moscow's development program on the grounds that it left Azerbaijani authorities in a position of control. Moreover, *Krunk* Committee members argued that economic reform detracted from their all-or-nothing political struggle. In November, Poghosyan conceded that many of their concerns were justified:

> I can unequivocally say that the plan for the socioeconomic development of the NKAO is being implemented badly, inadequately, and one-sidedly. We still do not know who will benefit from the resources allocated from the budget, through which sources they will be used, and which projects will be financed from which sources.[24]

The only remedy, according to Poghosyan, was a change in Mountainous Karabagh's status:

> The sixty-five years of the existence of Nagorno Karabakh within the structure of Azerbaijan . . . leaves no room for doubt that the oblast must without delay be taken out of the structure of Azerbaijan.[25]

In Baku, the struggle over Mountainous Karabagh was viewed as a war of attrition. Demographically, the Azerbaijanis were aided by a higher birth rate. Politically, they had the power to make life very difficult for the Armenians. To a greater or lesser extent, many of the dominant nationalities in the non-Russian republics had squeezed minority groups within their jurisdictions. The Georgians, for example, had long suppressed the separatist tendencies of the Abkhazians and Ossetians within their republic. Moldavians had tried to contain the aspirations of the Gagauz. Uzbeks had sought to limit the influence of the Tajiks, and the list went on. Stalin had served as a mentor in the ways of cultural genocide. Under his leadership, up to 3.5 million people were deported from their native lands. In the Caucasus and the Crimean peninsula alone, his regime uprooted eight small Muslim peoples during the mid-1940s.[26]

Within Azerbaijan, most of the republic's Muslim minorities—the Talish, Kurds, Tats, Avars, Tsakhourins, and others—were vulnerable to the forces of assimilation. In 1926, the Farsi-speaking Talish officially numbered 77,300. The 1979 census, however, made no mention of them. Although their population was estimated in the late 1980s to be from 350,000 to 500,000, the Talish were denied their own schools, newspapers, and clubs. Azerbaijan's more than 150,000 Kurds were also left out of the 1979 census and deprived of schools and newspapers.[27] The Muslim Lezgins, concentrated in the rugged mountains straddling the border between the Russian and Azerbaijani republics, were in a better position to resist Baku's efforts at homogenization.

The Armenian community in Baku was not viewed as assimilable. Nonetheless, Armenians were subjected to the same cultural repression as Azerbaijan's other minorities. During World War II, the city's seventy-six Armenian schools were shut down. Well-educated Armenians were passed over for top jobs. In the 1970s, when the community numbered more than 215,000, the Armenian theater, cultural center, pedagogical institute, and television programming section were closed.[28]

The case of the Karabagh Armenians was unique. In the early 1920s, the Azerbaijani authorities not only faced a people bearing scars from recent hostilities, but had to deal with the fact that the Karabagh

Armenians constituted 95 percent of the population in a compact autonomous oblast that shared a border with the Armenian republic. One of the few factors working in Baku's favor was the tendency of Lenin and his inner circle to disregard the staying power of nationalism. After completing his assignment in Mountainous Karabagh, Arkady Volsky observed:

> Our founding fathers in 1917 were romantics. They thought it didn't matter where the borders were—that the proletariat would triumph all over the world and the borders would fade away by themselves.[29]

The borders, of course, very much did matter, especially for a people such as the Azerbaijanis that had never known statehood prior to 1918. And while the authorities in Baku could not alter the demographics of their territory with the same ruthless finality employed by the Kremlin, they could nonetheless slowly chip away at the Armenian presence in their republic.

Clearly, Baku's efforts had as much to do with asserting Azerbaijani identity as with suppressing Armenian demands. The geographic juxtaposition of the two peoples went a long way toward explaining the development of Azerbaijani national consciousness. In large part, Azerbaijani identity began to crystallize in Baku during the boom years of the oil industry. The term "Azerbaijani" (*Azarbayjanli*) itself was not widely used until the rise of a nationalist intelligentsia in the late 1800s.[30] Before then, Muslim peasants in Transcaucasia had been known primarily as "Tatars" or "Tartars." The Shi'ite clergy and the landed gentry had shielded most of them from the forces of the modern age. As late as 1900, only 4 to 5 percent of the Azerbaijani population was literate.[31]

In Baku, however, workers from the countryside suddenly faced the capitalist world in its most rough-and-tumble form. Baku rode the first wave of the oil boom into the early years of the twentieth century.

Oil had been a commodity in ancient times on the Apsheron peninsula, where it naturally bubbled to the surface and formed in shallow pools around the area that became Baku. Modern drilling technology ushered in the growth years of the oil industry. Most significant was the arrival of Robert Nobel in Baku in 1873. Within a decade, the Nobel Company had emerged as the largest oil firm in Baku and had opened the gates to an outpouring of European investment. At its peak in 1901, the Baku area produced more oil than the United States.[32]

Armenian capitalists were well-positioned to reap the benefits of the oil bonanza. Until 1872, the Russian government maintained a monopoly over the Apsheron peninsula's oil fields. A Baku Armenian, I. M. Mirzoev, held the concession after 1863 and was quick to snatch up promising drilling sites when the state monopoly ended.[33] Mirzoev and his fellow Armenians were soon overshadowed by European investors, but as a group Armenian oilmen stayed well ahead of their Azerbaijani counterparts. They also provided employment for the thousands of Armenian laborers streaming in from the countryside.

A Western writer traveling in Transcaucasia in 1905 noted the contrasts between Armenians and Azerbaijanis in Baku:

> If it were not for them [the Armenians] the foreigners would soon have got the whole oil industry into their own hands, instead of being obliged to compete with capable, business-like, and energetic rivals. At the same time the Armenian workmen are much less tractable than the Tartars. They demand better food and higher wages, more comfortable lodgings, baths, reading rooms, etc. whereas the Tartars are content with anything that is given them. The Armenians belong to workmen's societies, and if they do not get what they want they organize strikes, and even take part in revolutionary movements.[34]

Azerbaijanis prospered in other areas of business. By the turn of the century, Azerbaijanis owned nearly half of Baku's merchant fleet. Traditional industries such as tobacco, silk, and carpet weaving, as well the area's largest textile factory, were also controlled by Azerbaijanis.[35] What rankled the growing circle of Azerbaijani intellectuals, however, was the belief that Baku had ceased to be an Azerbaijani city. Indeed, Azerbaijanis were poorly represented within Baku's governing bodies. By 1903, Russians had surpassed them as the city's largest ethnic group.[36]

Azerbaijanis had long felt that their Armenian neighbors were favored by Russian rule. Not only did Armenians and Russians share a religious affinity, but after the conquests of the tsar in Transcaucasia Armenians from Iran and the Ottoman Empire were welcomed into lands around Yerevan that had previously been dominated by Muslims. Unlike the Muslims of Transcaucasia, Armenians were allowed to serve in the army, and were well represented in the tsarist civil service. Likewise, Armenian clergy were subjected to fewer restrictions than their Azerbaijani counterparts.

Armenian professionals and skilled tradesmen came to dominate the growing cities of Transcaucasia in the 1800s. In noting the relative success of the Armenians, an Englishman observed:

> The Armenians have two points in common with the Jews: these are their extreme dispersion and their general superiority in

education, industry and enterprise over the population among whom they live and this made them both weak and strong.[37]

While at a disadvantage in competing with Armenians, the Azerbaijanis were among the most advanced Muslim peoples of the Russian Empire. Along with the Crimean Tatars, the Azerbaijanis developed their own secular intelligentsia around the turn of the century. The adornments of European civilization were imported as well. Baku, for example, was the site of the first modern theater and the first opera performance in the Muslim world.[38] In Elizavetpol (present-day Ganja), the forces of modernization were more likely to be channeled toward defining Azerbaijani nationalism. The term "Azerbaijani" was widely accepted in the area at a time when "Tatar" was still commonly used in Baku. Elizavetpol Azerbaijanis were also more likely to protest repressive features of Russian rule.[39] A common attachment to modernization even brought Azerbaijanis and Armenians together in support of the Young Turk revolution that took power in Istanbul in 1908 and the constitutional movement that shook Tabriz in 1908–09.[40]

By the early 1900s, Azerbaijani intellectual circles in Baku and Elizavetpol were increasingly dominated by a youthful middle class that had attended universities in Teheran, Kazan, and particularly Istanbul. While oriented primarily toward the Ottoman Empire, the emerging Azerbaijani elite could also claim its own intellectual role models. Among the most notable was Ali bey Huseynzade, a leading contributor to the formulation of pan-Turkism.

While studying medicine in Saint Petersburg, Huseynzade was impressed by the appeal of pan-Slavism among his fellow students. In 1889, he went to Istanbul and become a founding member of an opposition group called the Ottoman Union. Huseynzade and other proponents of pan-Turkism envisioned a vast *Turan* (or state encompassing the Turkic peoples) stretching from the Balkans to the Pacific. Their ideas, however, ran counter to the Ottoman Empire's official ideology of Ottomanism, which stressed the unity and equality of the sultan's subjects.[41] Upon returning to the Russian Empire, Huseynzade embarked on a career in journalism and in 1906 founded his own literary journal. Much of his energy was devoted to spreading the doctrine of pan-Turkism. He was particularly concerned that Azerbaijani nationalism would isolate his countrymen politically from other Turkic peoples. When the Young Turks—in many respects the ideological offspring of the Ottoman Union—came to power in the Ottoman Empire in 1908, Huseynzade and other prominent Azerbaijani intellectuals rushed to Istanbul. Several accepted positions in the Ottoman government or the ruling Committee of Union and Progress

(CUP). Huseynzade himself was appointed to the CUP's supreme council.[42]

Young Turk leaders favored tightening the bonds of cultural unity between Ottoman and Azerbaijani Turks as a first step toward achieving pan-Turkism's broader political goals. Back in the Russian Empire, however, pan-Turkism was caught up in competition with pan-Islamism and incipient Azerbaijani nationalism. At a mass level, the political philosophies of the educated classes made few inroads among Azerbaijani peasants and herders. Whereas the Armenian Revolutionary Federation won wide adherence among the Armenian population in the early 1900s, the vast majority of Azerbaijanis continued to ground their identity within Muslim Shi'ite culture. For most, Iran was the center of their universe. Persian remained the language of Azerbaijan's mullahs and nobles, while the Sunnism and new political currents of the Ottoman Empire stirred suspicion.

The agenda of the *Musavat* (Equality) Party, founded by Azerbaijanis in 1912, likewise gave precedence to promoting Muslim unity over pan-Turkism. *Musavat*ists, who quickly constituted their people's leading political party, were hesitant to openly challenge the tsarist government. The outbreak of World War I and the subsequent chaos of the Russian Revolution, however, introduced a new set of questions. The disintegration of the Russian army along the Anatolian front in 1917 demanded that the *Musavat* Party assume the responsibilities of national leadership. Whereas only a few years earlier Azerbaijani autonomy had seemed a far-fetched objective, by the time the Bolsheviks seized power in November 1917 the prospect of independent statehood was fast approaching.

With empires collapsing around them, many Azerbaijani leaders turned away from pan-Turkism and began thinking about independence in concrete terms, especially when the ill-fated Transcaucasian Federation unraveled in the early months of 1918. Relations between Azerbaijani and Ottoman officials cooled further when Ottoman Turkey hesitated in recognizing Azerbaijan's declaration of independence on 28 May 1918. At the same time, the fate of Mountainous Karabagh, Zangezur, and Nakhichevan were identified as key national issues by Azerbaijani policymakers.[43]

Ultimately, Sovietization decided the course of the Azerbaijani people. Azerbaijan became a de facto nation under Soviet rule, with secure borders and a state-approved culture distinct from the other Muslim peoples of the Soviet Union. Peasants who divided their loyalties between their local villages and the vast Islamic world were instructed to consider themselves Soviet Azerbaijanis. Contact with Turkey and Iran was cut off, religion squelched, and communism imposed as the official ideology of the elite. But with the process of national development arrested in its early stages, Azerbaijani identity had little on which to focus. Hostility toward Armenians served as one of the few salient features, particularly with memories still fresh of communal violence in Baku during 1918 between supporters of the *Musavat* Party and the Armenian-backed city soviet. The fate of compatriots across the border in northwestern Iran offered another common cause. Under Stalin, Azerbaijan's border with Iran was closed and Azerbaijanis with Iranian passports were expelled in 1938.[44] The collapse in 1946 of the Soviet-backed Autonomous Government of Azerbaijan, established on territory in northwestern Iran held by Soviet troops during World War II, nurtured a "literature of longing" based on the goal of uniting Azerbaijanis in the Soviet Union and Iran under a single government.[45]

Above all, Azerbaijanis grappled with a sense of insecurity and inferiority in facing the ancient cultures of the two other Transcaucasian republics. Even in respect to Shushi (known as Shusha among Azerbaijanis)—the focal point of Azerbaijani attachment to Mountainous Karabagh—the roots were relatively shallow. Azerbaijanis did not enter the area until the 1750s, when an ambitious Armenian *melik* invited an Azerbaijani tribal chieftain to join forces with him in opposing the other four Armenian *melik*s of Mountainous Karabagh. The chieftain, Panah Ali Khan, built a castle at Shushi, and his descendants extended their suzerainty over all of Mountainous Karabagh, but the *melik*doms and the region's overwhelming preponderance of Armenian inhabitants did not give way. During the decades before World War I, the Azerbaijanis remained a minority while Shushi emerged as the third largest city in Transcaucasia, with a population of 41,000. Of the city's twenty-one prewar newspapers and magazines, nineteen were published in Armenian and two in Russian.[46]

Rather than trying to flesh out the recent history of Azerbaijanis in Shushi or other areas of Mountainous Karabagh, Azerbaijani scholars turned to ethnography to bolster the Azerbaijani sense of nationhood. After the death of Stalin, special attention was given to questions surrounding the Caucasian Albanians. The academic tug-of-war that resulted was a typically Soviet dispute. With no other outlets to resolve tensions between national groups, battles were waged over obscure points of history. In the case of Azerbaijanis and Armenians, scholars from both sides first staked out their arguments in their respective national journals, and Moscow served as the ultimate arbiter by deciding which articles would be reprinted in leading Soviet publications.[47]

The controversy that brought the Caucasian Albanians back to life began with the claim that the Azerbaijanis were the genetic and cultural descendants of the ancient Albanians. Some scholars dated the emergence of the "ancient Azerbaijanis" to the third century B.C. Others took a different approach, asserting that large numbers of Turks migrated into the southern Caucasus as early as the sixth century and subsequently intermarried with Caucasian Albanians and other indigenous peoples.

In Azerbaijani scholarship, the Caucasian Albanians represented one of the oldest and richest cultures of the region. Z. Buniatov, for example, claimed that the Armenian clergy translated Albania's national literature into their own tongue and then destroyed the evidence, and that the Armenians of Mountainous Karabagh and Zangezur were in fact the descendants of assimilated Albanians. I. Aliev went still further, contending that the origins of the Caucasian Albanians predated those of the Armenians and that Albania was the first state in the region to adopt Christianity.[48]

The traditional Armenian portrait of the Caucasian Albanians was rooted in a very different premise. According to A. S. Mnatsakanyan and other Armenian scholars, an Albanian culture emerged only in the first centuries of the Christian era as a result of the intermingling of several tribes. Geographically, the Caucasian Albanians were confined to a relatively small area north of the Kur River, while the lands of what became Mountainous Karabagh were Armenian as far back as the seventh century B.C. After Armenia was divided between the Byzantine and Sasanid empires in 387 A.D., the Persian Sasanids extended the administrative boundaries of the Albanian province south of the Kur River to incorporate Artsakh and Utik in 428. Ethnically, however, the area remained Armenian. With the adoption of Christianity in the fourth century and the initial flowering of Armenian literature in the fifth century, Armenian culture naturally flowed across provincial divisions and was gradually adopted by the Albanian ruling class of southern (or "new") Albania, according to Armenian sources.[49] Armenians also noted that the three leading medieval works on the region, written by Persian and Azerbaijani historians of the seventeenth and eighteenth centuries, consistently referred to Karabagh as Armenian land. In the Soviet period, one of the most conclusive studies of the Caucasian Albanians was coauthored by Karabagh Committee member Alexander Hakobyan in 1987.

Even while contesting the history of the Caucasian Albanians, many Azerbaijanis remained convinced that the Soviet system was stacked against them. From the Azerbaijani viewpoint, communism did little to wash away historical Russian antipathy for the Turkic peoples. Whether based on a deep-seated fear going back to the Tatar conquests of Russia or the colonial mentality that accompanied tsarist armies into Central Asia and Transcaucasia, the prejudice of Russians toward their Turkic neighbors, the argument maintained, had yet to be overcome. A corollary of the same supposition held that Armenians were privileged in the Soviet Union. Not only was Azerbaijan's most famous communist revolutionary, Stepan Shahumyan, an Armenian descendent of one of Mountainous Karabagh's *melik* clans, but many Azerbaijani nationalists resented his stature in the Soviet pantheon for what they viewed as his brutal repression of Azerbaijani interests during his leadership of the ill-fated Baku soviet in 1918. In addition, other Armenians figured prominently among Soviet scientists and cultural figures. More grating still was the relatively open relationship between Armenia and its diaspora—in sharp contrast with the restrictions separating Azerbaijanis in the Soviet Union from their kinsmen in Iran.

Lenin had hoped that the development of Soviet Azerbaijan would send a message to non-Western peoples across Asia. Azerbaijan, he predicted, would be "the best agitation, the best propaganda for our affairs, throughout this huge multinational East."[50] Within Azerbaijan itself, however, there were few Azerbaijani communists to serve Lenin's vision. As late as 1925, only 43 percent of Communist Party members in the republic were Azerbaijani. (In Armenia at the same time, 93 percent of the communists were Armenian.)[51] Nariman Narimanov, the sole Azerbaijani on the Baku soviet and the first chairman of Soviet Azerbaijan's Revolutionary Committee, warned Stalin in 1923 that Armenian communists in the republic sought to carry out "*Dashnak* [Armenian Revolutionary Federation] work under the flag of communism."[52]

Even the creation of the Nagorno Karabakh Autonomous Oblast pricked Azerbaijani national pride. Narimanov argued that Armenian concerns in Mountainous Karabagh stemmed from a "general weakness of party and soviet work"—shortcomings that in his opinion did not justify the establishment of a separate administrative unit.[53] President of the *Sovnarkom* (Soviet People's Commissars) at the time, Narimanov headed the Azerbaijani-dominated state apparatus. He believed that the Azerbaijani Communist Party, led by Sergei Kirov (a Russian), had scant regard for Azerbaijani sensitivities. Azerbaijani nationalists would later contend that Narimanov's suspicions were validated by the party's decision to make Khankendi (later renamed Stepanakert) the administrative center of Mountainous Karabagh and to proclaim Armenian as the official language.

As in other non-Russian republics, Moscow sought to cultivate a new generation of local cadres in Soviet Azerbaijan. Under this process, Azerbaijanis gradually came to control the levers of power within the republic, often at the expense of Armenians.[54] In the big picture of Soviet nationalities policy, however, many Azerbaijanis felt manipulated by the Kremlin. In 1940, for example, the Cyrillic alphabet replaced the Latin alphabet for Azerbaijanis and other Turkic-speaking peoples in the Soviet Union. Azerbaijan had led the way in switching from Arabic script to Latin in 1924, but when Turkey followed suit Moscow feared that Latinization would invite the spread of Ankara's influence.[55] Some Azerbaijanis also saw malice in Moscow's decision in the late 1930s to change their people's official designation from "Turk" to "Azerbaijani." In the political sphere, the Kremlin maintained a firm grip over Azerbaijani nationalism. Under Stalin, First Secretary Mir Jafar Baghirov was more interested in self-preservation than in Azerbaijan's national development. As in other Muslim republics, Moscow appointed Russians to fill the second secretary post in Azerbaijan's Communist Party. And even though the Soviets promoted *korenizatsiia* (nativization), Azerbaijanis still comprised only 61 percent of the republic's Communist Party in the mid-1960s, while Armenians accounted for 16 percent of party membership.[56] (In the general population, Russians outnumbered Azerbaijanis in Baku until the 1960s.[57])

Events in the Gorbachev era further rankled Azerbaijani national feelings. First, Moscow scrapped its campaign against the central government in Iran, thereby cutting off moral support for any movement toward separatism among Azerbaijanis across the border. In the summer of 1987, Haidar Aliyev—former first secretary of Azerbaijan and the first member of his nationality to reach the Politburo—was removed from his post.[58] At the same time, Gorbachev included two Armenians—Georgi Shakhnazarov and Abel Aganbegyan—within his inner circle of advisers.

Like Armenians, Azerbaijanis were haunted by a sense of vulnerability. For Armenians, the image was of a beleaguered island of Christianity engulfed by a hostile Muslim sea. Among Azerbaijanis, pressure came from being hemmed in by Russia to the north, Armenia to the west, and Iran to the south—all nations with an interest in suppressing Azerbaijani political claims. The Turks were accepted as potential allies, but even their support was tempered by concern over Turkish designs on Azerbaijan.

With the first stirrings of the Karabagh movement, Azerbaijanis saw the issue as a slap in the face of their national honor. The movement not only rekindled a nearly 200-year-old inferiority complex, but also raised historical consciousness about the connection between the Shushi region and some of Azerbaijan's most revered literary and artistic figures.[59] As an Azerbaijani journalist told a Turkish newspaper, "It is as if the Armenian attitude has awakened the people and moved them to safeguard their rights." [60]

Azerbaijani intellectuals attacked Armenian claims on a number of fronts. In February 1988, a well-known poet, Bahtiyar Vahabzade and a historian, Suleiman S. Aliyarov, coauthored an open letter that challenged the historical bonds between Karabagh and its Armenian population. Vahabzade and Aliyarov argued that Karabagh was inhabited in ancient times by Caucasian Albanians and later became an independent khanate populated and ruled by Turks. They also contended that the decision in 1921 to place Mountainous Karabagh under Azerbaijan's jurisdiction was part of a quid pro quo in which Azerbaijan relinquished claims to Zangezur.[61] Azerbaijani nationalists later took this interpretation a step further, demanding administrative autonomy for Azerbaijanis within Armenia. Velayat M. Kuiev, an Azerbaijani writer and deputy director of the Azerbaijan Literary Institute, asserted that the Karabagh movement was part of a larger scheme to grab territory. Kuiev said:

> Lately the Armenian nationalists, including some quite influential people, have started talking again about "Greater Armenia." It's not just Azerbaijan. They want to annex parts of Georgia, Iran, and Turkey.[62]

On a more official level, Baku authorities replied to charges that they had stifled Mountainous Karabagh's development by producing statistics purporting to show that the oblast ranked ahead of Azerbaijan and Armenia in many quality-of-life indicators.[63] The figures pointed out that housing space and the number of hospital beds in Mountainous Karabagh were relatively high per capita, although there was no mention that the favorable rankings were attributable to the migration of Armenians out of the oblast.

As for conspiracy theories, Baku provided just as fertile an environment as Yerevan. Diaspora Armenians and the Armenian Apostolic Church were often held responsible in the Azerbaijani media for instigating the demonstrations in Yerevan and Stepanakert. Baku Radio claimed that American-Armenian lobbyists wielded substantial power in the American political system, even reporting (incorrectly) that Michael Dukakis's chief adviser on domestic affairs during the 1988 presidential campaign was Armenian.[64] At the same time, resentment was directed toward progressive intellectuals in the Baltics, Ukraine, Belorussia, and Moscow for sympathizing with the cause of the Armenians. Andrei Sakharov was reviled with particular venom. Finally, the reaction of the Western media to the Sumgait massacre served to substantiate the conviction that the Christian world was out to besmirch Azerbaijani culture.[65]

But even with tension mounting, Baku remained relatively calm throughout most of 1988. The first large demonstrations did not take place until mid-May, apparently with tacit government approval. In June, Azerbaijani First Secretary Abdul Rakhman Vezirov spoke to a gathering in Baku's Lenin Square at the same time that nearly a million Armenians were massed in the streets of Yerevan.[66] Like Suren Harutiunyan, Azerbaijani political leaders had learned from the mistakes of Demirchyan. In the *glasnost* era, the will of the people could not be completely ignored. But whereas Karabagh and corruption-fighting played well in Theater Square, Azerbaijani officials understood the power of Islam and wounded nationalism among their own population. More illustrative of Azerbaijan's political climate were the divisions among Azerbaijani intellectuals and political activists. As in other Soviet republics, there were enough reform-minded democrats in Azerbaijan to protest against the control of hard-line communists. In August 1988, they initiated the formation of the Popular Front of Azerbaijan in Support of *Perestroika*.[67] The creation of the front, however, marked the opening of a deeper struggle for the allegiance of the Azerbaijani people. In the months that followed, Westernized intellectuals continued to emphasize the establishment of a civil society and adherence to legal principles, but increasingly they faced militant nationalists who placed Mountainous Karabagh at the heart of their agenda. By the time the Azerbaijani Popular Front held its founding congress in July 1989, the strident nationalists had the upper hand. In retrospect, both sides would look back at the events of September 1988 as a turning point that did not bode well for the moderates.

Chapter 9

Campaign

Khachik Stamboltsyan presided over Theater Square in late September like a patron saint. After the clash at Khojalu, the bearded biophysicist began a hunger strike on behalf of his countrymen in Mountainous Karabagh. For the first few days of the fast, he paced about the square in characteristic fits of frenetic energy, but as time passed Stamboltsyan's strength waned. By October, Stamboltsyan rarely ventured beyond the bright orange canopy he had strung up beside the statue of Hovannes Tumanyan. At Stamboltsyan's side were four other hunger-strikers. Across the square, another group of four or five protesters kept a fast next to the Spendiaryan statue. Part circus, part holy rite, the hunger strike again made Theater Square a 24-hour shrine to the movement. The faithful came to receive inspiration from Stamboltsyan, his placid visage rendered more somber by his sunken cheeks and weary eyes. Artists offered new interpretations of political themes. Among the hunger-strikers, a Russian and a Yezidi became the objects of special veneration by the crowd.

Even as martyr, though, Stamboltsyan was working to achieve a well-defined political goal as a "candidate of the people" in running for a seat in the Armenian Supreme Soviet. Stamboltsyan, Ashot Manucharyan, and Rafael Ghazaryan were among the first political outsiders to test the limits of Gorbachev's *demokratizatsiya* (democratization). They had decided to put forward their candidacies in September after the Armenian government announced special elections to fill three vacancies in the republic's legislature. The matter had split the Karabagh Committee. Vazgen Manukyan, among others, feared that involvement in the electoral process would sidetrack the movement and allow the authorities to co-opt popular leaders. There was also the question of the elections themselves. In

159

the Baltics, reasonably fair balloting may have been possible, but few expected the Communist Party in Armenia to refrain from fraud and intimidation.

For Stamboltsyan and his fellow democrats, the special elections represented an opportunity to put the organizational principles of the Armenian National Movement into practice. Like their Baltic counterparts, they insisted on taking the laws governing the Soviet political system seriously, even to the point of challenging the underpinnings of communist power. In this effort, they had an unlikely ally in Suren Harutiunyan. Against Karen Demirchyan and his cronies, the ANM candidates would have been barred from campaigning altogether. But Harutiunyan was a champion of *perestroika*, and in theory he was committed to making the Soviet Union a society of laws.

At the same time, Harutiunyan had no intention of losing to the democrats. For the two elections scheduled to take place on 4 October, he fielded some of the party's most able candidates. In the town of Abovyan, ten miles northeast of Yerevan, Armenian Foreign Minister Anatoly Mkrtchyan, a prominent figure in the environmental movement, was slated to run against Manucharyan. In Yerevan, Armenian Interior Minister Husik Harutiunyan faced Stamboltsyan. Moreover, bureaucratic obstacles were thrown in front of Stamboltsyan and Manucharyan to prevent them from officially registering. The democratic candidates had no recourse but to tell their supporters to cross out the party candidates and write in the name of Stamboltsyan or Manucharyan on their respective ballots.

Of course, the leaders of the democratic movement were no longer novices to the political arena. As early as June, staff members at the Institute of Physics had voted to recall their deputy. Outside of Yerevan as well, activists had tried to jump-start the mechanisms of democracy. In the northern mining town of Alaverdi, for example, nearly 1,000 residents succeeded in removing the district party committee and winning the appointment of their own slate after making the 120-mile journey to Yerevan. District officials in Echmiadzin and Abovyan likewise fell to popular pressure.

The results of 4 October proved to be the most salient evidence yet of public indignation. In Yerevan, Stamboltsyan's write-in campaign received 78 percent of the vote, against 14 percent for the interior minister. Similarly, Manucharyan tallied 70 percent of the ballots in Abovyan in his contest against Mkrtchyan.

Party leaders were stunned by the results. A million demonstrators in Theater Square was one thing, but the authorities never expected that over two-thirds of the voters would turn out for an election. Officially, their initial reaction came on 9 October, when Armenian Supreme Soviet Presidium Chairman Hrant Voskanyan announced to a crowd gathered outside the legislature that the democratic candidates had failed to meet registration requirements. Moments later, Kristofer Mandalyan, chairman of the Armenian Supreme Soviet's Credentials Committee, emerged to report that a special committee meeting had voted to validate the elections. The next day, the drama shifted to a plenum of the Armenian Central Committee, which attributed the success of Stamboltsyan and Manucharyan to "election rigging" and nullified the decision of the Credentials Committee. In addition, Suren Harutiunyan pushed through a resolution to expel Mandalyan from the party and to reprimand Vladimir Galumyan for allowing the Credentials Committee to convene.[1] (In November, Galumyan was replaced as deputy chairman of the legislature.[2])

 Even with the first round of elections voided and the communist authorities on the alert, the democrats were not ready to abandon the process. Instead, they retraced their steps. By law, the government was compelled to hold new elections, and this time both Stamboltsyan and Manucharyan meticulously complied with the rules of the electoral commission. The authorities also changed their tactics. In a well-timed concession to public pressure, Harutiunyan announced on 8 October that the nuclear power plant at Medzamor would be closed. The party also put forward two new candidates who could pass as communist mavericks—actor Sos Sargsyan and Shavarsh Karapetyan, a former world champion in underwater swimming. In the end, though, Sargsyan and Karapetyan were perhaps too far beyond the grip of party discipline. The pair recognized the irresistible appeal of the democratic movement and withdrew from the race the day before the elections.[3]

 With Sargsyan and Karapetyan out of the running, one notable hurdle remained for the democrats. According to the law, a candidate had to win the support of a majority of the eligible voters in a district to be elected. In Stamboltsyan's Yerevan neighborhood, getting out the vote was not a problem, but in the town of Abovyan Manucharyan faced a difficult challenge. The weather on election day was blustery cold, and the authorities had done their best to discourage residents from going to the polls. When activists from Yerevan arrived in the late afternoon, only 40 percent of Abovyan's voters had turned out. Snow had begun to fall. Manucharyan's colleague from School #183, Ashot Dabaghyan, quickly divided up the town among his crew of volunteers and ordered them to comb each neighborhood for votes. *Zurna* players accompanied the teams of activists, drawing the attention of even the most apathetic citizens with their high-pitched reed instruments. Before the polls closed, Manucharyan had gained the votes he needed.[4] The Karabagh movement had elected its first two deputies.

Together, Manucharyan and Stamboltsyan promised to transform the temperament of the Armenian legislature. Each in his own style had played the role of moral conscience for the Karabagh movement. Manucharyan was the unbroken idealist who had refused to allow bitterness to erode a penetrating, analytical mind; Stamboltsyan was fueled by an emotional fire that could not be contained.

Like Manucharyan, Stamboltsyan brought a lifelong record of activism to the Karabagh movement. Born in 1940 in the town of Vardenis, not far from the southeastern shore of Lake Sevan, Stamboltsyan worked first as a lathe operator and tailor for a puppet theater before earning a degree in physics from Yerevan State University in 1969. Three years later, he joined the Institute of Experimental Biology as a research scientist. His work steered him toward an often lonely crusade to protect Armenia's environment. As the ecology movement gained acceptance in the mid-1980s, Stamboltsyan spearheaded a grass-roots effort to organize his fellow scientists to push for the closure of the Medzamor nuclear power plant and the Nairit chemical factory. Meanwhile, Stamboltsyan's intense religious faith led him to play a tireless role promoting the preservation and study of Armenian Christianity's ancient architectural tradition.

Long before February 1988, Stamboltsyan had acquired local celebrity in Yerevan. His bushy black beard and thick tangle of salt-and-pepper hair made him instantly recognizable, while his indefatigable sermonizing earned him affection, if not always converts. Stamboltsyan was too much the voice in the wilderness to be an insider on the Karabagh Committee. He nonetheless served as a powerful symbol in his own right. Stamboltsyan was the closest thing the movement had to an oracle—a people's catholicos without the robes. During his hunger strike, he formalized his role by announcing the establishment of a social service organization, *Gtutiun* (Charity), and gained government recognition for his creation on 8 October 1988.[5]

With the experience of Stamboltsyan and Manucharyan to draw on, the democratic forces regrouped in mid-October to campaign in a third special election in the town of Charentsavan, twenty miles north of Yerevan. The activists realized that as they moved farther away from Yerevan resistance from the authorities would be more difficult to overcome. Charentsavan, a picturesque highland valley settlement that straddles the Hrazdan River, proved to be the limit of their influence.

In Charentsavan, the party again brought in a strong candidate—in this case the chief of the organization department of the republic's Central Committee. There was also chicanery in the local electoral commission when local supporters of Karabagh Committee member Rafael Ghazaryan tried to register him as a candidate. The Charentsavan activists were told day after day that the electoral commission had postponed the registration procedure, until one day they were informed that the deadline had passed. Undeterred, they went ahead with a write-in candidacy for Ghazaryan. The party, however, pressed its advantage further. Officials threatened to close down the town's shops and cut telephone communication. Two days before the 16 October election, the militia sealed off Charentsavan. Ashot Manucharyan reported that he was first offered a bribe to divert him from the campaign and later received a death threat from two mafia enforcers when he stopped at a teahouse along the Yerevan–Sevan highway. At the time, Manucharyan was in fact on his way back to Yerevan. The threat changed his plans. "I told them I would be in the main square of Charentsavan the next day at 3 P.M., if they wanted to find me."[6]

On election day, according to Manucharyan, more than 200 party thugs were on hand to intimidate voters. Ghazaryan, who was at a physics conference in Bulgaria at the time of the election, charged that 900 ballots marked with his name were dumped in the trash.[7] When the results were finally tallied, Ghazaryan had won a plurality of the votes cast but had failed to gain the necessary majority. The authorities reported that voter turnout for the special election was 72 percent. The second round of balloting was delayed until 1989. For the moment at least, the momentum of the democrats had been halted.

While Charentsavan was hardly a setback, the election did bring to the surface the fundamental conflict between the Karabagh movement and the seamier side of the republic's power structure. "Mafia" was the popular term that served as Soviet shorthand for the complex web of corruption running through the entire command economy. The Soviets, of course, did not invent corruption, but their system of government-controlled monopolies—with all raw materials, investment funds, and finished goods passing through the hands of government officials—created opportunities for graft on an almost unimaginable scale. As the Brezhnev regime reached old age in the mid-1970s, organized greed worked its way into practically every facet of the economy. In Armenia, a long tradition of bazaar-level business smarts combined with Karen Demirchyan's plunder-now-pay-later approach to stamp the republic's economy with one of the worst reputations in the Soviet Union. As Manucharyan often emphasized, the mafia was not a problem within Armenia's government. It was Armenia's government.

" 'Mafia' is not the right word," Manucharyan would often point out if pressed for clarification:

> The [Soviet] mafia is inseparable from the central government. In Armenia the mafia is more respectable than in Uzbekistan, but these are different branches of the same tree, whose trunk and roots must be sought in Moscow—especially in Moscow.[8]

> In the homeland of the mafia, Italy, the revelation that a high-ranking police official or a single senator may be a mafia member is enough to jolt society. Now, imagine entire republics that are governed by the mafia. Ministers, secretaries of central committees, and judges are all members of the mafia. Imagine a country where high-ranking leaders are either bribed by the mafia, count themselves as members, or are paralyzed by fear to the point of being helpless against them.[9]

Stalin's terror had kept most administrators honest, if only for reasons of self-preservation, but as the party elite grew more smug during the 1950s and 1960s many began to openly partake of the fruits of the Soviet system. Officially, Moscow tried to break up the patronage circles that linked family, friends, and government corruption in the Transcaucasus. In the late 1960s and early 1970s, the Kremlin named new first secretaries in Azerbaijan, Georgia, and Armenia as part of a high-profile battle against corruption. Haidar Aliyev was promoted to the top spot in Azerbaijan in 1969 after heading the republic's KGB. In Georgia, Eduard Shevardnadze, who had worked his way up the ranks of the Georgian KGB and had served as the republic's minister of internal affairs, was awarded the first secretary position in 1972. Finally, Karen Demirchyan was brought in to lead the party in Armenia in 1974 with the same mandate to clean up the economy and restore the Kremlin's authority.[10] Moscow had already placed a Russian second secretary in the republic. (Among the non-Russian republics, only Armenia, Ukraine, Belorussia, and Estonia were permitted native first and second secretaries from 1954 to 1973.[11])

Demirchyan began by dismissing a number of leading officials associated with Armenia's previous first secretary, Anton "Diamond" Kochinyan. He also showed proper respect for Moscow's cultural leadership. The corruption, however, did not stop. It only became more centralized. The three first secretaries who preceded Demirchyan, dating back to the year of Stalin's death, had all made their careers in the Armenian party machine. No major purges had been undertaken to break up the republic's entrenched patronage networks. By the time Demirchyan came to power, the "shadow economy" was ready to realize its full potential: fabricated projects soaked up millions of rubles to turn out nonexistent products; payrolls were padded with workers who never showed up; embezzled state resources were diverted to off-the-record factories or wound up on the black market. Demirchyan was soon a leading beneficiary.

Vazgen Manukyan mapped out the interlocking layers of the system:

> [Suppose] I am appointed the director of a factory. . . . In order not to be fired, I have to share part of that income with my superior, and therefore, I have one binding relationship with him. Then there are groups which are involved in racketeering who exert pressure on me. I may need some people to scare those groups. In order to keep those people happy, I set up a store next to my factory and give it to the security people for income with the understanding that they will serve me. This way the pyramid of the power structure runs all the way down and creates a whole interrelated system which, in fact, is exploiting state property supposedly owned by the people. The authorities and the security people at the top and the thieves at the bottom join each other in one single group. We can call that group the mafia.[12]

The abuses of the mafia inevitably spilled over into other areas of society. On a day-to-day level, store clerks, waiters, taxi drivers, and almost everyone else handling money overcharged their patrons a few kopeks. Policemen collected five or ten rubles from hapless motorists. Factory workers pilfered a bag of cement. The choicest cuts of meat and the best cognac were available only at prices well above those set by the state, or were traded for other privileges. Professionals—doctors, dentists, architects—expected under-the-table fees for anything more than mediocre service. In relative terms, though, the people at the bottom of the food chain were left with small crumbs. Money in the mafia system tended to bubble up rather than trickle down.

Essentially, everything was for sale by those in power. Advancement on waiting lists for apartments and cars proceeded smoothly only with illicit payments. Applications to institutions of higher education were accompanied by substantial bribes, ranging from 7,000 to 10,000 rubles for admission to pedagogical institutes to approximately 25,000 rubles for entrance to medical school. Party leadership posts at the district level cost 150,000 to 400,000 rubles.[13] Even membership to the Communist Party came with a pricetag.

The heavyweights of the *kasharakerutiun* (literally the "eating of bribes") system were the managers of large retail stores and university rectors who often paid hundreds of thousands of rubles for their positions. By squeezing those beneath them, they had the opportunity to enrich themselves to the same degree as factory directors, labor union bosses, and government ministers. The occupants of the most unsavory layer of the mafia network—and the least inhibited in showing off their riches—were the open criminals who controlled prostitution, drug trafficking, gambling, protection rackets, and smuggling, and supplied the enforcement muscle against anyone challenging the system.

Of course, even the mafia could not completely squelch the public revulsion unleashed in the Gorbachev era. Haik Kotanjyan's speech to the Central Committee plenum 25 July 1987, and the increasingly harsh spotlight of the Soviet media indicated that Demirchyan was vulnerable. Armenia's leadership did not fare well in the new atmosphere of candidness about the Soviet economy. Authorities acknowledged that 18 percent of Armenia's able-bodied population was not officially working—a figure 50 percent above the union average. Moreover, theft of state property in the republic was reported to have increased sixfold in the previous decade, while embezzlement under Demirchyan in the 1980s was said to have doubled.[14] Even before Kotanjyan's speech, the district party boss in Hrazdan, S. G. Danielyan, had been dismissed after the exposure of ties connecting party officials, law enforcement, and the underworld in a long-running extortion operation. From there, the link to the Armenian first secretary was unavoidable. According to Kotanjyan, Demirchyan had not only filled the leadership of the republic with his family and friends, but had also fashioned "a conspiratorial circle of 'shadow taxation' and graft—a circle with its own code of silence."[15]

But while Kotanjyan had hoped that *perestroika* would root out the most entrenched benefactors of Demirchyan's rule, the real threat to the mafia was an end to the Communist Party's stranglehold on power. Manucharyan well understood the consequences of authentic electoral democracy:

> The mafia's holiest of holy principles is based on the system of appointing leading officials; namely, that it is possible to gain a sought-after position with the appropriate sum, which in turn gives the appointed official the means to enrich himself while sharing the spoils with his superior and amassing enough to purchase a higher position. Since even so-called "elected" offices are in fact filled by appointment, it is possible to understand the dangers facing the mafia from a truly democratic governmental hierarchy at every level applying democratic precepts to elections and appointments, as well as from true popular participation: that is, a critical, broad public

movement that exposes the existence of mechanisms by which the mafia allots official positions. Worse yet is the prospect of a movement that is not only critical, but also achieves its objectives.[16]

Manucharyan was certainly correct in arguing that the mafia could not survive in a truly democratic system. But perhaps more basic to the mafia's domination was the unspoken power of intimidation. Manucharyan took special pride in noting that one of the accomplishments of the Karabagh movement was the breakdown of fear. Although he himself was often accompanied by supporters to ward off reprisals, Manucharyan refused to back down. The mood of defiance had first taken hold in February, when many of the movement's impromptu orators railed against mafia bosses. Initially, their statements were tinged by concern and anxiety. Within a few months, they were openly mocking the power brokers. The sheepish servility that had kept workers in their place for decades had been smashed. Subcommittees of the Karabagh Committee in enterprises throughout the republic deprived the authorities of unchallenged control. When, at last, local bosses attempted to join the popular movement, it was too late. A heckler in Leninakan captured the new attitude when a factory manager tried to ingratiate himself with the people by raising the issue of aid for Sumgait refugees.

The heckler's response: "Why don't you make one of your dachas available to them?"[17]

Chapter 10

Explosion

*T*he reform effort launched by Mikhail Gorbachev was largely the story of unintended consequences. Loosening the reins of communist control led to the unraveling of the political and economic system. The process of democratization designed to grease the wheels of economic progress instead opened the door to an outpouring of national and social problems.

By the time the Karabagh movement was fully underway, the Soviet Union was caught up in a sort of post-totalitarian limbo. The Soviet state of 1988 still had the strength to suppress popular demands and to limit violence within its borders, but the security apparatus was no longer the overbearing force of old. Furthermore, the leadership of Mikhail Gorbachev lacked the vision and the will to resolve the assortment of national conflicts sprouting up throughout the USSR. Rather than developing a coherent approach for resolving disputes, the Kremlin preferred to look the other way. When neglect was no longer possible, Gorbachev reached into a bag of ad hoc half-measures—reshuffling local leaders, dangling economic incentives, intimidating critics of the system, or, occasionally, making a show of force.

Mountainous Karabagh offered a case study of the ramifications of the Soviet Union's tortuous disintegration. Without the presence of the declining Soviet state, the Mountainous Karabagh dispute would have likely sparked an open war between Armenia and Azerbaijan in 1988. Or, as optimists of the Karabagh Committee maintained, truly sovereign Armenian and Azerbaijani republics may have peacefully settled their differences through diplomacy. As it was—unable to fight or negotiate—the conflict festered. A war of words and gestures filled the vacuum left by

Moscow's waning power. In November, a major symbolic skirmish in the ongoing struggle was fought over a hillside in Mountainous Karabagh visible from the outskirts of Shushi. The place was known as Topkhana to the Azerbaijanis; Topkhan to Armenians.

In itself, Topkhan had no particular importance. Separated from Shushi by a ravine, the hillside in the Askeran district was home to a single tree and a few scraggly bushes. The site first surfaced in connection with the Mountainous Karabagh conflict early in November, when a convoy of vehicles from Armenia delivered a supply of building materials to the hillside. Two earthmovers soon began carving out a foundation on a plot of land, and plans for the construction of a small workshop were drawn up.

In fact, Topkhan was but one more move in a high-stakes chess game. A few days before the arrival of the building materials, Azerbaijan's first secretary announced that a single span bridge would be erected over a river to link Shushi with the surrounding countryside. Armenians saw the decision as an Azerbaijani intrusion onto lands they had long considered their own. An Azerbaijani project to construct incongruous multistory buildings in the village of Khojalu had already raised suspicions.[1] In turn, the Armenian-controlled city soviet of Askeran designated fifteen acres of farm land at Topkhan as the site of a vacation resort for workers from Yerevan's Kanaker aluminum factory. Authorities in Baku were incensed that the Karabagh Armenians had not asked their permission to begin construction. Ultimately, the Azerbaijani government put a stop to the building, and even undertook efforts to restore the hillside, but not before Topkhan had contributed to the ever-widening rift between the Armenian and Azerbaijani communities.[2]

After a relatively calm October, Topkhan triggered a new round of massive protests in Yerevan and Baku. Huge demonstrations in Armenia, of course, were hardly novel, but November marked a turning point in Azerbaijan. Topkhan was a fitting spark. On the one hand, the construction plans reinforced the argument that Armenians would resort to underhanded means to deprive Azerbaijanis of Mountainous Karabagh. On the other, Topkhan permitted Azerbaijani nationalists to infuse another symbol into the historical consciousness of their people. What was otherwise a rather nondescript hill became a sacred forest in the Baku media. According to Azerbaijani radio, Topkhan was a "historical natural monument" and the site of an Azerbaijani fortress erected to resist Iranian invaders.[3]

More accurately, Topkhan was a product of Transcaucasia's overheated political atmosphere. As a Soviet journalist noted: "The sense of proportion is beginning to fail residents of both sides, even the best of them. They view even the most trifling conflict in the light of inter-ethnic relations."[4]

There were other potentially volatile events in November as well. The Soviet Supreme Court handed down the first death sentence in the Sumgait trials on 21 November, condemning Akhmed Akhmedov to execution by firing squad. In Stepanakert, Armenians began another series of strikes to protest what they viewed as Azerbaijani attempts to inflate the population of Shushi. At the union level, the Presidium of the Supreme Soviet affirmed that Mountainous Karabagh should remain within Azerbaijan. In addition, an extraordinary session of the Supreme Soviet was scheduled for the end of the month to consider a number of constitutional amendments proposed by Gorbachev to enhance the power of the central government.

In Baku's Lenin Square, an around-the-clock demonstration began on 17 November. Like their counterparts in Yerevan, protesters in Baku accused the Soviet media of ignoring or distorting their cause. On 25 November, pressmen in Baku refused to print that day's edition of *Izvestia* and other Soviet newspapers. There were other similarities to Armenian rallies as well, including chants of "Ka-ra-bagh," student walkouts, headbands inscribed with the word "Karabakh," logos from packs of "Karabakh" cigarettes, and a display of homemade banners and posters. Groups advocating the protection of Azerbaijan's environment and broader study of Azerbaijani language and history gained new exposure, while efforts to construct a popular front received a boost. Many of those in the square fasted.[5]

At the same time, the Baku demonstrations had their own distinct tone. As demonstrators kept vigil through the night, the huge, sprawling square was lit up by scattered bonfires. Sheep were slaughtered in nearby parks. As the days passed, the green flag of Islam became more prominent, while portraits of Iran's Ayatollah Ruhollah Khomeini were hoisted above the crowd.[6] Chants of "Death to the Armenians" and "Russians and Armenians out of Azerbaijan" were also heard. Regular coverage by republican television and sympathetic articles in the Azerbaijani press transmitted the story of the demonstrations to people throughout Azerbaijan.[7]

Scholars and literary figures dominated the speaker's platform in Baku's Lenin Square, but a 26-year-old lathe operator, Nemat Panakhov, won the crowd's favor. Like his counterparts in Yerevan, Panakhov directed much of his resentment toward the authorities. Specifically, he condemned the "passiveness" of Azerbaijani officials in response to the Karabagh movement. Panakhov also echoed the Karabagh Committee's support for "the principles of democracy, *glasnost*, and respect for the law." For the moment, Panakhov placed three issues at the top of the Azerbaijani national agenda: gaining autonomy for Azerbaijanis living in

Armenia; transferring criminal cases related to the Sumgait massacre back to Azerbaijan; and guaranteeing the safe return of Azerbaijani refugees from Mountainous Karabagh.[8]

The Baku demonstrations brought the city's volatile mixture of class and ethnicity to the boiling point, leaving the Armenian community especially vulnerable. Armenians in Baku generally ranked above their Azerbaijani counterparts in terms of professional status and education. Many Armenian families had lived in the city for generations, and shared little in common with the hundreds of thousands of Azerbaijanis who had moved to Baku from the countryside in recent decades. As one newspaper reported:

> It used to be that men coming from outlying areas to work at the plant would live in dormitories and their wives and children couldn't even get residence permits to join them. . . . Gradually, other problems snowballed as well. There was a demand that those responsible for this situation be found. And found they were—in the person of representatives of the Armenian nationality, who were said to be undeservedly using things that there weren't enough of for the Azerbaijanis themselves.[9]

While the atmosphere in Baku may have been potentially explosive, in Kirovabad (present-day Ganja) it was deadly. MVD troops were called out in the city of 200,000 to guard the Armenian quarter and thwart attacks on Communist Party offices after mobs beat an Armenian priest and toppled a statue of Marshal Hovannes (Ivan) Bagramyan. On 22 November, a lieutenant and two enlisted soldiers were killed by a grenade lobbed from an unruly crowd that had surrounded Kirovabad's party headquarters.[10] Ultimately, MVD troops set up a barrier on the Ganjachai River to prevent mobs from entering a district where approximately 40,000 Armenians lived. Roads leading into the city were sealed off, and military helicopters evacuated hundreds of Armenian residents. General Viktor Omelchenko, the military commander of Kirovabad, recorded "more than seventy attempts to organize pogroms" against the city's Armenian community. Roving gangs remained on the offensive for several nights, seeking to set fire to Armenian neighborhoods. Soviet sources reported that sixty Armenian houses were burned down during the riots.[11]

Although MVD troops eventually restored order to Kirovabad, the violence there set off the chain reaction that had long been feared. Anti-Armenian riots soon spread to Nakhichevan, which in turn triggered intercommunal clashes in Zangezur. Finally, attacks against Azerbaijanis living in the Ararat plain and northern Armenia also flared up.

Vigilante roadblocks were thrown up overnight around key flashpoints in both republics. Rail traffic came to a halt on the line that snaked through southern Azerbaijan, Zangezur, Nakhichevan, and the Ararat plain along the Arax River. Before the end of November, streams of refugees were trudging through the icy mountain passes that defined the border between the two republics.

No violence took place in Yerevan, although the city was the scene of a series of demonstrations beginning 16 November. The Karabagh Committee initially organized the rallies to voice concern over Gorbachev's efforts to amend the constitution. The committee also called for a one-day strike on 18 November, kicking it off by dumping a wagonload of hay at the gates of a Yerevan factory. The message: only a donkey would not join the strike.[12] Earlier in the month, the committee had made use of the symbolism of 7 November—the official anniversary of the 1917 Bolshevik Revolution—to vent popular frustration. The ceremony had begun in a fairly routine fashion, with government leaders, party bosses, and generals taking their usual places on a platform set up in Lenin Square. The proceedings were hardly underway, however, when rows of orderly marchers poured into the square hoisting banners bearing the slogans of the Karabagh movement. While Suren Harutiunyan stood by in stunned silence, column after column passed before the reviewing stand, each falling back to make way for more protesters. Harutiunyan eventually called on the demonstrators to disperse, but to no avail. Instead, many sat down. Levon Ter Petrosyan then stepped up to a microphone set up below the official rostrum and ran down a list of key items on the democratic platform: Mountainous Karabagh, environmental pollution, democratization, the Sumgait trials. Looking up at the rostrum, he added:

> The government must decide. Is it with the people or not? If it is with the people, then stop obediently carrying out orders from the town with the ruby stars [a reference to the ornaments atop the Kremlin towers]. Use your heads. If you are not with the people, resign and make way for those who really care.[13]

With their election successes and the sustained energy of the Karabagh movement, the democratic forces in Armenia were increasingly acquiring a recognized political power base. "We lead totally open lives," Levon Ter Petrosyan told a reporter for *Time*. "If they [the authorities] arrested us, they'd have an insurrection on their hands."[14]

When a sixteen-member commission was formed on 14 November by the Armenian Council of Ministers to address refugee issues, Vazgen Manukyan and Khachik Stamboltsyan were among the appointees.

The chairman of the Armenian Presidium, Hrant Voskanyan, and the Central Committee secretary for ideology, Galust Galoyan, felt compelled to participate in a rally that attracted nearly one million demonstrators to Theater Square on 18 November. Moreover, the movement's newly elected deputies, Ashot Manucharyan and Khachik Stamboltsyan, used their popular support to shape the agenda of the Armenian Supreme Soviet session scheduled to meet on 22 November. By adhering to the constitution and the mechanisms of *perestroika*, the Karabagh Committee had outgrown the government's conventional measures to contain it. Even within the Supreme Soviet, many of the working-class deputies, who realized few privileges from their positions, were attracted to the message of Manucharyan and Stamboltsyan. Central Committee officials were suddenly confronted with the possibility of an independent parliament.

Before the legislature convened on 22 November, Voskanyan suggested that the session appeal to the USSR Supreme Soviet to support the unification of Mountainous Karabagh with Armenia and to acknowledge the Sumgait massacre. Once the deputies took their places, they proved similarly eager to placate public opinion. With little discussion, they voted to declare 24 April an official day of commemoration and to appeal to the Soviet legislature to recognize the 1915 genocide. The session was about to turn to the subject of Mountainous Karabagh and Gorbachev's proposed constitutional amendments when Arkady Volsky reported on the escalating anti-Armenian violence in Azerbaijan.[15]

News of the pogroms derailed the session, prompting Volsky to suggest that the deputies quickly accept the constitutional amendments put forward by Gorbachev and then return to their home districts to prevent further outbreaks of violence. Manucharyan agreed to an adjournment, but won acceptance of a proposal to reconvene the session as soon as possible to consider the remainder of the agenda.[16] Two days later, Manucharyan led efforts to assemble a quorum inside the opera house as 500,000 people gathered in Theater Square. Although the presidium refused to authorize the meeting, messengers brought back deputies one by one from their home districts during the afternoon. The less compliant were subjected to *deputatavorsordutiun* (deputy-hunting), a term coined to describe the tracking down of deputies by ad-hoc citizen groups. One deputy was even escorted into Theater Square while still inside his Volga sedan. Each new arrival was greeted with tumultuous applause, until by evening nearly 200 of the 340 deputies were present.[17]

At 6 P.M., the Supreme Soviet session got underway. Manucharyan and Stamboltsyan took the lead in pressing for the adoption of resolutions on closing the Medzamor nuclear power reactors and safeguarding Armenians in Azerbaijan. Each decision was met by approval in the square, but the mood of the evening was hardly boisterous. Overhead, MVD helicopters were moving troops into position. Tanks and armored personnel carriers rumbled onto the city's main thoroughfares. Late in the evening, martial law was announced over television. The crowd in Theater Square was told that a curfew would take effect at midnight. Vazgen Manukyan insisted that the session should continue until the agenda was concluded. The half million people in the square stood their ground as well until the session finished at 1 A.M. Activists then called on the crowd to disperse in groups to avoid being caught alone by MVD troops. Later that day, the Armenian Presidium declared the session illegal.[18]

The crackdown in Yerevan was part of a concerted effort by Moscow to clamp down on disorder in Azerbaijan and Armenia. The main concern in Armenia had been the influence of the two democratic deputies over the Supreme Soviet. At the same time, demonstrations in Baku were taking an increasingly anti-Soviet bent, while in Kirovabad attacks on Communist Party offices had occurred. The response was the imposition of a 10 P.M. to 6 A.M. curfew on Yerevan, Baku, Kirovabad, and Nakhichevan.[19]

The USSR Supreme Soviet session that took place at the end of November raised the possibility of still stronger measures. Gorbachev set the tone 26 November at a Presidium meeting when he denounced Estonia's push for economic autonomy as "political adventurism." Moving on to Transcaucasia, he insisted on the need to "stop demagogues, those who embark on political speculation by taking advantage of the processes of democratization and *glasnost*."[20] Gorbachev's words were meant in part for the presidents of Armenia and Azerbaijan, who used the Supreme Soviet session to air their contrasting interpretations of the violence in their two republics. Azerbaijan's Suleyman Tatliev blamed Armenians for igniting the conflict by continuing their protests. Hrant Voskanyan retorted that his Azerbaijani counterpart was "categorically rejecting any compromise," prompting a round of applause from the deputies.[21]

On 1 December, a highly charged report by Arkady Volsky jolted the Supreme Soviet gathering. "When the law is being violated and blood is being spilled, the state cannot stand aside," Volsky said, contending that both Azerbaijan and Armenia continued to "literally boil." Meanwhile, the functions of a special task force to curb ethnic and racial hostility were made clearer. According to Alexander Katusev, deputy prosecutor general and head of the task force, efforts would be made to arrest and try popular leaders held responsible for provoking violence. The official spin, once again played up in the central media, asserted that Armenian activists were stirring up local unrest to cover up their involvement in corruption, bribery, and embezzlement.[22] A few days later, the Council of

Ministers directed officials in Armenia and Azerbaijan to bring criminal charges against strike organizers. To emphasize the Kremlin's resolve, Gorbachev summoned the first secretaries of Armenia and Azerbaijan to Moscow and warned that he was prepared to take even more decisive action in the two republics.[23] The general secretary said:

> It has been noted that the party and Soviet agencies of the Nagorno Karabakh Autonomous Oblast, Armenia and Azerbaijan have, to one extent or another, lost control of events. This is a result not merely of confusion but of a lack of principle. Fear of "losing the people's confidence," as well as assenting to nationalistic sentiments, has led to a situation in which part of the party *aktiv* has departed from internationalist positions.[24]

The hammer came down hardest in Mountainous Karabagh. For the first time, Soviet authorities aimed at established leaders of the Armenian community in hopes of decapitating the movement. A number of prominent *Krunk* activists were arrested, including one of the oblast's most widely respected figures, Arkady Manucharov. Manucharov was the director of the Stepanakert Construction Materials Combine. As a young deputy in the oblast soviet in 1965, he was one of thirteen authors of a petition addressed to Moscow that carried 45,000 signatures from Mountainous Karabagh. The repercussions drove Manucharov out of the oblast, but he returned in 1977 from Armenia with a solid professional record and a long list of contacts. Considering his reputation for integrity, the official charges against him were viewed as especially malicious: accepting bribes, embezzlement, and even squeezing money for erecting tombstones.[25] In fact, he was targeted largely for challenging Volsky's tendency to run roughshod over local authority in Mountainous Karabagh. When troops came to arrest Manucharov, several of his supporters attempted to intervene. A few thousand of Manucharov's neighbors soon gathered around the house, leading MVD forces to use truncheons and shovels against the crowd. Seven civilians as well as one soldier were injured in the melee.[26]

In Yerevan, the special status imposed by the authorities met scant resistance. A partial strike sputtered along for a few days until the Karabagh Committee called on workers to return to their jobs. (The committee's request to broadcast an appeal for calm over Armenian television was rejected.) More than 1,400 people were detained in Yerevan for curfew violations. In contrast to Yerevan, the curfew in Baku seemed only to aggravate tension. MVD troops were forced on several occasions to fire warning shots into the air. Thousands of Azerbaijanis maintained a 24-hour vigil in Lenin Square despite repeated orders to disperse. Young demonstrators took charge of controlling access to the square to prevent the infiltration of provocateurs. Finally, a phalanx of MVD soldiers swept through the square in the early morning darkness of 5 December and cleared out the demonstrators. All the while, sporadic attacks against Armenians in the city continued.[27]

The most lasting consequence of November's turmoil was the refugee crisis. By the end of the month, Armenian officials reported that 30,907 Armenians had crossed into the republic while 40,652 Azerbaijanis had left Armenia. Baku put the number of Azerbaijani refugees at 55,000.[28] The Kremlin tried to stop the hemorrhaging by setting up a special commission of Armenian and Azerbaijani representatives, along with Politburo members, and threatened criminal penalties against officials found promoting "the mass nature of dismissals from work because of nationality." But in December the refugee traffic only accelerated.[29] Despite official efforts, few of the refugees were eager to return to their homes any time soon. On the contrary, by the end of the year the great majority of the approximately 300,000 Armenians in Azerbaijan outside of Mountainous Karabagh had either left or were planning to leave as quickly as possible.[30] The same was true for Armenia's more than 160,000 Azerbaijanis.

The population exchange created tremendous dislocation in both republics. Armenian refugees came primarily from Baku and Kirovabad. Many were well-educated, with jobs in management and technical fields. Moreover, they were generally more Russified than their countrymen in Armenia. Baku had been deprived of Armenian-language schools since World War II and children within the community were educated in Russian. Mountainous Karabagh had been a distant concern for most of them until the Sumgait massacre.

Meanwhile, the Azerbaijanis fleeing Armenia were typically farmers. Their absence was initially felt in the free markets of Armenia's cities, where Azerbaijanis had found a niche selling fresh fruits and vegetables, and salty cheese. The villages they left behind in Zangezur, the Ararat plain, and north of Lake Sevan were populated only reluctantly by Armenian refugees from Baku. It was also not long before Yerevan's approximately 2,300 Azerbaijani residents departed. The Armenian capital's small Azerbaijani community had passed largely unnoticed until 1988. Its members had always been on the periphery of the city's life, although the Armenian government made provisions for two Azerbaijani schools, an Azerbaijani theater, an Azerbaijani philology department, and an Azerbaijani division at the pedagogical institute. Verbal threats and a few incidents of arson in November convinced many Azerbaijanis that their best option was to exchange apartments with Armenians leaving Baku.[31]

"Azerbaijanis feel that they are not wanted here," complained a longtime Azerbaijani resident of Yerevan. "The Armenians only want their own kind."[32] Another Azerbaijani living in Armenia was more philosophical in his observations to an American reporter: "Our years of living with Armenians are over. Now they have their struggles and we have ours."[33]

In terms of human suffering, November 1988 marked the most agonizing month of the Karabagh movement to date. Separation of Armenians and Azerbaijanis—a dynamic that had gathered momentum throughout the twentieth century—was now complete, and few expected that it would soon be reversed. An editor at Armenpress, Armenia's official news agency, remarked:

> We are Eastern people, the Armenians and Azerbaijanis. Emotional people, inclined toward panic and rumors. Speaking realistically, it will be generations before relations are really normal again.[34]

In addition to redrawing the demographic map of Transcaucasia, the events of November 1988 brought on yet another reassessment of how nearly two centuries of Russian rule had shaped Armenian–Azerbaijani relations. Many of the assertions heard in Baku's Lenin Square echoed the upheavals of the nineteenth century, especially claims that relatively well-off Armenians were occupying scarce housing while Azerbaijanis lived in cramped dormitories, and that the Karabagh movement was part of larger scheme to deprive Azerbaijan of territory.[35] Armenians also noted the parallels between the November crisis and the Armenian–Azerbaijani conflict of 1905–06. Like their Azerbaijani counterparts, many believed that Moscow had a hand in precipitating the violence in both cases.

But as refugees abandoned their homes and headed toward unknown destinations, there were both Armenians and Azerbaijanis who found something positive in the massive transfer of population. In the span of a few weeks, minority issues had been swiftly, albeit tragically, simplified in both republics. A problem that had smoldered for decades had been suddenly erased.

Armenians had long fretted over numbers. From the formation of the Soviet Union, Armenia had been the most ethnically homogeneous of the republics. Although many Armenian officials shared the desire of their counterparts in Azerbaijan and Georgia to limit the growth of minority groups, Armenia's demographics afforded them little cause for implementing heavy-handed policies. Of course, Armenia was also the smallest of the Soviet republics, a limitation contributing to the fact that for decades a higher proportion of Armenians lived outside their native republic than any other republican nationality. (The Tajiks surpassed the Armenians in this category in the 1980s.) According to the 1989 census, after decades of a steady flow of Armenians into Armenia, nearly 30 percent of Armenians in the Soviet Union remained outside their homeland.[36]

There were other factors feeding Armenian demographic concerns. Soviet Armenia's birth rate peaked in 1958 at 41.1 births per 1,000 inhabitants. By 1984, it was approaching the relatively low standard of the USSR's Slavic peoples, with 18.4 births per 1,000 residents.[37] Armenia in the 1980s was still growing slightly, but the boom that took the republic's population from 1,320,000 in 1940 to 3,031,000 in 1979 was over. The larger truth was that Armenia had run out of room. That conclusion was at least partially affirmed by the tremendous movement of residents out of the republic. Between 1979 and 1989, 321,000 more people left Armenia than came in, by far the highest rate of outward migration for any Soviet republic.[38]

Most worrisome was the departure of Armenians abroad once restrictions on emigration eased in the late 1980s. By the last quarter of 1987, U.S. embassy officials reported that they were receiving 1,400 applications monthly from Armenians seeking admission to the United States as refugees.[39] From 1987 to 1990, 29,382 Soviet Armenians arrived in the United States for good, with approximately 85 percent settling in the Los Angeles area.[40] All this was occurring while the Azerbaijani population surged. As late as 1959, Azerbaijanis in the USSR outnumbered Armenians by only 153,000. In 1989, though, the gap had widened to nearly 2.2 million.[41] Armenians were especially sensitive to the growth of the Azerbaijani population in Armenia, which increased from 108,000 in 1959 to 161,000 nearly two decades later. Proportionally, the Azerbaijani population in the republic actually declined during the twenty-year span, but the growing Azerbaijani presence in the countryside raised concern.[42] Armenians under Soviet rule abandoned the rural areas of their homeland at a rapid rate, and according to the most fearful scenarios the republic would eventually consist of Armenian urban enclaves surrounded by Azerbaijani villages.

The demographic situation in Mountainous Karabagh was still more distressing from the Armenian perspective. The Armenian majority of the region had steadily eroded under Soviet rule, falling from 94.4 percent in 1923 to 75.9 percent in 1979.[43] The demographic watershed was World War II, when more than 22,000 men from the oblast died fighting Nazi Germany. The number of Armenians in Mountainous Karabagh in 1988 had yet to reach 1939 levels. But while Armenian growth rates stagnated, the number of Azerbaijanis jumped from 18,000 in 1959 to 37,300 in 1979 (22.9 percent of the oblast's total population). As in Armenia, the shift was most noticeable in the countryside, where dozens of Armenian villages disappeared.[44] The worst-case scenario for Karabagh Armenians was all too apparent in the fate of Nakhichevan. In 1917, Armenians made up almost 40 percent of the area's population. The proportion fell precipitously in the 1920s after the Nakhichevan Autonomous Republic was created and Baku forbade the return of Armenian refugees driven out of their homes by the strife of 1918–20. By 1979, only 3,400 Armenians were left—1.4 percent of the total population.[45]

Chapter 11

Earthquake

*T*he Armenian homeland straddles an active seismic zone that begins in the Atlantic, runs through the Mediterranean, and continues on into Central Asia. Medieval chroniclers in the ninth century recorded the tremors that destroyed Dvin (southeast of present-day Yerevan), the Armenian capital that had been built by the Arshakuni dynasty more than 500 years earlier. The first-century pagan temple at Garni, a few miles north of Yerevan, was leveled by an earthquake in the 1600s. In 1926, Leninakan was jolted by a powerful quake. Five years later, Zangezur was hit by a still stronger temblor.

The magnitude of the earthquake that struck northern Armenia on 7 December 1988 was not extraordinary. At its epicenter fifteen miles northeast of Leninakan near the town of Spitak, the earthquake measured 6.9 on the Richter scale (or 10.5 on the twelve-point Soviet scale). Seismologists identified it as a shallow-force earthquake, meaning that its shock waves were concentrated relatively close to the earth's surface in a small area. The death and destruction left by the temblor were staggering. More than 25,000 people died as a result of the earthquake; 530,000 people were left homeless. The disaster idled one-quarter of Armenia's industry. Total damage was estimated at 13 billion rubles ($20 billion).[1]

Geology, poor construction, and unfortunate timing magnified the impact of the earthquake. The water table in much of the earthquake zone lay only a few feet below a layer of moist, alluvial soil. The seismic waves of the earthquake shook the region like a bowl of jelly. Eyewitnesses to the disaster reported that the earthquake was punctuated by two strong tremors spaced about thirty seconds apart. In many cases, buildings that withstood the first jolt collapsed from the second shock. Most vulnerable were buildings that had been constructed in the 1970s and 1980s. Children were among the most likely victims. The earthquake struck at 11:41 A.M. on a Wednesday. Elementary and secondary school students were in their classrooms, many of which had been recently built.

Like few other natural disasters, the tragedy of the Armenian earthquake registered around the world. On 7 December, Mikhail Gorbachev was in New York speaking at the United Nations. The Soviet leader pledged to reduce the troop strength of his country's armed forces by 500,000 men, and to withdraw 50,000 soldiers and 5,000 tanks from Eastern Europe. Later in the day, he met with President Reagan and affirmed that the tensions of the Cold War were melting. Gorbachev's international reputation was at its zenith.

The Armenian earthquake served to illustrate the new relationship between East and West. For the first time since World War II, the Soviets opened themselves up to outside assistance. Regulations governing foreign access to Soviet airspace were waived to make way for relief flights. Visa restrictions and customs inspections were set aside. The international community responded with unprecedented generosity. In the frantic days immediately following the earthquake, 3,600 foreigners from 26 countries helped rescue and care for the survivors. Over the next months, $552 million from 113 foreign countries was provided for relief and reconstruction—the single largest outpouring of aid for a natural disaster to date. Italy led donors with contributions valued at $95 million. West Germany was second ($84 million), and the United States third ($42 million).[2] Three airplanes transporting supplies and relief workers crashed while trying to land in Armenia. One of them, carrying an emergency team from Azerbaijan, had departed from Sumgait.[3]

For a few days after the earthquake, Armenia held the world's attention. Television crews from abroad beamed back images from towns in the northern part of the republic that had previously known few foreign visitors. Italians arrived with all-terrain vehicles and a 30-man dog team. British firefighters came with heat-sensitive probes to locate buried survivors. Czechoslovakia set up a fully equipped field hospital. Kenya donated ten tons of tea and three tons of coffee, while Turkey sent twenty helicopters and fifteen cranes. Italians, Norwegians, Austrians, Swiss, Hungarians, British, Poles, Germans, French, Yugoslavs, Bulgarians, Americans, and others manned construction projects in the earthquake zone. Foreign health-care specialists staffed newly built hospitals and rehabilitation centers. For a people that had long prided itself on its ties to the world beyond Soviet borders, Armenians were suddenly playing host to a cross section of the international community.

The unsolicited celebrity did not last long. The earthquake story eventually ran its course in the international media. There were a few miraculous tales of survival after the first week passed, as well as outlandish hoaxes. As the supply of news was exhausted in Leninakan, Spitak, and other towns, a handful of journalists explored outlying villages for new angles on the tragedy. On 21 December, the explosion of a PanAm flight over Lockerbie, Scotland, offered the public in the West a fresh media disaster to ponder.

Once Armenians again turned inward, they were confronted with the issues raised by the earthquake. The design and quality of construction in the earthquake zone was among the leading topics of discussion. Rescue workers were the first to fully appreciate the shoddiness of the building practices. In many cases, multistory apartment buildings and schools had literally disintegrated, burying victims alive in mounds of rubble. Rescuers found few pockets of air where survivors might be hidden.

The collapsed structures revealed a legacy of corruption, incompetence, and indifference. The prefabricated concrete slabs that were commonly used in construction were responsible for most of the deaths. As the debris of the earthquake showed, workers had substituted sand for cement. Reinforcing steel bars were of insufficient strength or lacking altogether. Workmanship was poor.

Armenians were forced to shoulder most of the blame. From party officials to struggling pensioners, Armenians knew that the missing construction materials had entered the shadow economy. Project directors had grown rich building private houses on the side. Ordinary workers had seen no harm in helping themselves to supplies of cement to patch up a few cracks at home or line a courtyard barbecue pit. Less comprehensible were the decisions of urban planners to allow the construction of fourteen-story high rises in an active seismic zone. As Armenians realized in the earthquake's aftermath, they had forgotten the lessons of their forbearers.

Ronald Altoon, a Los Angeles architect who led a U.S. team to Armenia to work with the Soviets on plans to rebuild Spitak, observed:

> Every single multistory building built in Gorbachev's, Chernenko's, Andropov's, Brezhnev's, and Khrushchev's time was totally destroyed. Those built in Stalin's time withstood the initial shock and therefore saved lives, but will have to be destroyed because they are not repairable. The buildings constructed in Lenin's time survived with superficial structural damage and are repairable and habitable. Those buildings built in the time of the tsar had absolutely no damage whatsoever. In those days you built the way your ancestors built.[4]

A letter published in *Pravda* two months after the earthquake by a senior scientist from Leningrad's Hydrometeorological Institute supported Altoon's observations. The scientist noted that seismological teams had downgraded the dangers posed by earthquakes in Transcaucasia based on studies conducted in the 1970s and thus recommended laxer construction standards. Underlying the weakening of the building code, according to the scientist, were cost-cutting pressures and local corruption.[5]

Among the construction projects of the 1970s were the nuclear reactors at Medzamor, less than fifty miles from the epicenter of the earthquake. The Medzamor plant had been built to withstand earthquakes registering up to eight points on the twelve-point Soviet scale. The strongest tremor recorded on 7 December was 5.5. Nonetheless, the earthquake heightened public support for a shut-down of the reactors.

Even without Medzamor to worry about, Armenians needed little to rouse their fears. Many were indeed convinced that the earthquake had been man-made. In the days following the disaster, two theories emerged regarding its origin. One linked the tremor to Moscow's efforts to snuff out the Karabagh movement. The other hypothesized that Turkey had somehow tunneled into Armenian territory and set off an explosion. Among those less inclined toward conspiracy theories, there was nonetheless widespread suspicion that Moscow had withheld information predicting the earthquake.[6]

There were also concerns that Soviet authorities were deliberately minimizing the death toll so as to dampen international sympathy for Armenia and not draw attention to the influx of Armenian refugees from Azerbaijan in the weeks preceding the earthquake. Officially, the number of deaths resulting from the earthquake approached 25,000 by the end of December. In contrast, a United Nations report first estimated that 50,000 to 60,000 had died. Meanwhile, many Armenians were quick to put the figure at 80,000 or higher. (A study later conducted under the auspices of Armenia's Ministry of Health found that the figure of 25,000 dead was more or less correct.)[7]

A Soviet television announcer further exacerbated tensions by suggesting that families throughout the USSR would be willing to adopt children orphaned by the earthquake. Although meant as a gesture of solidarity, the comment sparked controversy in light of the earthquake's especially cruel toll on Armenia's children. A few discerned a plan to deprive Armenia of its sons and daughters, and denounced efforts to relocate orphans, even temporarily, outside of the republic.

Gorbachev arrived in Armenia on 10 December, the official day of mourning for earthquake victims, after cutting short his visit to the United States. Gorbachev's two-day mission to the republic was humanitarian. The general secretary was there to offer his condolences and to express the government's commitment to quickly rebuild damaged areas. But while Gorbachev's popularity on the world stage had prompted the outpouring of aid from the international community, the Soviet leader was hardly welcomed as a hero in Armenia.

His tour through the earthquake zone was derailed unceremoniously in Leninakan, where the general secretary stumbled into a shouting match with earthquake survivors. Exhausted from his transatlantic travels and shaken by the devastation in northern Armenia, Gorbachev was drawn off course by demands that he address the Karabagh issue. There were also insults hurled at his wife. Gorbachev reacted angrily. He shook his finger in the direction of his critics and condemned what he saw as an attempt to derive political gain from human suffering.

After returning to Yerevan, Gorbachev directed especially harsh words toward the Karabagh Committee, blaming the activists for fanning tensions in the aftermath of the earthquake. In an interview with television journalists, the general secretary said:

> What kind of morals do these people have, I ask? People should know what sort of clique it is that uses concern for the people and for the nation to conceal what it is doing. This clique is grabbing for power. It must be stopped using all our strength, both political and administrative.[8]

Before leaving Leninakan, Gorbachev promised that the earthquake zone would be rebuilt within two years. Prime Minister Nikolai Ryzhkov was named chairman of a Politburo commission to oversee reconstruction. Before the end of the year, the Soviets adopted a comprehensive recovery plan for northern Armenia. Officials estimated that reconstruction would cost \$16.5 billion and require 150,000 workers.[9] Although Gorbachev returned to Moscow with his reputation further tarnished in Armenia, Ryzhkov won broad popular support for his no-nonsense emphasis on quick results and stern warnings against corruption. Faith in Ryzhkov, however, could not change the fact that Soviet projections were unrealistic. Even in the best of circumstances, rebuilding northern Armenia in two years would have been an impressive accomplishment. In the Soviet Union of the late 1980s, it was well-nigh impossible.

The political atmosphere in Armenia was likewise not conducive to a massive rebuilding effort. Indeed, the earthquake widened the gulf between Karabagh movement activists and the authorities. During the first few days after the earthquake, members of the Karabagh Committee had found themselves thrust into the role of relief organizers. On 7

December, many of them headed for the earthquake zone. Those remaining behind established an office at the Writers' Union in central Yerevan to coordinate rescue operations. Starting with the evening of 7 December, sixty to seventy busloads of volunteers were dispatched each day to the earthquake zone. At the same time, earthquake survivors without shelter were transported to Yerevan and other safe areas. Thousands of Yerevanis registered at the Writers' Union to take in those left homeless by the disaster. Karabagh Committee members also sought to quash rumors that the origins of the earthquake were man-made.[10]

   According to Ashot Manucharyan, the committee had intended to serve as an arm of the government's rescue and relief efforts. By the evening of 8 December, however, hopes for cooperation had been dashed. Instead, Manucharyan later explained, government relief operations were hampered by a lack of organization, transportation bottlenecks, and an absence of leadership, even as hotels in Yerevan were filling up with officials from Moscow.[11] The foreign aid only added to the confusion. Rather naively, the committee appealed to two well-known diaspora Armenians—French singer Charles Aznavour and California governor George Deukmejian—to coordinate relief activities abroad.[12] (Deukmejian had requested that Reagan make use of his 7 December meeting with Gorbachev to urge the Soviet leader to "take whatever steps are necessary" to stop violence against Armenians in Azerbaijan.[13]) Where the committee's efforts were more effective was on the ground in the earthquake zone. The network of activists that had formed during the Karabagh movement helped channel relief directly to where it was most needed. Mountain villages that had been bypassed by Soviet and foreign crews were reached for the first time.[14]

   On 10 December, the committee became embroiled in public concern over the status of children orphaned by the earthquake after hundreds of women gathered in front of the Writers' Union. Yerevan was still under martial law, with tanks and troops guarding the main roads and controlling access to Lenin Square. The continuation of the military presence in the aftermath of the earthquake had already strained relations between the authorities and ordinary Yerevanis. The crowd at the Writers' Union was particularly agitated. With the agreement of the district military commander, Manucharyan appeared before those assembled to assure them that the orphans would remain in Armenia. The crowd formed again two hours later, and Manucharyan requested that the women return home. That evening at 6 P.M, the district military commander showed up at the Writers' Union—located two blocks away from where Gorbachev was spending the night—and demanded that the approximately 1,000 volunteers present stop working. Manucharyan asked for another hour, but within twenty minutes the district commander came back with the MVD general who had recently been appointed to oversee martial law in Yerevan. Committee members were again ordered to disperse the volunteers immediately. They refused. A few minutes later the seven committee members inside and fifteen other activists were arrested.

After midnight, Manucharyan was questioned by MVD officers at the military commander's station. The officers acknowledged that as a deputy of the Armenian Supreme Soviet Manucharyan would be released. Manucharyan also pressed for the release of the other activists, recounting how the Karabagh Committee had cooperated with Yerevan's previous military commander to calm the city's residents. The officers seemed conciliatory. "Receiving the appropriate assurances and reaching an agreement," Manucharyan wrote later that month while in hiding, "I departed from the authorities on good terms, convinced that the conflict had been resolved." [15]

The problems for the Karabagh Committee, however, were only beginning. The next morning, Manucharyan learned that the other committee members were still in custody, based on a Supreme Soviet decree issued 23 November 1988. According to the new law, the authorities were empowered to detain "persons who incite national strife through their actions" for up to thirty days in areas where a curfew had been imposed.[16]

A public meeting was arranged, and Manucharyan explained the circumstances of the arrests. Next, Manucharyan led a march through the center of Yerevan to spread the word about the detention of the committee members. MVD tanks blocked the demonstrators as they walked down Abovyan Street. A few blocks away, MVD troops set upon the marchers, beating them with batons. Manucharyan was clubbed in the back when he tried to wedge himself between the troops and the marchers.

At the time, Manucharyan did not fully appreciate that the tactics of the MVD troops and the previous evening's arrests were the start of a broad government crackdown on the Karabagh movement. Six committee members—Babgen Ararktsyan, Samvel Gevorgyan, Samson Ghazaryan, Alexander Hakobyan, Vazgen Manukyan, and Levon Ter Petrosyan—had been taken into custody at the Writers' Union. On 13 December, Vano Siradeghyan returned from the earthquake zone and turned himself over to the authorities. Hambartsum Galstyan, Manucharyan, and Davit Vardanyan went into hiding in Yerevan, while 64-year-old Rafael Ghazaryan was put under tight surveillance. The four were arrested 7 January at an apartment in Yerevan. In addition, nearly 200 other activists were rounded up.

In January, the eleven committee members, along with Khachik Stamboltsyan, and three other activists, were transferred to Moscow to await trial. Igor Muradyan was held in Kirovabad, Azerbaijan, until being sent to Moscow in late February. Members of the Karabagh Committee were all charged with breaking article 206–3 of the Soviet criminal code (organizing group actions that violate the public order) and faced a maximum three-year sentence if convicted. In addition, Manucharyan, Manukyan, and Ter Petrosyan were accused of violating the public order in meetings and demonstrations. Soviet authorities singled out Manucharyan by charging him with violating the equality of the rights of nationalities and races. He was also the subject of an article in Armenia's *Kommunist*, in which he was quoted as urging "armed struggle" to gain Mountainous Karabagh.

At the same time, the central press again inferred a connection between the Karabagh Committee and the local mafia. *Pravda* wrote:

> The "Karabagh Committee" leaders are at work, but corrupt wheeler-dealers of various sorts, the godfathers of the local mafia, are skimming the cream. They are very cozy and comfortable hiding behind the backs of political demagogues.[17]

Speculation about the rationale behind the arrest of the Karabagh movement's leading advocates began circulating even before the group was transferred to Moscow. The fact that the first wave of arrests coincided with Gorbachev's visit to Armenia suggested that the decision had come from the central government. If nothing else, the inescapable drumbeat for the unification of Mountainous Karabagh that Gorbachev had heard in the earthquake zone dovetailed with the general secretary's view that the Karabagh Committee was out to manipulate public opinion for its own political ends. Some observers imagined that the imprisonment of the Karabagh Committee would be the first step in an all-union crackdown on dissent in the non-Russian republics. Indeed, hundreds of local officials in Armenia and Azerbaijan were dismissed or disciplined for failing to control the ethnic violence that had raged in the last weeks of 1988.

Other analysts stressed the local angle in explaining the arrests. Although the Karabagh Committee had long been a thorn in the side of the authorities in Armenia, the earthquake created both a need and an opportunity to move against the activists. According to this interpretation, the ability of the committee to mobilize volunteers and collect relief supplies stood in sharp contrast to the local government's ineptitude. The arrival of the international media exposed the government to a worldwide audience. Under such circumstances, second-guessing at home could not be tolerated. The bonanza of international assistance for Armenia further raised the stakes. As members of the Karabagh Committee pointed out before their imprisonment, a strictly monitored system of aid distribution was necessary to avert corruption. With the most prominent watchdogs out of the picture, there were no real checks on the power of local officials as they began to administer reconstruction projects.

Assuming this scenario, the activists could expect relatively short prison terms. Even optimists, however, expected that they would be held at least until 26 March 1989, the day elections for the Congress of Peoples Deputies were scheduled. The truth was that in the closing days of 1988 no one knew for sure.

Epilogue

The year 1989 marked a watershed in the history of the twentieth century. Beginning with Poland and Hungary, the Soviet Union's satellites in Eastern Europe broke free of Moscow's control. The Berlin Wall—the most salient symbol of the divisions of the Cold War—was breached by throngs of euphoric Germans. In the Soviet Union, the appeal of national movements spread from the Baltics and Transcaucasia to virtually every corner of the country. By the end of 1989, legislatures in five republics had asserted the primacy of republican law over the laws of the USSR. (The Armenian Supreme Soviet approved a similar measure in January 1990.) The Communist Party of Lithuania went so far as to declare its independence from the all-union party. Meanwhile, reform leaders in the Slavic republics and Central Asia were increasingly challenging the authority of the center.

The year 1989 was eventful in Armenia as well. But whereas the Armenians had occupied center stage among the Soviet nationalities movements for much of 1988, by 1989 they were merely one among several national actors. The developments that had drawn the spotlight to Armenia in 1988—huge demonstrations, articulate democratic activists, conflict with the authorities, ethnic strife—were now being replicated in other republics. Moreover, the breakup of the Soviet empire in Eastern Europe and the broadening of national movements in the Soviet Union redefined the context of the Karabagh movement. With the Baltic republics setting the pace, concrete political goals came to dominate the agenda of the Karabagh movement and other national movements in the Soviet Union. Activists made wresting power away from local, hard-line leaders their first priority. Once their initial objectives were achieved, they could then set their sights on the struggle against Moscow to gain control over the affairs of their respective republics. The Karabagh movement—which had simultaneously taken on the authorities in Yerevan, Moscow, and Baku—

had not followed a clearly marked roadmap to power. Now it found itself floating along with the main current of change in the Soviet Union.

The aftereffects of the earthquake and the arrest of the Karabagh Committee set the tone of events in Armenia in early 1989. With martial law still in place and Yerevan swollen with refugees from both the earthquake zone and Azerbaijan, the winter months in Armenia's capital were grey and sullen. Public political activity was confined to an unofficial demonstration on behalf of the Karabagh Committee on International Women's Day and, three days later, on 11 March, spontaneous calls for the release of the activists at a soccer match in Hrazdan Stadium. A handful of Armenians celebrated International Women's Day by hanging bundles of lingerie on the fence surrounding the Armenian Central Committee to let Suren Harutiunyan know that they considered him a weak leader. Meanwhile, the authorities made sure that the jailed activists were cut off from their supporters in Armenia, as well as from each other. After committee members were transferred to Moscow in January, they eventually wound up at the notorious Butyrka prison. There, they were subjected to the standard Soviet regimen for political prisoners: isolation from fellow dissidents, occasional beatings, rotten food, and lack of outside news.

Gradually, however, news from Butyrka began to reach Armenia. The activists raised money for earthquake survivors among other inmates, most of whom were common criminals. Khachik Stamboltsyan provided spiritual counseling to convicted murderers. Hambartsum Galstyan staged a sixteen-day hunger strike and was punished by confinement in an isolation cell and threatened with forced feeding. At the same time, Andrei Sakharov, Amnesty International, Helsinki Watch, and dozens of other human rights groups created a public relations embarrassment for *glasnost* by campaigning for the release of the activists. The French city of Montpeilier awarded Galstyan honorary citizenship. Even African American leader Jesse Jackson expressed his concern about the political prisoners during a visit with a startled Harutiunyan in February.

Elections to Gorbachev's new parliament, the Congress of Peoples Deputies, offered another rallying point. Several Karabagh Committee members were nominated by grass-roots committees, although officials refused to place them on the ballot. More noteworthy was the campaign of Galina Starovoitova, a Russian ethnologist who was chosen by defense plant workers to represent their Yerevan district. Starovoitova, who had lived most of her life in Leningrad and Moscow, became a popular favorite in Armenia after writing a letter in February 1988 supporting the self-determination of Karabagh Armenians. Along with Sakharov, she worked relentlessly to ensure that the case of the Karabagh Committee remained before the public eye. When the authorities declined to register her candidacy, a majority of voters in Starovoitova's district boycotted the 26 March elections.

By May, the mood was shifting in Yerevan. Supporters of the Karabagh Committee had announced that they would carry on the work of the Armenian National Movement (ANM) while their fellow activists were imprisoned. They were soon attracting hundreds of thousands of Yerevanis to rallies in front of the Matenadaran. After a nearly two-month delay in her district's election, Starovoitova won 80 percent of the vote to gain a seat in the Congress. On 19 May, factories in Yerevan were shut down by a strike on behalf of the Karabagh Committee. In Moscow, pressure was building as well. The imprisonment of the committee was becoming a *cause célèbre* for liberal-minded intellectuals, thanks largely to Sakharov and Starovoitova. Gorbachev was counting on this same elite circle to rally support for his reforms and was keenly sensitive to their opinions.

The new round of activity on behalf of the Karabagh Committee ended abruptly on 31 May, when the activists were suddenly released from prison and flown back to Yerevan. There, they were left in the custody of befuddled KGB officials, who in turn released them to a crowd that had quickly gathered in the center of the city. The activists received a hero's welcome, as supporters carried them on their shoulders to take part in a midnight rally of 20,000 people in Theater Square. As one committee member observed, he and his associates had gone to prison as unassuming critics of the government and had returned as living martyrs.

In Mountainous Karabagh, Armenians did not share Yerevan's celebration. *Krunk* Committee member Arkady Manucharov, who had been jailed in November, was to remain imprisoned another full year. More important, the oblast's network of Armenian party bosses and government officials had been further isolated by Moscow's latest measures in the region. On 12 January 1989, the Presidium of the Supreme Soviet had established provisional "special administrative status" in Mountainous Karabagh. According to the Presidium's decision, the oblast was to remain part of Azerbaijan but would be governed directly by Moscow. Arkady Volsky was named to head a joint Armenian–Azerbaijani committee that would replace local authority.

Mountainous Karabagh's special status satisfied no one. Azerbaijanis viewed it as an infringement on their republic's sovereignty. Armenians resented that Henrik Poghosyan had been forced to step down as first secretary and that other Armenian officials in the oblast had been deprived of their authority. For his part, Volsky tried to play the role of even-handed viceroy. He cut through red tape to accelerate the oblast's economic development and attended the dedication ceremony of a monument in Stepanakert commemorating the Sumgait massacre. At the same time, he regularly reported to Baku and responded to the needs of Mountainous Karabagh's Azerbaijani community. Tensions in the oblast, however, continued to mount. After a series of work stoppages in Stepanakert, Armenians in Mountainous Karabagh launched a general strike on 2 May 1989 to reinstate the oblast's party apparatus. More ominous was a clash later in the month between Armenians and Azerbaijanis near Stepanakert—the first incident in what was to be a year of spiraling communal violence.

The worsening strife in Mountainous Karabagh was to define the course of political activism in both Armenia and Azerbaijan, while Moscow's policies only aggravated the dispute. In late May 1989, the inaugural session of the Congress of People's Deputies delegated the task of resolving the Mountainous Karabagh question and other minority problems to the newly elected Supreme Soviet. Galina Starovoitova also presented Gorbachev with the signatures of 168 deputies on a petition demanding the release of the Karabagh Committee.[1] The Congress session was followed by a meeting between Gorbachev and deputies from Mountainous Karabagh in which the Soviet leader made clear that Volsky would be given additional powers. In July, the first members of the Supreme Soviet's commission on Mountainous Karabagh arrived in the oblast to conduct yet another round of meetings with local officials. Even as Moscow continued to pursue its official plan of mediation, however, the situation on the ground was growing more polarized.

In early July 1989, clashes near Stepanakert resulted in the deaths of two Azerbaijanis and one Armenian. In addition, an Armenian was killed in Mardakert, the oblast's northernmost district. More small-scale battles soon followed. Most were confined to exchanges of gunfire between Armenians and Azerbaijanis armed with hunting rifles and shotguns, but Soviet army weapons were also beginning to show up in the oblast. The violence reflected, and in turn fueled, a deepening militancy on both sides of the conflict. In Azerbaijan, the Azerbaijani Popular Front (APF) had been formed in the spring of 1989. Like members of the Karabagh Committee, many of the group's leading figures had been jailed following the demonstrations in Baku at the end of 1988. With the founding congress of the APF in July 1989, the group's influence in the republic quickly expanded. The APF demanded that the special administrative status in Mountainous Karabagh be abolished, and threatened to press for Azerbaijan's independence if the Kremlin did not relent.

In August, the APF's stridently nationalist wing organized strikes that cut off rail traffic to Armenia and closed down key factories in Baku, Sumgait, and other major cities. Mountainous Karabagh had long suffered from a transportation blockade, but for Armenia the experience was much more serious than the interruptions that had occurred in late November and early December of 1988. Eighty-five percent of the rail traffic reaching Armenia passed along the line that ran south along the Caspian Sea before veering west toward Armenia. Along with Estonia and Tajikistan, Armenia had the highest level of intra-union imports among the republics of the USSR. Moreover, 40 percent of Armenia's enterprises were tied to the Soviet military-industrial complex.[2]

Armenia's dependence on the railway, as well as its reliance on two natural gas pipelines passing through Azerbaijan, brought home with sudden urgency the republic's vulnerability to an economic blockade. More important was Moscow's failure to break the stranglehold. Despite the Kremlin's claims to have resolved the blockade through negotiations in October 1989, rail traffic to Armenia in the following months was reduced to a trickle. Reconstruction in the earthquake zone soon came to a halt. Soviet construction crews from outside of Armenia returned to their home republics, often with little to show for their efforts. Armenian industries were also idled by the blockade. The cutoff of fuel shipments plunged Armenia into an energy crisis, aggravating the crimp in electricity supplies caused by the shutdown of Medzamor's nuclear reactors in the winter of 1989.[3]

While the rail blockade jolted Armenia, in Azerbaijan it affirmed the power of the APF's hard-line nationalists. In September, the APF's public pressure campaign forced the government to convene a special session of the Azerbaijani Supreme Soviet. With APF members taking part in the debate, the Azerbaijani legislature voted to dissolve Volsky's special commission and reassert its rule over Mountainous Karabagh. Nine days later, the Azerbaijani Supreme Soviet proclaimed the republic "sovereign within the USSR." In acknowledgment of its political clout, the APF won official recognition by the Azerbaijani government in early October.

The openly intransigent tone in Baku was matched by the steely determination of Karabagh Armenians. The clearest evidence of the Armenian community's outlook was the formation of an Armenian National Council on 16 August 1989. The seventy-eight member council declared that it would represent Mountainous Karabagh's Armenians until the restoration of the oblast's government. Eight days after its creation, the council announced Mountainous Karabagh's secession from Azerbaijan and unification with Armenia. The secession declaration drew immediate condemnation from Baku and Moscow. In Shushi, a crowd of Azerbaijanis vented their anger by holding three visiting MVD generals hostage for a few hours. Volsky characterized the situation in the oblast as being "on the brink of civil war."[4] The Karabagh National Council concurred with Volsky's assessment, calling on the United Nations Security Council to send UN forces to protect Armenians in the oblast.

In Armenia, Mountainous Karabagh's troubles were followed attentively, but at an undeniable distance. The political current in Yerevan was heading in a different direction. Two days after the release of the Karabagh Committee, 500,000 people gathered in front of the Matenadaran to hear Levon Ter Petrosyan pledge the committee's support for democratization and restructuring, and to discuss Armenia's place in the large scheme of Soviet reform. On 16 June, 310 delegates from unofficial reform groups in Armenia met at Yerevan State University to define the goals of the Armenian National Movement. Plans were announced to hold a general meeting of the ANM in the fall. As in a number of other Soviet republics, the ANM had staked out a central role for itself in Armenian politics. Democratic, Western-oriented, supportive of *perestroika*'s goals but mistrustful of the Kremlin, the ANM was positioned to act as both a cooperative partner and a potential rival for Armenia's government. On 28 June, the group was granted official recognition by the Armenian Supreme Soviet.

While the Karabagh Committee was in prison, the Armenian government had sought to join in the national renaissance that had been initiated in 1988. The early months of 1989 saw the authorities enact a string of symbolic measures ringing with national pride: 24 April was proclaimed a legal holiday in the republic; the Armenian Communist Party replaced the Russian word *sovet* (soviet or council) with the Armenian *khorhurd*; 28 May, the day when the Armenian Republic declared independence in 1918, and the red, blue, and orange tricolor were recognized as symbols of Armenia's sovereignty. In an interview with *Le Monde*, Levon Ter Petrosyan noted the convergence of interests between the party in Armenia and the ANM, and praised Suren Harutiunyan for raising the Mountainous Karabagh issue at the Congress of People's Deputies. He added that the Karabagh Committee did not have "any intentions to take the place of the official leadership at the moment." [5]

The Karabagh movement, however, remained split along philosophical lines. A debate within the Armenian Supreme Soviet in June 1989, which featured the participation of non-members, illustrated the basic division. On one side, Zori Balayan framed the Karabagh movement as a struggle against pan-Turkism. On the other side, Khachik Stamboltsyan insisted that the issue be cast in terms of self-determination and accused Balayan of inciting anti-Azerbaijani sentiments. What brought the two mindsets closer together was the quickening tempo of Armenian–Azerbaijani violence.

In October 1989, Karabagh Committee members called for the creation of self-defense units in Armenia to protect border areas from Azerbaijani attacks, and appealed to Armenian conscripts to serve within the republic rather than report to the Soviet army. A few days earlier, discussions between the committee members and the APF had failed to promote reconciliation on the future of Mountainous Karabagh. Mediation efforts by the Inter-Regional Group of deputies in the democratic Congress to break the impasse also led nowhere.

The ANM's founding congress, held 4–5 November 1989, marked another milestone in the maturation of the democratic movement, but offered nothing new on the question of Mountainous Karabagh. If anything, the congress confirmed the desire of Karabagh Committee members to place themselves at the hub of Armenian politics. The proceedings contained something for everyone: Paruir Hairikyan opened the session with a prerecorded address taped in the United States; representatives of Armenian diaspora organizations and reform movements from Eastern Europe and other Soviet republics were in attendance; even Suren Harutiunyan had his turn at the microphone. The more than 1,000 delegates to the congress approved a program that focused on advancing democratization in Armenia. Not much had changed conceptually since Vazgen Manukyan's first draft of the ANM platform in August 1988. Structurally, the ANM incorporated the eleven-man Karabagh Committee into a new thirty-six member executive body.

The major news in November was made in Moscow, not Yerevan. On 28 November, the USSR Supreme Soviet voted 348–5 to end Mountainous Karabagh's special administrative status and restore Azerbaijani control over the oblast. Although the Supreme Soviet adopted additional measures to bolster Mountainous Karabagh's autonomy and to reestablish the authority of the oblast's soviet, observers in Armenia and Azerbaijan saw Moscow's decision largely as a victory for Baku. Gorbachev's hope was that the decision would somehow rid him of one of the *glasnost* era's most intractable problems. In September 1989, he had reiterated his opposition to changing the USSR's internal borders at a Central Committee plenum on nationalities. A few days later, at a session of the USSR Supreme Soviet, Gorbachev gave Armenian and Azerbaijani officials two days to end the rail blockade and to develop a process for resolving the dispute over Mountainous Karabagh. Otherwise, he warned, Moscow would have to take stronger measures. In fact, another unit of MVD troops was dispatched to the oblast to supplement the 4,000-man force already in place.

Gorbachev's tough tone, however, intimidated neither the Armenians nor the Azerbaijanis. On the contrary, the dissolution of Volsky's commission—which in its eleven-month existence had done little to resolve the dispute in the oblast—opened the way for an intensification of the conflict. On 1 December, the Armenian Supreme Soviet took its boldest action yet on Mountainous Karabagh in a special joint session with the

Karabagh National Council. Rejecting the validity of the USSR Supreme Soviet resolution, the Armenian legislature voted to unify Armenia with Mountainous Karabagh and to extend citizenship rights to the oblast's population. In January 1990, the Armenian Supreme Soviet incorporated Mountainous Karabagh's finances into the overall budget of the Armenian republic. The Armenian Supreme Soviet's decision reflected a major shift in the political winds of the republic. Although a great majority of the deputies in the legislature had been loyal agents of the Soviet system, they were in essence staking their political future on representing the interests of Armenia, not Moscow. In Baku, where similar conclusions about the Soviet Union's prospects were being drawn, the Azerbaijani Supreme Soviet condemned the Armenian decision, voted to place Mountainous Karabagh under direct Azerbaijani control, and declared the Zangezur region of southeastern Armenia to be part of Azerbaijan.

In mid-January 1990, the worst outbreak of violence since Sumgait exploded in Baku. After three days of rallies, mobs in the Azerbaijani capital rampaged through Armenian neighborhoods. Of the roughly 25,000 Armenians who had remained in Baku, more than 50 were killed. Nearly all the others fled the city. World chess champion Garry Kasparov (whose mother was Armenian) chartered a plane to fly himself and his relatives to safety. At the same time, well-armed Azerbaijani units attacked Armenian-populated areas in and around the towns of Shahumyan and Khanlar, just north of Mountainous Karabagh. The assault—spearheaded by helicopters and armored vehicles—constituted a serious escalation of the fighting between Armenians and Azerbaijanis. A few days later, Azerbaijani forces struck in northern Armenia, not far from Ijevan, and near the Nakhichevan border in the Ararat plain.

Although Moscow did little to stop the pogrom against Armenians in Baku, the Kremlin moved decisively to quell a threat to Azerbaijan's government. On 20 January 1990, Soviet troops stormed the central city, killing at least eighty-three Azerbaijanis. Gorbachev justified the action by claiming that the APF sought "to seize power by force in the Azerbaijani republic." APF members, especially those in the movement's beleaguered democratic wing, saw the events of January as part of a Communist Party plot to discredit proponents of independence. Indeed, Soviet Defense Minister Dmitri Yazov told journalists in Baku that the objective of government forces was to destroy the organizational structure of the Popular Front. APF members also noted the contrast with Moscow's response to the situation in Lithuania, where the Lithuanian Supreme Soviet had established a commission to explore means for attaining independence and had rescinded the article in the republic's constitution that upheld the supremacy of the Communist Party. Gorbachev himself had paid a visit to

Vilnius in January 1990, pledging that the draft of a new law on secession would soon be released. At the same time, the Soviet leader took to the streets of the Lithuanian capital to press his campaign for preserving the union. Kremlin hard-liners had urged Gorbachev to show his teeth in Lithuania, but the Soviet leader was apparently concerned that the use of force in the Baltics would damage his reputation in the West. The Transcaucasus, however, was a different story. And although Gorbachev's intervention in Baku came too late for the city's Armenian community, it demonstrated Moscow's resolve to preserve the union.

The crackdown against the APF afforded the authorities in Baku and Moscow an opportunity to reimpose order in Azerbaijan. The relative calm in the streets of Baku, however, came at the expense of the Armenians in Mountainous Karabagh. Throughout much of the winter and spring of 1990, MVD forces helped Azerbaijani officials reassert Baku's control over the oblast. In mid-January, a state of emergency was declared in Mountainous Karabagh. Nearly one-fifth of the oblast's population was detained in a house-to-house search that netted more than 3,000 weapons.[6] In the months that followed, ad hoc Armenian militias throughout the oblast were systematically disarmed and their leaders arrested. With MVD forces in Stepanakert beefed up, Azerbaijani officials were again able to establish Baku's hold on the airport and highways leading to the oblast capital. The Yerevan–Stepanakert helicopter link that had operated since 1988 was virtually severed. In addition, thousands of Armenians were deported from the regions to the north of Mountainous Karabagh.

The trials of Mountainous Karabagh's Armenian community inevitably tarnished the credibility of the communist regime in Armenia, while bolstering the stature of the ANM. In March 1989, Armenia had recorded the lowest voter turnout among the republics for elections to the Congress of People's Deputies. The 53 percent showing in Yerevan was particularly embarrassing for the authorities. ANM members believed that they could take advantage of the regime's waning appeal in upcoming electoral contests. In August, Rafael Ghazaryan and Levon Ter Petrosyan won seats to the Armenian Supreme Soviet, along with two Karabagh Armenians, Robert Kocharyan and Arkady Manucharov.[7] In an indication of the Karabagh movement's credibility among the Supreme Soviet deputies, Ghazaryan, Ter Petrosyan, and Kocharyan were elected to the Armenian legislature's Presidium in February 1990. Ghazaryan was selected as vice chairman of the body. At the same time, the ANM made plans to field a full slate of candidates for the elections to the Armenian Supreme Soviet in May 1990.

The escalation of violence in January 1990 brought the ANM closer to the levers of power. ANM representatives served in a crisis management team with government and party officials, and also took the lead in organizing volunteers into self-defense brigades. The ANM's head-quarters was designated as a collection site for weapons. In early February, four members of the ANM executive committee—Hambartsum Galstyan, Ashot Manucharyan, Davit Vardanyan, and School #183 director Ashot Bleyan—took part in informal talks with APF representatives in Riga, under the auspices of the Baltic Council. On the second day, the discussions fell through after the ANM delegation received word that Azerbaijani officials, as well as APF leaders, had demanded that Armenian villagers in Azat and Kamo, north of Mountainous Karabagh, abandon their homes. Although the ANM members returned to a barrage of criticism in Yerevan, they brushed off the charge that they had been duped. Galstyan said:

> [The ANM's] position is a corollary to the incontestable truth that the Azerbaijanis and the Armenians have to live with each other in the region. If, through such meetings, we can save the life of at least one or two persons without compromising our just cause, then it is immoral not to do so.[8]

The winter of 1990 had indeed cast a grim pall over Armenia. The Soviet economy was in a free fall. The economic situation in Armenia, complicated by the blockade, the earthquake, and the refugee crisis, was calamitous. Shortages of even the most basic items, such as soap and sugar, were becoming common. Hopes for Mountainous Kara-bagh were growing dimmer as well. Most Armenians were convinced that the Kremlin had opted to resolve the problem by forcing out the oblast's Armenian community. Over the horizon, many saw a future of unabated hostility with Azerbaijan.

The prospect of political gains by the ANM had scant effect on the mood of the republic. The fault did not lie in the electoral contest itself. By all accounts, the campaign for the May 1990 elections to the Armenian Supreme Soviet was the most important in the history of Soviet Armenia—and spiced with political drama. Among the candidates running under the ANM banner were two corruption-fighting former prosecutors from Moscow—Telman Gdlyan and Nikolai Ivanov. Before being dismissed, the pair had implicated Brezhnev's son-in-law in a kick-back scheme. There were also plenty of accusations that the authorities in Armenia were attempting to block the registration of ANM candidates. Meanwhile, a new first secretary, Vladimir Movsisyan, had been named to replace Suren Harutiunyan at the head of the Armenian Communist Party in April 1990. Movsisyan quickly adopted many of the ANM's themes.

The reality, however, was that neither party officials nor

the ANM were capable of controlling the streets in Yerevan and nearby towns. The volunteer militias that had gained prominence during the border clashes in January were increasingly taking the law into their own hands. In early May, the most powerful group—the Armenian National Army—seized the offices of the Yerevan city soviet and the headquarters of the republic's Komsomol. A few days later, fighting between rival militias in Artashat resulted in four deaths. The worst bloodshed came on 27 May, when MVD troops battled Armenian volunteers after gunfire broke out at Yerevan's train station. Both sides blamed the other for provoking the fighting. The death toll was twenty-six: twenty-three militiamen and three MVD soldiers.

In comparison to the growing turmoil in the republic, the Armenian Supreme Soviet elections were uneventful. Voter turnout was a dismal 50 percent. (In Mountainous Karabagh, 94 percent of eligible Armenians voted for the twelve seats allotted to the oblast in the Armenian legislature.) The results held few surprises: ANM candidates did well in Yerevan and other big cities, while Communist Party officials prevailed in the countryside. In electoral districts where voter turnout was below 50 percent, or where no candidate had received a majority, another round of elections was scheduled. The upshot was that the electoral process dragged on through the summer. A new legislature was not seated until 20 July 1990.

Ultimately, the elections gave the ANM and its prospective coalition partners a narrow majority within the Armenian Supreme Soviet. The ANM, however, was itself a dubious vehicle for political power. Like other grass-roots dissidents in the Soviet bloc, the founders of the ANM saw themselves mainly as critics of the political system, not as participants. When the opportunity to compete for power came, many within the ANM were reluctant to transform their movement into a formal political party. As evidenced by the ANM's founding congress in November 1989, the goal was to make room for just about everyone under the ANM banner. The 1990 elections reflected the ANM's ad hoc organization. Among the ANM supporters elected to the Armenian Supreme Soviet, there was a solid core of democratic activists connected to the Karabagh Committee. However, the ANM had also endorsed a disparate collection of candidates who had little to do with the committee. Thus, the ANM bloc within the new Armenian Supreme Soviet included single-minded nationalists, former communists eager to jump on the ANM bandwagon, and liberal, Western-oriented democrats. The notion of party discipline was out of the question.

When the Armenian Supreme Soviet convened on 20 July 1990, the ANM could more or less count on the support of 35 percent of the deputies. Representatives from Mountainous Karabagh and smaller political groups held 12 percent of the seats, while one-third of the legislature was composed of loyal communists. In addition, 40 of the body's 260 seats remained to be filled in upcoming elections. The main item on the agenda of the legislature was the election of a president, or chairman of the Presidium—an office that had meant little when political power was concentrated in the hands of the Communist Party but in constitutional terms represented the top position in the government. Within the ANM, a handful of Karabagh Committee veterans—Rafael Ghazaryan, Ashot Manucharyan, Vazgen Manukyan, and Levon Ter Petrosyan—were the most likely contenders for the presidency. They made the final decision regarding the ANM's nominee in a closed-door meeting in late July. Ter Petrosyan was to be the presidential candidate, while Manukyan would be put forward for the office of prime minister. Meanwhile, Vladimir Movsisyan was chosen as the presidential candidate of the Armenian Communist Party.

The legislature took up the matter of selecting a president on 3 August. Ter Petrosyan and Movsisyan were each given a turn at the podium to present their respective platforms. In appearance, the democratic activist and the communist *apparatchik* seemed to share little in common. Ter Petrosyan, his shirtsleeves rolled up, spoke to the gathering wearing neither necktie nor jacket. Movsisyan, with his ill-fitting suit and heavy, lumbering gait, represented another generation. In their presentations, however, the differences were not nearly as striking. Many of the ANM's guiding principles—support for multiparty democracy, a pledge to put Armenia's interests ahead of Moscow, commitment to economic restructuring—had found a place in Movsisyan's platform. During his address, Ter Petrosyan acknowledged that a common language of reform had come to dominate the political landscape in the Soviet Union:

> If we compare the concrete measures included in the array of declarations on independence or sovereignty accepted by Soviet republics, then we see that, except for the details, essentially they do not differ from one another. Virtually all of the republics first and foremost underline the following measures as part of their national program.[9]

Ter Petrosyan went on to enumerate the core elements of the Soviet Union's reform movements, including republican-level control over the local economy, natural resources, foreign relations and defense, and support for multiparty democracy, free-market economics, sweeping reform of state institutions, and the revitalization of language and culture. As Ter Petrosyan noted, the items had been features of the ANM platform from the outset. What Ter Petrosyan emphasized, however, was that he could be trusted to guide Armenia toward the future.

The first ballot, cast at 10 P.M., indicated that the Armenian Supreme Soviet was divided in two camps. Ter Petrosyan's nomination received 112 votes in favor and 107 opposed (131 votes—a majority of the legislature's seats—were needed for victory). Movsisyan's nomination drew 93 votes in favor and 124 opposed. A second ballot at midnight gave Ter Petrosyan twelve more votes, but the session was adjourned without a conclusive result. On 4 August, the legislature reconvened. Four additional candidates—Rafael Ghazaryan, Paruir Hairikyan, Vazgen Manukyan, and Hrachik Simonyan—had been nominated for the presidency. All but Hairikyan promptly withdrew. In the third round of balloting Hairikyan received only eight votes, while support for Ter Petrosyan and Movsisyan remained virtually unchanged. After another round of speeches on behalf of the two leading candidates, the fourth round of balloting proved decisive. Ter Petrosyan received 140 votes, compared to 76 for Movsisyan. Armenia had a non-communist president.[10]

The news of Ter Petrosyan's election was greeted by an outburst of celebration in front of the legislative building. The crowd that had circulated outside the chamber for two days sang *Mer Hairenik* (Our Fatherland), the anthem of the 1918–20 republic. Inside the auditorium, Ter Petrosyan cast his election not as a victory for himself or the ANM, but for the people of the republic, the ideals of democracy, and the restoration of state institutions. He later addressed a gathering in Freedom Square (formerly Lenin Square). In between chants of "Le-von! Le-von!" Ter Petrosyan stressed that his first order of business would be to stabilize Armenia's internal situation.

The proceedings within the Armenian Supreme Soviet had not halted the republic's slide toward chaos. Despite attempts to unify the volunteer militias under an autonomous self-defense council, fighting among the armed groups intensified in July. On 25 July 1990, Gorbachev outlawed volunteer militias throughout the Soviet Union and warned that MVD troops would confiscate their weapons if the units did not disarm within fifteen days. Armenians assumed that Gorbachev's decree was aimed largely at their republic. Tensions worsened a few days later when the Armenian Supreme Soviet rejected Gorbachev's deadline, and militiamen seized weapons from an ammunition depot near Yerevan.

Three days after his election, Ter Petrosyan flew to Moscow and convinced Soviet authorities to extend the deadline for disarming Armenia's volunteer militias. Moreover, the Kremlin agreed to let the Armenian government take on the task. Ter Petrosyan's policy was to integrate the militias into the republic's security forces. Ter Petrosyan's conciliatory approach, however, gave way to stronger measures after a representative from the ANM's executive committee and a guard were shot to death at the end of August 1990 as they approached the Yerevan headquarters of the Armenian National Army (ANA). Ter Petrosyan responded by imposing a curfew in Armenia and ordering members of the ANA to surrender their weapons. The day following his announcement, Ter Petrosyan instructed government forces to occupy ANA headquarters throughout the republic. ANA leaders surrendered peacefully, and appealed to their comrades to cooperate with the new government in a videotaped message broadcast on Armenian television.

While Ter Petrosyan's election proved a force for stability in Armenia, the Soviet Union itself continued to plot an unsteady course. In April 1990, the Supreme Soviet had passed a new law governing the right of the USSR's republics to secede from the union. The decision required that two-thirds of the voters in an independence-minded republic opt for secession in a referendum. Other conditions included a five-year transition period, approval by the Congress of People's Deputies, and financial assistance in resettling those who wished to leave. Within the republics where support for independence was strongest—principally the Baltics, Azerbaijan, Georgia, and Moldavia—the Supreme Soviet's decision was largely dismissed as a Kremlin-designed roadblock. In Armenia, however, the law on secession meshed with the republic's unique position. Sandwiched between Azerbaijan and Turkey, and lacking an outlet to the sea, an Armenian state detached from the Soviet Union would find itself in a more precarious situation than any other republic. Even proponents of independence recognized Armenia's vulnerability. Within the Ter Petrosyan government, many welcomed the five-year waiting period built into the new law on secession. In addition, the law created a legal framework for realizing independence. Just as Karabagh Committee member Ter Petrosyan had stressed the importance of adhering to legal norms, so President Ter Petrosyan pledged that Armenia's road to independence would not stray from the path of the constitution.

On 24 August 1990, Armenia issued a carefully worded declaration *on* independence, or, as the body of the document explained, "the beginning of the process of establishing independent statehood." By this time, Ter Petrosyan had brought a number of his colleagues from the ANM into the government. Babgen Ararktsyan had been appointed vice-president, while Vazgen Manukyan had been elected prime minister. Manukyan was particularly instrumental in drafting the declaration on independence. He also succeeded in scuttling two competing declarations, while gaining passage for his middle-of-the-road version in the Armenian Supreme Soviet by a vote of 183–2.

Uncertainty clearly lay ahead, but at the end of August 1990 members of the Ter Petrosyan government could nonetheless look back with satisfaction at their remarkable odyssey. In two and a half years, the democratic movement in Armenia had swept aside one of the Soviet

Union's most stagnant regimes, changed the political culture of the republic, and catapulted its leaders to the highest positions in the government. The declaration on independence, a document that was the movement's crowning achievement, differed little in tone from the first ANM manifesto Vazgen Manukyan had drafted in August 1988.

Whatever its shortcomings, the democratic movement in Armenia had been at the forefront of change in the Soviet Union. If not completely cognizant of the democratic values they had endorsed at the ballot box, the people of Armenia had at least been among the first in the USSR to openly discuss the issues and choices that would dominate their future. Moreover, the sense of national purpose that had been forged in the early days of the Karabagh movement would serve them well as the basis for social stability during the fitful disintegration of the Soviet system.

Conclusion

In July 1994, the Noyan Tapan news agency assembled a panel of sixteen journalists and political insiders to identify the most influential people in Armenia. The top five spots on the list that was produced were occupied by former Karabagh Committee members.[1]

The results of the survey, the first of its kind conducted by Noyan Tapan, should not be seen as an indication of the Karabagh Committee's metamorphosis into a unified political force or as evidence that committee members had replaced the Communist Party elite at the top of a static political hierarchy. Far from it. The committee had begun fragmenting even before the collapse of the Soviet Union, and politics in the independent Republic of Armenia were anything but stable and predictable. Rather, the rating reflected the political staying power of the Karabagh Committee's individual members and the realization among Armenians that they continued to live with the repercussions of 1988. From the conflict over Mountainous Karabagh to the troubled infancy of newly born democratic institutions, Armenia was passing through a historical era that had begun in Theater Square. Indeed, Levon Ter Petrosyan in 1994 was the only remaining non-communist leader in the Commonwealth of Independent States to have taken office before the downfall of the USSR.

The personalities and locus of the republic's political stage had changed little over six years, except that Karabagh Committee members now filled both the government and the opposition. At rallies in Theater Square in 1994, Ashot Manucharyan accused President Ter Petrosyan, Interior Minister Vano Siradeghyan, and Parliament Chairman Babgen Ararktsyan of subverting democracy and fueling corruption. Siradeghyan in particular was held personally responsible for graft and heavy-handed security measures. "Vano is not [the] Vano we used to know," Manucharyan told demonstrators in July 1994. "He has become a monster on [the] people's throat."[2] Hambartsum Galstyan's critique of the government was even more damning. He accused Siradeghyan of sanctioning thirty politically moti-

204

vated murders and denounced Ter Petrosyan for tolerating political terror.[3] (When Galstyan himself was murdered in Yerevan in December 1994, suspicions immediately focused on Siradeghyan.) Manucharyan, Galstyan, and two other former Karabagh Committee members, Vazgen Manukyan and Davit Vardanyan, were among the most prominent founders of a new political party—the National Democratic Union—formed in 1994 to challenge the power of the Armenian National Movement.

Ter Petrosyan responded to his critics by charging them with fomenting instability. According to the Armenian president, the behavior of his former associates was especially reckless in light of the crisis gripping Armenia. The republic, Ter Petrosyan asserted, risked drifting into the same maelstrom of political turmoil that had wrecked the fortunes of Georgia and Azerbaijan. "If we want to lose Karabagh plus Zangezur and some other territories," Ter Petrosyan warned, "there is no shorter path to that." [4] He also came to the defense of Siradeghyan and his other ministerial appointees, labeling his opponents in the National Democratic Union as "mentally disequilibrated people."

The disintegration of the Karabagh Committee, even the accompanying rancor, was hardly a surprise. Throughout the former Soviet bloc, the political coalitions that brought down communist regimes soon succumbed themselves to infighting and factiousness. Movements in Central Europe that were once applauded for their vision, courage, and egalitarianism—Solidarity in Poland, the Civic Forum in Czechoslovakia, and the Hungarian Democratic Forum in Hungary—fell apart within a few years of taking power. The fate of democratic movements within former Soviet states was still more discouraging.

The expectations generated by political revolution were partly to blame for the disillusionment. The twentieth century contains many siren songs of false utopias. In addition, the bitterness within the former USSR was tainted with a peculiarly Soviet flavor. Decades of superpower status had blinded many former Soviets to the backwardness of their industry and technology in the global market. Seventy years of communist rule and intellectual isolation had trapped their societies in the standards and mindsets of the Soviet system.

In Armenia as well, the leadership that emerged from the Karabagh movement was unable to transcend its Soviet origins. The transparency of the demonstrations in Theater Square soon gave way to the opacity of the Soviet system. The curtains were again drawn on the political process. As in other former Soviet states, the concerns of security and stability came to preoccupy the Ter Petrosyan government. The rulers almost instinctively mistrusted private initiative and too often depicted political opponents as threats to Armenia's very nationhood. The ruled, in turn, still looked to the state to solve their problems, and yet viewed politics with cynicism and disgust.

The shackles of the past undermined the legitimacy of parliamentary elections held in July 1995. The ruling ANM engineered an overwhelming victory at the polls, but at the expense of Armenia's reputation in the West. International observers characterized the campaign as unfair, citing numerous government violations of democratic principles.

There were voices of protest in Yerevan, but most Armenians shrugged off the results with indifference. A quotation from Otto von Bismarck engraved on a pillar flanking the grave of Hambartsum Galstyan seemed to capture the historical lesson drawn by the electorate. The inscribed words of the master of *Realpolitik* read: "Romantics plan revolutions, fanatics implement them, and villains benefit from them."

What, then, remained of the legacy of the Karabagh movement? Or, of equal significance, where does one search for the meaning of the movement?

The place to begin looking is not the battlefields of Mountainous Karabagh or the Armenian political arena. The movement, after all, was made by the people—the hundreds of thousands who turned out for rallies and meetings. Members of the Karabagh Committee readily conceded that they were only barometers of the popular will, not its masters.

For the people of Armenia in the mid-1990s, contemplating the legacy of the Karabagh movement was difficult. A string of winters without heat, hot water, and only a couple of hours of electricity a day had dimmed the hopes of even the most indefatigable optimists. By 1995, as many as one million Armenians had left the republic, mostly to Russia, in search of work and better living conditions. Under the strain of such hardships, looking back to the euphoria that once reigned in Theater Square was likely to bring only pain, if not indignation.

At the same time, there existed in Armenia a more thoughtful, balanced perspective. Many of the deprivations wracking Armenia were attributable to the breakdown in the Soviet economic system. The energy and transportation blockade imposed by Azerbaijan and Turkey, the chronic instability of Georgia, the burden of the conflict over Mountainous Karabagh, and the aftermath of the 1988 earthquake in northern Armenia further aggravated the republic's problems. However, what distinguished Armenia among the countries of the former Soviet Union during its first years of independence was the republic's social stability. Armenia's politicians hardly deserve credit for the common sense of the citizenry. The feuds within influential circles in Armenia were often just as nasty and petty as elsewhere in the former Soviet Union. Political thuggery, perhaps even as-sassination, was not unknown. And yet the people of Armenia served as a restraining force on their own political leaders. There were no attempted coups, no regional warlords, no audience for militaristic demagogues. The people of Armenia took the task of building their state seriously, even as they questioned the competence and honesty of government officials.

The Karabagh movement contributed to the resilience of the populace, offering a legacy of both success and failure. The movement did not achieve the unification of Armenia and Karabagh through constitu-tional means, nor did it eliminate corruption or instill popular faith in the rejuvenative powers of democracy. But disappointment proved to be an instructive teacher. Armenians were among the first peoples of the Soviet Union to learn that they could not count on Gorbachev or on many of their own political leaders. The initial steps toward independence were taken with a sober understanding of the trials that lay ahead. Unlike many other republic capitals in the last years of Gorbachev's rule, Yerevan entertained few illusions about the challenges of statehood.

What remains of the Karabagh movement is thus most readily found in the worldview of ordinary Armenians. The sense of purpose and broadly felt consensus that emerged in 1988 galvanized Armenians to withstand the blows that struck in later years. The shoulder-to-shoulder camaraderie in Theater Square, even if only fleeting, helped heal the divi-sions that had separated longtime urbanites from peasant transplants, Yere-vanis from Leninakanis, and native Armenians from post-World War II repatriates. Finally, the people of Armenia came to believe in their collective strength—a self-image seared into Armenian consciousness during the mass rallies in Theater Square. The sea of raised fists, the home-made placards, the handwritten questions channeled toward the speaker's platform, and ulti-mately the discipline, determination, and shared commitment left a lasting impression on the citizens of the struggling republic. Of course, by the mid-1990s the slogans had changed. *Gha-ra-ba-ghe mer ne!* (Karabagh is ours!) and *Yelk ch'ka!* (There's no turning back!) were seldom heard on the streets of Yerevan. Rather, Armenians took heart from an expression that sprang from their long history: *Piti dimanank* (We will endure).

Notes

All references to books and to magazine and journal articles are abbreviated. Full publication details can be found in Works Cited.

1. Stepanakert

1. Yuri Rost, *Armenian Tragedy*, p. 15.
2. Avedis K. Sanjian, *Colophons of Armenian Manuscripts, 1301–1480*, pp. 124–125.
3. George A. Bournoutian, *Eastern Armenia in the Last Decades of Persian Rule: 1807–1828*, pp. 73–74. Eastern Armenia consists of historical Armenian lands east of the Akhurian River, including present-day Armenia, Nakhichevan, and Mountainous Karabagh.
4. Ibid., pp. 74 and 89.
5. Bournoutian, *A History of the Armenian People, Volume II*, pp. 69–70.
6. Richard G. Hovannisian, "Nationalist Ferment in Armenia," p. 30.
7. Claire Mouradian, "The Mountainous Karabagh Question," pp. 4–5.
8. Bournoutian, *Eastern Armenia in the Last Decades of Persian Rule*, p. 75.
9. Ibid., p. 101.
10. Ibid., pp. 41 and 101.
11. Hovannisian, *Armenia on the Road to Independence, 1918*, p. 15; Christopher J. Walker, ed., *Armenia and Karabagh*, p. 85. Russian colonization schemes added to the ethnic diversity of the Caucasus. Under the administration of Count Vorontsov–Dashkov, for example, 20,000 Russians were settled in what is now southeastern Azerbaijan. Although irrigation was brought to the dry steppe of the region, most of the Russian villages failed to take root. Firuz Kazemzadeh, *The Struggle for Transcaucasia*, p. 23.
12. Hovannisian, "Nationalist Ferment in Armenia," p. 30; Luigi Villari, *Fire and Sword in the Caucasus*, p. 169.
13. Ronald Grigor Suny, *Looking toward Ararat*, pp. 66–67.
14. Ibid., p. 45.
15. Hovannisian, *Armenia on the Road to Independence, 1918*, p. 18; Walker,

Armenia: The Survival of a Nation, p. 70; Walker, ed., *Armenia and Karabagh*, p. 31.

16. Villari, *Fire and Sword in the Caucasus*, p. 5.
17. Walker, ed., *Armenia and Karabagh*, p. 31; Hovannisian, *Armenia on the Road to Independence*, pp. 18–21.
18. Villari, *Fire and Sword in the Caucasus*, pp. 169, 195, and 198.
19. Suny, *The Baku Commune 1917–1918: Class and Nationality in the Russian Revolution*, pp. 36–37; Anahide Ter Minassian, "The Revolution of 1905 in Transcaucasia," p. 9.
20. Walker, *Armenia: The Survival of a Nation*, pp. 73–74; Stepan H. Astourian, "On the Rise of Azerbaijani National Identity," pp. 42–43.
21. Walker, *Armenia: The Survival of a Nation*, pp. 76–77; Walker, ed., *Armenia and Karabagh*, pp. 86–87.
22. Hovannisian, *Armenia on the Road to Independence*, p. 22.
23. Ibid., p. 21.
24. Hovannisian, "The Armeno–Azerbaijani Conflict," pp. 34–39; Walker, *Armenia: The Survival of a Nation*, pp. 306–318.
25. Bournoutian, "Karabagh in Political Perspective," p. 23.
26. Bournoutian, *A History of the Armenian People, Volume II*, p. 63.
27. The title *bek*, a Turkish word meaning "lord" or "prince," was taken by the brothers and other close male relatives of the Mountainous Karabagh *meliks*.
28. *Yuzbashi*, meaning "commander" in Turkish, was the title given to the military leaders in each of Mountainous Karabagh's five *melik*doms.
29. Bournoutian, *A History of the Armenian People, Volume II*, pp. 35–38; Walker, *Armenia: The Survival of a Nation*, pp. 38–40.
30. Bournoutian, "Karabagh in Political Perspective," p. 24.
31. Walker, ed., *Armenia and Karabagh*, pp. 91–92.
32. Hovannisian, *Armenia on the Road to Independence*, pp. 241–42; Hovannisian, "The Armeno–Azerbaijani Conflict," pp. 11–16.
33. Gerard J. Libaridian, ed., *The Karabagh File*, p. 155.
34. G. A. Galoyan and K. S. Khudazerdyan, eds., *Nagornyi Karabakh* (Mountainous Karabakh), pp. 25–26.
35. Ibid., pp. 28–29.
36. Ibid., p. 31.
37. Audrey L. Altstadt, *The Azerbaijani Turks*, p. 117; Libaridian, ed., *The Karabagh File*, pp. 35–36.
38. Galoyan and Khudzaerdyan, eds., *Nagornyi Karabakh*, p. 34; Libaridian, ed., *The Karabagh File*, pp. 42–43; United States Department of State, *Soviet Nationalities Survey*, at 1.
39. Walker, *Armenia: The Survival of a Nation*, pp. 325–326.
40. Ibid., p. 373.
41. Bohdan Nahaylo and Victor Swoboda, *Soviet Disunion*, p. 60.
42. Mouradian, "The Mountainous Karabagh Question," p. 9; Nahaylo and Swoboda, *Soviet Disunion*, p. 76; Libaridian, ed., *The Karabagh File*, pp. 40–41; Walker, *Armenia: The Survival of a Nation*, 342–343.
43. Libaridian, ed., *The Karabagh File*, pp. 44–45.

44. Suny, "Nationalism and Democracy in Gorbachev's Soviet Union," pp. 484–485; "Chronology of Events 1920–1988 in Nagorno–Karabakh," *Glasnost*, no. 16–18, p. 11; Libaridian, ed., *The Karabagh File*, pp. 42–43.
45. Suny, *Looking toward Ararat*, p. 188; Interview with Vigen Hairapetyan, Yerevan, Armenia, 24 June 1992.
46. B. S. Mirzoian, "Nagornyi Karabakh: Statistical Considerations," p. 13.
47. Galoyan and Khudazerdyan, eds., *Nagornyi Karabakh*, pp. 46–47.
48. Mirzoian, "Nagornyi Karabakh," pp. 18–19.
49. Ibid., pp. 22–23.
50. Vladimir Y. Khojabekyan, *Artsakhe Portsutyan Zhamin* (Artsakh in the Time of Trial), pp. 60 and 54.
51. Mouradian, "The Mountainous Karabagh Question," p. 9.
52. FBIS–SOV (Moscow Television Service), 25 July 1988, at 52.
53. Shahen Mkrtchian, "Witnesses to History," p. 40.
54. Haroutiun Gayayan, "The Disappearance of Rugs from Armenian Artzakh–Karabagh," p. 55; Levon Chorbajian, *Karabakh and the U.S. Press*, p. 2; Libaridian, ed., *The Karabagh File*, p. 82.
55. Igor Muradyan, "Glasnost and Nagorno–Karabakh: The Public Speaks," pp. 19–20; Khojabekyan, *Artsakhe Portsutyan Zhamin*, p. 26; Interview with Vigen Hairapetyan.
56. Muradyan, "Glasnost and Nagorno–Karabakh," p. 20; *Asbarez*, 13 Feb. 1988, p. 18; Altstadt, *The Azerbaijani Turks*, p. 195.
57. "Chronology of Events," *Glasnost*, p. 12; *Asbarez*, 13 Feb. 1988, p. 27; *New York Times*, 11 Mar. 1988, p. 1.
58. Andrea Chandler and Charles F. Furtado, Jr., eds. *Perestroika in the Soviet Republics: Documents on the National Question*, p. 403.
59. Interview with Vigen Hairapetyan.
60. Rost, *Armenian Tragedy*, p. 13; "Chronology of Events," *Glasnost*, pp. 12–13; U.S. Department of State, *Soviet Nationalities Survey*, at III.
61. Rost, *Armenian Tragedy*, p. 13; U.S. Department of State, *Soviet Nationalities Survey*, at III.
62. FBIS–SOV (*Izvestia*), 14 July 1988, at 44.
63. "Chronology of Events," *Glasnost*, p. 13; U.S. Department of State, *Soviet Nationalities Survey*, at III; Suny, "Nationalism and Democracy in Gorbachev's Soviet Union," pp. 487–488.
64. V. B. Arutiunyan, *Sobytiya b Nagornom Karabakhe* (Events in Mountainous Karabagh), p. 27.
65. Ibid., p. 38.
66. Interview with Vigen Hairapetyan.

2. Yerevan

1. Alfred Erich Senn, *Lithuania Awakening*, pp. 33–34.
2. FBIS–SOV (Moscow TASS in English), 24 Feb. 1988, at 36; United States Department of State, *Soviet Nationalities Survey*, at IV.

3. L. A. Abramian (Levon H. Abrahamyan), "Archaic Ritual and Theater," p. 57.
4. Bournoutian, *Eastern Armenia in the Last Decades of Persian Rule, 1807–1828*, pp. 62–63 and 145.
5. Philip P. Ketchian, "Air Pollution in Yerevan," 1 Aug. 1992, p. 6.
6. Suny, "Modernization Soviet Style: The Case of Armenia," p. 40.
7. Nora Dudwick, "The Karabagh Movement," p. 67; "Chronology of Events 1920–1988 in Nagorno–Karabakh," *Glasnost*, no. 16–18, p. 14.
8. Libaridian, ed., *The Karabagh File*, p. 93.
9. Mark Malkasian, "A Report from Armenia," p. 16.
10. U.S. Department of State, *Soviet Nationalities Survey*, at V; Chandler and Furtado, eds. *Perestroika in the Soviet Republics*, p. 404.
11. Nahaylo and Swoboda, *Soviet Disunion*, pp. 255–256.
12. "Chronology of Events," *Glasnost*, no. 16–18, pp. 14–15; U.S. Department of State, *Soviet Nationalities Survey*, at V; Malkasian, *Armenian Weekly*, 30 July 1988, p. 16.
13. Interview with Ashot Dabaghyan, Providence, RI, Mar. 1991.
14. *New York Times*, 29 Feb. 1988, p. 8.
15. Aliyev culminated a political comeback in 1993, becoming president of Azerbaijan after orchestrating a coup against the country's popularly elected leader, Abdulfez Elchibey.
16. Rost, *Armenian Tragedy*, pp. 11–12.
17. "Chronology of Events," *Glasnost*, p. 20; Interview with Ashot Dabaghyan. Yuzbashyan was replaced as Armenia's KGB chief by Valery Badamyants in Oct. 1988. In 1994, Yuzbashyan was murdered in Yerevan.
18. Levon H. Abrahamyan, "The Karabagh Movement as Viewed by an Anthropologist," p. 71; Rost, *Armenian Tragedy*, p. 22.
19. Libaridian, *The Question of Karabagh*, p. 14; *Artsakhyan Taregrutiun* (Artsakh Annals), p. 169.
20. Malkasian, *Armenian Weekly*, 25 July 1988, p. 8; FBIS–SOV (Yerevan Domestic Service in Russian), 25 Feb. 1988, at 40.
21. FBIS–SOV (Paris AFP in English), 25 Feb. 1988, at 40; *New York Times*, 25 Feb. 1988, p. 6; *Artsakhyan Taregrutiun*, p. 169.
22. Malkasian, *Armenian Weekly*, 23 July 1988, p. 8.
23. FBIS–SOV (Yerevan Domestic Service in Russian), 26 Feb. 1988, at 42; *Los Angeles Times*, 26 Feb. 1988, p. 2.
24. U.S. Department of State, *Soviet Nationalities Survey*, at VI.
25. Malkasian, *Armenian Weekly*, 23 July 1988, p. 8.
26. Mouradian, "The Mountainous Karabagh Question," p. 22. In December 1994, Galstyan was murdered in Yerevan. His murder sparked a political crisis in Armenia.
27. Thomas J. Samuelian, "Cultural Ecology and Gorbachev's Restructured Union," p. 200.
28. Suny, *Looking toward Ararat*, p. 227.
29. *Asbarez*, 11 June 1988, p. 28.
30. Dudwick, "The Karabagh Movement," *Armenian Review*, pp. 67–68.
31. Abrahamyan, "The Karabagh Movement as Viewed by an Anthropologist," p.

71; Corbin Lyday, "A Commitment to Truth-Telling"; Malkasian, *Armenian Weekly*, 23 July 1988, p. 8; "Armenian Self-Discipline Avoided Clashes, Witness Says," Reuters, 28 Feb. 1988.

32. Malkasian, *Armenian Weekly*, 16 July 1988, p. 11; Libaridian, *The Question of Karabagh*, p. 7; Dudwick, "The Karabagh Movement," p. 68.
33. Open letter by Rafael Ghazaryan to General Secretary Mikhail Gorbachev, Yerevan, Armenia, 5 May 1989.
34. Lyday, "A Commitment to Truth-Telling."
35. U.S. Department of State, *Soviet Nationalities Survey*, at IV; "Chronology of Events," *Glasnost*, p. 13.
36. Robert Cullen, "Roots," p. 65; Rost, *Armenian Tragedy*, pp. 20–21.
37. Suny, "Nationalism and Democracy in Gorbachev's Soviet Union," p. 488.
38. Nahaylo and Swoboda, *Soviet Disunion*, pp. 153, 212, and 265–266.
39. Cullen, "Roots," *New Yorker*, p. 66.
40. Malkasian, *Armenian Weekly*, 23 July 1988, p. 10; Rost, *Armenian Tragedy*, pp. 21–22.
41. Libaridian, *The Question of Karabagh*, p. 6.

3. Sumgait

1. *New York Times*, 2 Mar. 1988, p. 10.
2. Theodore Shabad, *Basic Industrial Resources of the USSR*, pp. 156–157.
3. Altstadt, *The Azerbaijani Turks*, p. 164.
4. Samvel Shahmuratian, ed., *The Sumgait Tragedy*, p. 5; FBIS–SOV (TASS), 7 Mar. 1988, at 44; FBIS–SOV (Baku Domestic Service), 7 Mar. 1988, at 44; Rost, *Armenian Tragedy*, pp. 26–27.
5. Shahmuratian, *The Sumgait Tragedy*, p. 3; V. B. Arutiunyan, *Sobytiya b Nagornom Karabakhe*, pp. 39–40.
6. Ibid., p. 4; United States Department of State, *Soviet Nationalities Survey*, at VI; Rost, *Armenian Tragedy*, p. 28.
7. Ludmilla Alexeyeva, "Unrest in the Soviet Union," p. 70; "Riots Were Planned Genocide, Armenian Communist Newspaper Says," Reuters, 5 Nov. 1988.
8. Malkasian, "A Report from Armenia," *Armenian Weekly*, 30 July 1988, p. 10.
9. Lyday, "A Commitment to Truth-Telling"; Rost, *Armenian Tragedy*, pp. 28–29.
10. Ibid., p. 28; Lyday, "A Commitment to Truth-Telling."
11. Ibid.
12. FBIS–SOV (*Pravda*), 2 Mar. 1988, at 44; FBIS–SOV (*Pravda*), 7 Mar. 1988, at 47; FBIS–SOV (Moscow Television Service), 11 Mar. 1988, at 26.
13. FBIS–SOV (TASS), 7 Mar. 1988, at 44.
14. *New York Times*, 27 Apr. 1988, p. 12; Lyday, "A Commitment to Truth-Telling."
15. "An Appeal to Scholars, Creative Artists, Journalists," *Glasnost*, no. 16–18, p. 21.
16. Dudwick, "The Karabagh Movement," p. 64.
17. Rost, *Armenian Tragedy*, pp. 31–32.
18. Malkasian, "A Report from Armenia," p. 10.
19. "The Human Drama of Nagorno–Karabakh," *Glasnost*, no. 16–18, p. 24.

20. Malkasian, "A Report from Armenia," p. 10.
21. FBIS–SOV (Baku Domestic Service), 7 Mar. 1988, at 44; FBIS–SOV (Baku Domestic Service), 7 Mar. 1988, at 45.
22. Mark Saroyan, "The 'Karabagh Syndrome' and Azerbaijani Politics," p. 18.
23. Malkasian, "A Report from Armenia," p. 10.

4. Dormancy

1. "Armenians Resume Protests after Moscow Hints at Tough Line," Reuters, 21 Mar. 1988; *New York Times*, 21 Mar. 1988, p. 1.
2. FBIS–SOV (TASS), 22 Mar. 1988, at 62–63.
3. Malkasian, "A Report from Armenia," p. 10.
4. Silva Kaputikyan, "An Open Letter," p. 28.
5. "A Chronology of Events 1920–1988 in Nagorno–Karabakh," *Glasnost*, no. 16–18, p. 15.
6. Nahaylo and Swoboda, *Soviet Disunion*, p. 290.
7. FBIS–SOV (*Izvestia*), 24 Mar. 1988, at 43.
8. "Gorbachev Accuses West of Meddling in Soviet Regional Dispute," Reuters, 5 Apr. 1988.
9. FBIS–SOV (*Pravda*), 4 Apr. 1988, at 39.
10. FBIS–SOV (*Bakinskiy Rabochiy*), 12 Apr., 1988, at 52.
11. United States Department of State, *Soviet Nationalities Survey*, at VII–VIII; "Chronology of Events," *Glasnost*, p. 16.
12. FBIS–SOV (*Izvestia*), 6 Apr. 1988, at 37; Malkasian, "A Report from Armenia," p. 10.
13. Martha B. Olcott, ed., *The Soviet Multinational State*, p. 569.
14. FBIS–SOV (*Kommunist*), 12 Apr. 1988, at 50; *Artsakhyan Taregrutiun*, p. 177.
15. FBIS–SOV (*Kommunist*), 8 Apr. 1988, at 47.
16. Malkasian, "A Report from Armenia," p. 10; Kaputikyan, "An Open Letter," p. 29.
17. Malkasian, "A Report from Armenia," *Armenian Weekly*, 6 Aug. 1988, p. 10.
18. Nahaylo and Swoboda, *Soviet Disunion*, p. 287; U.S. Department of State, *Soviet Nationalities Survey*, at VII.
19. Nahaylo and Swoboda, *Soviet Disunion*, p. 288; "Gorbachev Warmly Greeted in Yugoslavia, Speaks Out on Unrest," Reuters, 14 Mar. 1988.
20. *Asbarez*, 19 Dec. 1987, p. 17.
21. "Chronology of Events," *Glasnost*, p. 16.
22. Interview with Ashot Dabaghyan, Providence, RI, Mar. 1991.
23. Rost, *Armenian Tragedy*, pp. 59–61.
24. Nadia Diuk and Adrian Karatnycky, *The Hidden Nations*, p. 156.
25. "Chronology of Events," *Glasnost*, p. 17.
26. FBIS–SOV (*Pravda*), 4 Apr. 1988, at 38; FBIS–SOV (*Kommunist*), 26 Apr. 1988, at 49.
27. FBIS–SOV (DPA), 25 Mar. 1988, at 37.

5. Renewal

1. United States Department of State, *Soviet Nationalities Survey*, at XI; *Artsak-hyan Taregrutiun*, p. 184.
2. "First Defendant in Sumgait Riots Sentenced to 15 Years," Reuters, 16 May 1988.
3. Interview with Gurgen Boyajyan, Providence, RI, Dec. 1994.
4. Rost, *Armenian Tragedy*, p. 44; Malkasian, "Report from Armenia," *Armenian Weekly*, 6 Aug. 1988, p. 10; Interview with Ashot Dabaghyan, Providence, RI, Mar. 1991; Interview with Levon H. Abrahamyan, Yerevan, Armenia, June 1992.
5. Malkasian, "A Report from Armenia," p. 10.
6. Rost, *Armenian Tragedy*, p. 45.
7. FBIS–SOV (*Komsomolskaya Pravda*), 25 July 1988, at 46–47; Abrahamyan, "The Karabagh Movement as Viewed by an Anthropologist," p. 69.
8. The members of the Karabagh Organizing Committee in Armenia after the group was reorganized in May 1988 were: Babgen Ararktsyan, born 1944 in Yerevan, chairman and professor of the Department of Applied Mathematics at Yerevan State University; Hambartsum Galstyan, born 1956 in Yerevan, researcher at the Yerevan City Soviet and the Institute of Ethnology of the USSR Academy of Sciences; Samvel Gevorgyan, born 1949 in Yerevan, host of the television program, *Yerevan and Its Inhabitants*; Rafael Ghazaryan, born 1924 in Armavir, Krasnadar region of Russia, professor of physical sciences at the Polytechnic Institute of Yerevan, chairman and professor of the Department of Physics of the Armenian Academy of Sciences; Samson Ghazaryan, born 1953 in Yerevan, teacher of history at School #183 in Yerevan; Alexander Hakobyan, born 1955 in Yerevan, researcher at the Oriental Studies Institute in Caucasology and Byzantinology at the Armenian Academy of Sciences; Ashot Manucharyan, born 1954 in Yerevan, vice-principal of School #183 in Yerevan; Vazgen Manukyan, born 1946 in Yerevan, professor of applied mathematics at Yerevan State University; Vano Sira-deghyan, born 1946 in Shavarshavan, Armenia, editor of *Yeregoyan Yerevan* (Evening Yerevan), *Sovetakan Haiastan* (Soviet Armenia), and *Haiastani Ashkhatavor* (Armenian Worker); Levon Ter Petrosyan, born 1945 in Aleppo, Syria, director of research of the Institute of Ancient Armenian Manuscripts at the Armenian Archival Library; Davit Vardanyan, born 1950 in Yerevan, chairman and professor of the Department of Biology at Yerevan State University.
9. Interview with Ashot Dabaghyan; Interview with Levon H. Abrahamyan.
10. Louise Manoogian Simone, "A Discussion with Vasken Manoukian," p. 11.
11. Malkasian, "A Report from Armenia," 23 July 1988, p. 8.
12. Lyday, "A Commitment to Truth-Telling."
13. Malkasian, "Yerevan School Takes Perestroika to the Limits," p. 9.
14. Interview with Ashot Dabaghyan.
15. Pashtpanutyan Khorhurd (Defense Council), "Teghekagir" (Report).
16. Malkasian, "A Report from Armenia," 23 July 1988, p. 8.

17. Libaridian, *The Question of Karabagh*, pp. 1–2.
18. Ibid., p. 16.
19. Taline Voskeritchian, "Looking in from the Inside," p. 36.
20. L. A. Abramian (Levon H. Abrahamyan), "Chaos and Cosmos," p. 73.
21. Malkasian, "A Report from Armenia," 6 Aug. 1988, p. 10.
22. Ibid., p. 59.
23. Rost, *Armenian Tragedy*, pp. 46–47.
24. Abramian, "Chaos and Cosmos," p. 56.
25. Malkasian, "A Report from Armenia," 6 Aug. 1988, p. 10.
26. FBIS–SOV (*Kommunist*), 17 June 1988, at 34; Malkasian, "A Report from Armenia," 6 Aug. 1988, p. 10.
27. FBIS–SOV (*Izvestia*), 14 July 1988, at 42.
28. Mouradian, "The Mountainous Karabagh Question," p. 11.
29. FBIS–SOV (*Pravda*), 6 June 1988, at 71; FBIS–SOV (*Izvestia*), 14 July 1988, at 42–43.
30. FBIS–SOV (*Izvestia*), 29 July 1988, at 48.
31. Suny, "Nationalism and Democracy in Gorbachev's Soviet Union," p. 486; Malkasian, "A Report from Armenia," 16 July 1988, p. 16; "The Secrets of Soviet Glasnost," *Glasnost*, no. 16–18, p. 65.
32. FBIS–SOV (*Izvestia*), 29 July 1988, at 48.
33. "An Appeal to Scholars, Creative Artists, Journalists," *Glasnost*, no. 16–18, p. 21.
34. Malkasian, "A Report from Armenia," 23 July 1988, p. 9.
35. Lyday, "A Commitment to Truth-Telling."
36. Kaputikyan, "An Open Letter," p. 28.
37. Malkasian, "A Report from Armenia," 23 July 1988, p. 9.
38. Ibid., p. 9. Tumanyan (1869–1923) based most of his writings on popular Armenian folk tales and fables. He was also deeply involved in humanitarian and political activities on behalf of Armenia. Sevak (1924–1972) was one of Soviet Armenia's leading poets and literary scholars, as well as a strong critic of Moscow's cultural policies. His death in an automobile accident raised suspicions of government involvement.
39. *Artsakhyan Taregrutiun*, p. 191.
40. *Los Angeles Times*, 20 June 1988, p. 1.
41. Malkasian, "A Report from Armenia," 6 Aug. 1988, p. 11.
42. Ibid.
43. Ibid.
44. Galoyan and Khudazerdyan, eds., *Nagornyi Karabakh*, pp. 92–93.
45. Malkasian, "A Report from Armenia," 6 Aug. 1988, p. 11.
46. Chandler and Furtado, eds., *Perestroika in the Soviet Republics*, p. 408.
47. *Los Angeles Times*, 21 June 1988, p. 6.
48. FBIS–SOV (AFP), 24 June 1988, at 26.
49. *Artsakhyan Taregrutiun*, p. 197; U.S. Department of State, *Soviet Nationalities Survey*, at XIII; FBIS–SOV (*Trud*), 29 June 1988, at 32.

6. Collision

1. "Gorbachev Denounces Appeals to Redraw Armenian Borders," Reuters, 28 June 1988.
2. Nahaylo and Swoboda, *Soviet Disunion*, pp. 305–308.
3. Ibid., p. 305.
4. *Artsakhyan Taregrutiun*, p. 198.
5. Malkasian, "A Report from Armenia," *Armenian Weekly*, 23 July 1988, p. 8.
6. Rost, *Armenian Tragedy*, pp. 53.
7. Ibid., p. 54.
8. Ibid.
9. Matthew Der Manuelian, "Chronology of July Events in Yerevan," 27 Aug. 1988, p. 10.
10. Ibid.
11. Ibid.; Rost, *Armenian Tragedy*, p. 55.
12. Ibid., p. 57; Der Manuelian, "Chronology of July Events in Yerevan," 27 Aug. 1988, p. 10.
13. *New York Times*, 11 July 1988, p. 2.
14. FBIS–SOV (*Pravda*), 7 July 1988, at 55; FBIS–SOV (*Izvestia*), 7 July, at 55.
15. FBIS–SOV (*Vremya*), 8 July 1988, at 54.
16. FBIS–SOV (Moscow Television Service), 18 July 1988, at 49.
17. Rost, *Armenian Tragedy*, pp. 55–56.
18. Der Manuelian, "Chronology of July Events in Yerevan," 27 Aug. 1988, p. 10.
19. Ibid.
20. Ibid., p. 11.
21. Rost, *Armenian Tragedy*, p. 55.
22. Der Manuelian, "Chronology of July Events in Yerevan," 27 Aug. 1988, p. 10.
23. Der Manuelian, "Chronology of July Events in Yerevan," 3 Sept. 1988, p. 11.
24. Ibid.
25. Der Manuelian, "Chronology of July Events in Yerevan," 27 Aug. 1988, p. 11; FBIS–SOV (*Izvestia*), 11 July 1988, at 62.
26. FBIS–SOV (Armenpress), 15 July 1988, at 59.
27. FBIS–SOV (Yerevan International Service), 13 July 1988, at 57.
28. Der Manuelian, "Chronology of July Events in Yerevan," 27 Aug. 1988, p. 10.
29. Edmund M. Herzig, "Armenians," p. 159.
30. FBIS–SOV (*Argumenty i fakty*), 15 July 1988, at 54.
31. United States Department of State, *Soviet Nationalities Survey*, at XIV.
32. FBIS–SOV (AFP), 18 July 1988, at 54; FBIS–SOV (AFP), 18 July 1988, at 60.
33. FBIS–SOV (*Komsomolskaya Pravda*), 21 July, 1988, at 54; FBIS–SOV (*Izvestia*), 22 July 1988, at 38.
34. FBIS–SOV (*Izvestia*), 22 July 1988, at 37–38; FBIS–SOV (TASS), 21 July 1988, at 57.
35. The article that appeared in *Izvestia* on 22 July 1988 attributed distribution of the leaflets to "Provocateurs who might have nothing to do with the 'Karabakh' Committee organizationally."

36. Suny, *Looking toward Ararat*, p. 188; Nahaylo and Swoboda, *Soviet Disunion*, p. 38.
37. Teresa Rakowska–Harmstone, "Nationalities and the Soviet Military," p. 87.
38. *Asbarez*, 1 Oct. 1988, p. 17.
39. Suny, *Looking toward Ararat*, p. 153.
40. Gertrude E. Schroeder, "Nationalities and the Soviet Economy," pp. 45-48, and Suny, "Transcaucasia," p. 238.
41. Malkasian, "A Report from Armenia," 30 July 1988, p. 10.
42. Suny, "Transcaucasia," p. 238.
43. Libaridian, ed., *Armenia at the Crossroads*, p. 26.
44. Nahaylo and Swoboda, *Soviet Disunion*, p. 189. Demirchyan's words echoed those of an Armenian member of the Kadet Party, Kristofor Vermishev, in 1917: "The attacks upon the so-called Russian imperialism are completely incomprehensible," Vermishev said. "In the Caucasus that imperialism has created law and order and the secure life which the Armenians did not have before. . . . And when I see that the Russians are afraid of that word and everybody renounces it, I as an Armenian grow sick at heart at the rejection of Russia's past." Kazemzadeh, *The Struggle for Transcaucasia*, p. 44.
45. Suny, *Looking toward Ararat*, p. 184.
46. Nahaylo and Swoboda, *Soviet Disunion*, p. 188; Diuk and Karatnycky, *The Hidden Nations*, p. 75.
47. Suny, "The Soviet South," p. 70.
48. Libaridian, ed., *Armenia at the Crossroads*, p. 26.
49. The total number of deputies in the Mountainous Karabagh oblast soviet was 150. Of the 102 deputies who attended the 12 July 1988 session, 101 voted in favor of secession while one abstained.
50. "Arms Seizure Reported in Disputed Soviet Region," Reuters, 13 July 1988; FBIS–SOV (TASS), 13 July 1988, at 55.
51. FBIS–SOV (TASS), 19 July 1988, at 59.
52. FBIS–SOV (*Pravda*), 20 July 1988, at 52–53.
53. *New York Times*, 20 July 1988, p. 1.
54. FBIS–SOV (*Pravda*), 20 July 1988, at 53.
55. Ibid., at 46–47.
56. Lyday, "A Commitment to Truth-Telling."
57. FBIS–SOV (*Pravda*), 20 July 1988, at 54.
58. Ibid., at 55. In 1994, Petrosyan was murdered in Yerevan.
59. Ibid., at 42–58.
60. FBIS–SOV (Moscow Television Service), 20 July 1988, at 40.
61. Der Manuelian, "Chronology of July Events in Yerevan," 3 Sept. 1991, p. 11; U.S. Department of State, *Soviet Nationalities Survey*, at XVI.
62. Der Manuelian, "Chronology of July Events in Yerevan," 3 Sept. 1988, p. 11.
63. FBIS–SOV (AFP), 20 July 1988, at 60; *New York Times*, 20 July 1988, p. 1.
64. FBIS–SOV (AFP), 19 July 1988, at 67; "Nagorno-Karabakh Ends Strike, Armenian Rallies Attacked," Reuters, 25 July 1988; U.S. Department of State, *Soviet Nationalities Survey*, at XVII; *Artsakhyan Taregrutiun*, p. 208.

65. "Soviet Decree Gives Interior Ministry Troops Broad Powers," Reuters, 26 Aug. 1988; Nahaylo and Swoboda, *Soviet Disunion*, p. 311.
66. FBIS–SOV (AFP), 21 July 1988, at 59; FBIS–SOV (Budapest Domestic Service), 2 Aug. 1988, at 49; FBIS–SOV (TASS), 2 Aug. 1988, at 50.
67. FBIS–SOV (Armenpress), 25 July 1988, at 34–36.
68. Der Manuelian, "Chronology of July Events in Yerevan," 3 Sept. 1988, p. 11.
69. Libaridian, *The Question of Karabagh: An Overview*, p. 2.
70. *Wall Street Journal*, 23 Sept. 1988, p. 1.
71. Andrei Sakharov, "An Open Letter to Mikhail Gorbachev."
72. Suny, "Nationalist and Ethnic Unrest in the Soviet Union," pp. 513–514.
73. Senn, *Lithuania Awakening*, p. 23.
74. Steven L. Burg, "Nationality Elites and Political Change in the Soviet Union," p. 31.
75. *New York Times*, 3 Oct. 1988, p. 1.
76. *Asbarez*, 17 Sept. 1988, p. 25; Der Manuelian, "Chronology of July Events in Yerevan," 3 Sept. 1988, p. 11.
77. FBIS–SOV (Armenpress), 23 Aug. 1988, at 42; "Soviet Official to Advise Parliament on Troubled Region," Reuters, 6 Oct. 1988.
78. Following the collapse of the Soviet Union, Volsky emerged as head of the Russian Union of Industrialists and Entrepreneurs. The union, representing mostly old-guard managers of state enterprises, sought to block the free-market reforms of the Yeltsin government and maintain subsidies for state industries.
79. *The Current Digest of the Soviet Press*, 18 Jan. 1989, p. 16.
80. *Armenian Update*, Jan. 1989, p. 4.
81. *Asbarez*, 10 Dec. 1988, p. 25; FBIS–SOV (*Moscow News*), 24 Aug. 1988, at 34.
82. *Asbarez*, 3 Dec. 1988, p. 29; *Asbarez*, 10 Dec. 1988, p. 25; Rost, *Armenian Tragedy*, p. 67.

7. Respite

1. Der Manuelian, "Chronology of July Events in Yerevan," 3 Sept. 1988, p. 11.
2. Pashtpanutyan Khorhurd, "Teghekagir."
3. Ibid.
4. FBIS–SOV (*Daily Telegraph*), 21 Sept. 1988, at 50.
5. Pashtpanutyan Khorhurd, "Teghekagir."
6. *Asbarez*, 17 Sept. 1988, p. 26.
7. *New York Times*, 5 Sept. 1988, p. 1.
8. Khojabekyan, *Artsakhe Portsutyan Zhamin*, p. 92; Libaridian, ed., *The Karabagh File*, p. 104. The Yezidi religion combines elements from Islam, Judaism, Christianity, and other ancient faiths.
9. Nahaylo and Swoboda, *Soviet Disunion*, pp. 79–80.
10. *Asbarez*, 17 Sept. 1988, p. 25.
11. *Los Angeles Times*, 11 July 1988, p. 4; Senn, *Lithuania Awakening*, pp. 90 and 120.

12. Nahaylo and Swoboda, *Soviet Disunion*, p. 297; Misiunas, "The Baltic Republics," pp. 209–210.
13. *Asbarez*, 8 Oct. 1988, p. 17; "Popular Front Created in Armenia to Help Ease Ethnic Crisis," Reuters, 29 Sept. 1988.
14. *Asbarez*, 26 Dec. 1987, p. 53.
15. Ketchian, "Air Pollution in Yerevan," 1 Aug. 1992, pp. 6–7.
16. Ibid.; Ketchian, "Air Pollution in Yerevan," 8 Aug. 1992, p. 7.
17. Ketchian, "Nayirit," p. 8.
18. Ketchian, "Air Pollution in Yerevan," 8 Aug. 1992, p. 6.
19. Ketchian, "Nayirit," pp. 8–10.
20. As a result of the Sevan–Hrazdan hydroelectric project, Lake Sevan's water level dropped eighteen meters. Completion of a thirty-mile canal to channel water from the Arpa River to Lake Sevan raised the lake's water level in the 1980s. *Asbarez*, 18 Jan. 1992, p. 16.
21. *Asbarez*, 26 Dec. 1987, p. 53; *Asbarez*, 26 Dec. 1987, p. 49.
22. *Asbarez*, 27 Feb. 1988, p. 18.
23. Komitas (1869–1935) studied music in Europe after being ordained a celibate priest in the Armenian Apostolic Church. Traveling from village to village, he conducted research on folk songs throughout the Middle East. Komitas was driven mad by the atrocities he witnessed during the 1915 genocide. Although he escaped death, Komitas spent the remainder of his life in mental institutions.
24. Alexeyeva, *Soviet Dissent*, pp. 124–25; Paruir Airikyan (Hairikyan), "Solving Nationality Problems," p. 8.
25. Alexeyeva, *Soviet Dissent*, pp. 125–26.
26. Ibid., pp. 127–29.
27. Ibid., pp. 131–32.
28. Mouradian, "The Mountainous Karabagh Question," p. 15.
29. Nahaylo and Swoboda, *Soviet Disunion*, p. 280; *Asbarez*, 10 Sept. 1988, p. 17.
30. Libaridian, *The Question of Karabagh*, p. 9.
31. "U.S. Denounces Soviet Expulsion of Armenian Dissident," Reuters, 21 July 1988.
32. Rafael Ghazaryan was born in Armavir in the North Caucasus.
33. *Asbarez*, 8 Oct. 1988, p. 17.

8. Khojalu

1. Ludmilla Alexeyeva, "Unrest in the Soviet Union," p. 71.
2. FBIS–SOV (Madrid *Diario*), 29 Sept. 1988, at 53.
3. *Artsakhyan Taregrutiun*, p. 213; Olcott, ed., *The Soviet Multinational State*, p. 593.
4. *New York Times*, 16 Sept. 1988, p. 8.
5. *Artsakhyan Taregrutiun*, p. 214; *New York Times*, 20 Sept. 1988, p. 3.
6. Rost, *Armenian Tragedy*, p. 63.
7. FBIS–SOV (Armenpress), 3 Oct. 1988, at 56.

8. FBIS–SOV (*Argumenty i fakty*), 3 Oct. 1988, at 59.
9. L. A. Abramian (Levon Abrahamyan), "Archaic Ritual and Theater," p. 58.
10. "All-Night Protest in Armenian Capital, Troops Seal Off Center," Reuters, 23 Sept. 1988; FBIS–SOV (AFP), 22 Sept. 1988, at 39; FBIS–SOV (*Pravda*), 26 Sept. 1988, at 58.
11. FBIS–SOV (AFP), 20 Sept. 1988, at 41; FBIS–SOV (*Daily Telegraph*), 22 Sept. 1988, at 40.
12. FBIS–SOV (*Daily Telegraph*), 23 Sept. 1988, at 46.
13. FBIS–SOV (AFP), 26 Sept. 1988, at 63; FBIS–SOV (Armenpress), 30 Sept. 1988, at 34–35.
14. *Chicago Tribune*, 27 Sept. 1988, p. 5.
15. Interview with Levon Abrahamyan.
16. *The Washington Post*, 12 Sept. 1988, p. 13.
17. *The Daily Telegraph*, 28 Sept. 1988, International Section.
18. FBIS–SOV (*Izvestia*), 23 Sept. 1988, at 42.
19. FBIS–SOV (*Selskaya Zhizn*), 7 Oct. 1988, at 35–37; FBIS–SOV (Moscow Domestic Service), 18 Oct. 1988, at 52.
20. "Students Occupy Teacher-Training College in Nagorno-Karabakh," Reuters, 20 Oct. 1988.
21. FBIS–SOV (*Kommunist*), 17 Nov. 1988, at 47–48.
22. FBIS–SOV (Armenpress), 1 Nov. 1988, at 64–66.
23. FBIS–SOV (TASS), 1 Nov. 1988, at 67; FBIS–SOV (*Kommunist*), Dec. 6, 1988, at 40.
24. FBIS–SOV (*Kommunist*), 17 Nov. 1988, at 49.
25. British Broadcasting Corporation (*Sovetakan Hayastan*), 4 Nov. 1988.
26. Nahaylo and Swoboda, *Soviet Disunion*, p. 97.
27. Khojabekyan, *Artsakhe Portsutyan Zhamin*, pp. 81 and 92; Berberian, "Regional Rivals," pp. 28–29.
28. Khojabekyan, *Artsakhe Portsutyan Zhamin*, p. 249; Mark Saroyan, "The 'Karabakh Syndrome,' " pp. 15–16.
29. Cullen, "Roots," p. 68.
30. Tadeusz Swietochowski, *Russian Azerbaijan, 1905–1920*, p. 191; Suny, "The Problematic Neighbor," p. 32.
31. Astourian, "On the Rise of Azerbaijani National Identity," p. 37.
32. Altstadt, *The Azerbaijani Turks*, pp. 21–22.
33. Suny, *The Baku Commune 1917–1918*, pp. 4–5; Altstadt, *The Azerbaijani Turks*, p. 21.
34. Villari, *Fire and Sword in the Caucasus*, p. 189.
35. Altstadt, *The Azerbaijani Turks*, pp. 23–24.
36. Ibid., pp. 31–32.
37. Swietochowski, "Azerbaijan," p. 36.
38. Edmund M. Herzig, "Armenians," p. 164.
39. Altstadt, *The Azerbaijani Turks*, p. 67.
40. Swietochowski, "Azerbaijan," p. 37.
41. Swietochowski, *Russian Azerbaijan, 1905–1920*, p. 33.
42. Ibid., p. 59 and pp. 70–71.

43. Walker, ed., *Armenia and Karabagh*, pp. 87–88; Astourian, "On the Rise of Azerbaijani National Identity," p. 36; Swietochowski, "Azerbaijan," pp. 37–38.

44. Herzig, "Armenians," p. 166.

45. Swietochowski, "Azerbaijan," pp. 39–40; Mouradian, "The Mountainous Karabagh Question," pp. 20–21.

46. Galoyan and Khudazerdyan, eds., *Nagornyi Karabakh*, pp. 17–22.

47. Mouradian, "The Mountainous Karabagh Question," p. 10; Dudwick, "The Case of the Caucasian Albanians," p. 377.

48. Robert H. Hewsen, "Ethno-History," pp. 27–28; Dudwick, "The Case of the Caucasian Albanians," pp. 379–381; Tamara Dragadze, "The Armenian–Azerbaijani Conflict," p. 68.

49. Hewsen, "Ethno-History," pp. 29–30; Dudwick, "The Case of the Caucasian Albanians," pp. 378–379.

50. Altstadt, *The Azerbaijani Turks*, p. 165.

51. Ibid., p. 122.

52. Ibid., p. 123.

53. Ibid., pp. 117–118.

54. Saroyan, "The 'Karabagh Syndrome' and Azerbaijani Politics," p. 16.

55. Altstadt, *The Azerbaijani Turks*, p. 124.

56. Ibid., p. 168.

57. Serge Afanasyan, "The Demographic Evolution in Azerbaijan SSR, 1959–1979," p. 18.

58. Swietochowski, "Azerbaijan," p. 42.

59. Diuk and Karatnycky, *The Hidden Nations,* p. 164. The first opera in the Muslim world was authored by two Azerbaijani brothers from Shushi. Altstadt, *The Azerbaijani Turks*, p. 54.

60. Saroyan, "The 'Karabagh Syndrome' and Azerbaijani Politics," p. 18.

61. Altstadt, *The Azerbaijani Turks*, pp. 195–196.

62. Suny, *Looking toward Ararat*, p. 199.

63. Ibid., p. 199.

64. FBIS–SOV (Baku Domestic Service), 1 Dec. 1988, at 59–60.

65. "The Answer from Baku," *Glasnost*, no. 16–18, p. 29; Swietochowski, "Azerbaijan," pp. 43–44; Mouradian, "The Mountainous Karabagh Question," pp. 27–28.

66. FBIS–SOV (Baku Domestic Service), 20 May 1988, at 25; FBIS–SOV (AFP), 20 May 1988, at 26; FBIS–SOV (Baku Domestic Service), 15 June 1988, at 39.

67. Helsinki Watch Report, *USSR: Human Rights under Glasnost*, pp. 19–20; Swietochowski, "Azerbaijan," pp. 44–45.

9. Campaign

1. *New York Times*, 12 Oct. 1988, p. 3; FBIS–SOV (*Daily Telegraph*), 13 Oct. 1988, at 47; FBIS–SOV (*Izvestia*), 12 Oct. 1988, at 56.

2. FBIS–SOV (Yerevan Domestic Service), 23 Nov. 1988, at 42.

3. Rost, *Armenian Tragedy*, p. 66.

4. Interview with Ashot Dabaghyan.
5. Pashdpanutyan Khorhurd, "Khachik Vardanovich Stamboltsyan."
6. Hedrick Smith, *The New Russians*, p. 331.
7. FBIS–SOV (Madrid *Diario*), 14 Feb. 1989, at 55; Rafael Ghazaryan, "Open Letter to General Secretary Mikhail Gorbachev."
8. FBIS–SOV (Madrid *Diario*), 14 Feb. 1989, at 56.
9. Ashot Manucharyan, "Inchpes Yeghav" (How It Happened).
10. Suny, "Transcaucasia," pp. 230–231.
11. Ibid., p. 249.
12. Simone, "A Discussion with Vasken Manoukian," p. 10.
13. Pohlmann, "Socialism in Armenia," p. 65; Smith, *The New Russians*, p. 330.
14. FBIS–SOV (*Pravda*), 20 Sept. 1988, at 42; FBIS–SOV (*Izvestia*), 29 July 1988, at 47.
15. "The Secrets of Soviet Glasnost," p. 65.
16. Manucharyan, "Inchpes Yeghav."
17. *Asbarez*, 25 June 1988, p. 21.

10. Explosion

1. Rost, *Armenian Tragedy*, pp. 75–76.
2. FBIS–SOV (Baku Domestic Service), 1 Dec. 1988, at 63.
3. FBIS–SOV (Baku Domestic Service), 21 Nov. 1988, at 59; Rost, *Armenian Tragedy*, p. 78.
4. *The New York Times*, 16 Sept. 1988, p. 8.
5. Suny, "Nationalism and Democracy in Gorbachev's Soviet Union," p. 499; FBIS–SOV (*Pravda*), 1 Dec. 1988, at 50; Altstadt, *The Azerbaijani Turks*, p. 201; Suny, *Looking toward Ararat*, p. 207.
6. "Moscow Says 28 Dead in Latest Transcaucasian Unrest," Reuters, 1 Dec. 1988.
7. FBIS–SOV (Hamburg DPA), 25 Nov. 1988, at 39.
8. British Broadcasting Corporation (report from *Izvestia*, 28 Nov. 1988), 5 Dec. 1988.
9. Suny, *Looking toward Ararat*, p. 208.
10. FBIS–SOV (TASS), 28 Nov. 1988, at 63; Rost, *Armenian Tragedy*, pp. 82–83; "Soldiers Put Down Azerbaijani Attempts to Massacre Armenians," Reuters, 26 Nov. 1988.
11. FBIS–SOV (TASS), 28 Nov. 1988, at 65; "Soldiers Put Down Azerbaijani Attempts to Massacre Armenians," Reuters, 26 Nov. 1988; "Two Killed as Violence Spreads to Armenia," Reuters, 25 Nov. 1988; *Los Angeles Times*, 27 Nov. 1988, p. 1; Rost, *Armenian Tragedy*, p. 81.
12. Rost, *Armenian Tragedy*, p. 79; "Armenians Appeal on Nagorno–Karabakh ahead of Parliament," Reuters, 19 Nov. 1988.
13. Rost, *Armenian Tragedy*, pp. 76–77.
14. *Time*, 28 Nov. 1988, p. 48.
15. FBIS–SOV (AFP), 21 Nov. 1988, at 58; "Armenian Parliament Suspended After Reports of Ethnic Clashes," Reuters, 22 Nov. 1988.

16. Rost, *Armenian Tragedy*, pp. 80–81.
17. Rost, *Armenian Tragedy*, p. 83; *Asbarez*, 3 Dec. 1988, p. 17.
18. FBIS–SOV (*Kommunist*), 8 Dec. 1988, at 66; Rost, *Armenian Tragedy*, p. 84; Interview with Ashot Dabaghyan.
19. "Dusk-to-Dawn Curfew Takes Force amid Tension in Azerbaijan," Reuters, 24 Nov. 1988; FBIS–SOV (AFP), 25 Nov. 1988, at 41; FBIS–SOV (Yerevan Domestic Service), 25 Nov. 1988, at 38.
20. Nahaylo and Swoboda, *Soviet Disunion*, p. 316.
21. "Transcaucasian Ethnic Row Spills Over into Soviet Parliament," Reuters, 30 Nov. 1988.
22. *Financial Times*, 29 Sept. 1988, p. 2.
23. *Los Angeles Times*, 2 Dec. 1988, p. 1; FBIS–SOV (*Izvestia*), 5 Dec. 1988, at 87.
24. *The Current Digest of the Soviet Press*, 4 Jan. 1989, p. 13.
25. Walker, ed., *Armenia and Karabagh*, p. 119; FBIS–SOV (TASS), 1 Dec. 1988, at 45; FBIS–SOV (Moscow Domestic Service), 2 Dec. 1988, at 58.
26. Arutiunyan, *Sobytiya b Nagornom Karabakhe*, p. 150.
27. FBIS–SOV (Moscow Domestic Service), 6 Dec. 1988, at 44; Rost, *Armenian Tragedy*, pp. 84–88; Altstadt, *The Azerbaijani Turks,* p. 202; FBIS–SOV (Moscow Television Service), 1 Dec. 1988, at 64.
28. FBIS–SOV (Yerevan Domestic Service), 1 Dec. 1988, at 65; FBIS–SOV (*Pravda*), 1 Dec. 1988, at 50.
29. "Mass Firing of Workers Reported in Armenia, Azerbaijan," Reuters, 5 Dec. 1988.
30. From November 1988 to April 1989, 180,000 Armenians left Azerbaijan. Another 30,000 departed in July and August of 1989. Khojabekyan, *Artsakhe Portsutyan Zhamin*, p. 96.
31. Ibid., p. 249; Galoyan and Khudazerdyan, eds., *Nagornyi Karabakh*, p. 58; *New York Times*, 12 Sept. 1988, p. 3.
32. *New York Times*, 12 Sept. 1988, p. 3.
33. *Washington Post*, 12 Sept. 1988, p. 13.
34. *New York Times*, 11 Sept. 1988, p. 3.
35. Suny, "Nationalism and Democracy in Gorbachev's Soviet Union," pp. 489, 499.
36. Samuelian, "Cultural Ecology and Gorbachev's Restructured Union," p. 200.
37. Walker, ed., *Armenia and Karabagh*, p. 11.
38. Diuk and Karatnycky, *The Hidden Nations*, p. 267.
39. "Sharp Increase in Armenians Seeking Refuge in U.S. —Newspaper," Reuters, 6 Mar. 1988.
40. *Armenian Mirror–Spectator,* 25 Jan. 1992, p. 9.
41. Suny, "Transcaucasia," p. 236; Diuk and Karatnycky, *The Hidden Nations*, p. 265.
42. Serge Afanasyan, "The Demographic Evolution in Azerbaijan SSR, 1959–1979," *Asbarez*, 13 Aug. 1988, p. 18.
43. Galoyan and Khudazerdyan, eds., *Nagornyi Karabakh*, p. 45.
44. Ibid., pp. 46–47; Walker, ed., *Armenia and Karabagh*, p. 115.
45. Galoyan and Khudazerdyan, eds., *Nagornyi Karabakh*, p. 55.

11. Earthquake

1. *International Bulletin for the Reconstruction & Development of Armenia* (Dec. 1989), pp. 1–3.
2. Ibid., pp. 3–5; Tony Halpin, "Disaster and Recovery," p. 8.
3. Rost, *Armenian Tragedy*, p. 151.
4. Halpin, "Disaster and Recovery," p. 14.
5. *Armenian Update*, Feb. 1989, p. 1.
6. Rost, *Armenian Tragedy*, pp. 105–106.
7. Halpin, "Disaster and Recovery," p. 10.
8. "Gorbachev—Television Interview in Armenia," Press release issued by the Soviet Embassy, Information Department, 12 Dec. 1988; *The Current Digest of the Soviet Press*, 11 Jan. 1989, p. 5.
9. *Armenian Update*, Jan. 1989, p. 3.
10. Rost, *Armenian Tragedy*, p. 165; Manucharyan, "Inchpes Yeghav."
11. Ibid.; Rost, *Armenian Tragedy*, pp. 97–98.
12. Manucharyan, "Inchpes Yeghav."
13. *Los Angeles Times*, 4 Dec. 1988, p. 3.
14. Rost, *Armenian Tragedy*, p. 165.
15. Manucharyan, "Inchpes Yeghav."
16. *The Current Digest of the Soviet Press*, 18 Jan. 1988, p. 7.
17. *The Current Digest of the Soviet Press*, 25 Jan. 1989, p. 12.

Epilogue

1. Interview with Galina Starovoitova, Providence, RI, 2 Feb. 1995.
2. Suny, *Looking toward Ararat*, p. 244.
3. The newer of Medzamor's two reactors was reactivated in 1995 to ease independent Armenia's chronic energy shortage.
4. Chandler and Furtado, eds., *Perestroika in the Soviet Republics*, p. 622; *Armenian Update*, Sept. 1989, p. 1.
5. *Armenian Update*, July 1989, p. 2.
6. Ibid., Jan. 1990, p. 3.
7. The election of Manucharov, who was still in prison at the time of the balloting, was invalidated by the Armenian Supreme Soviet.
8. *Armenian Update*, Mar. 1990, p. 7.
9. *Haik*, 9 Aug. 1990, p. 3.
10. In October 1991, Ter Petrosyan received 82 percent of the vote in winning Armenia's first popular election for president in the post-Soviet era.

Conclusion

1. "Survey of Most Influential People in Armenia," Armenian Information Service Daily News Summary—AGBU, 16 Aug. 1994. Individuals were ranked on a scale of one to ten according to their level of influence, either positive

or negative, on Armenia's current policies. Panelists determined that the five most influential Armenians were: 1. President Levon Ter Petrosyan (8.31); 2. former presidential adviser on national security Ashot Manucharyan (8.20); 3. Interior Minister Vano Siradeghyan (8.12); 4. Parliament Chairman Babgen Ararktsyan (7.43); 5. former prime minister and defense minister Vazgen Manukyan (6.89).

2. "NDU Meeting in Yerevan," *Aragil Electronic News Bulletin*, 4 July 1994.

3. "Ex-Yerevan Mayor Warns about Government Corruption, Violation of Human Rights," Armenian Information Service—AGBU, 30 June 1994.

4. "Detailed Account of President Levon Ter-Petrossian's and State Minister Vazgen Sarkissian's Speeches at the Meeting of Law Enforcement Bodies," *Noyan Tapan*, 9 Aug. 1994.

Works Cited

Levon H. Abrahamyan, "The Karabagh Movement as Viewed by an Anthropologist," *Armenian Review* 43: 2–3 (Summer/Autumn 1990).

L. A. Abramian (Levon H. Abrahamyan), "Archaic Ritual and Theater: From the Ceremonial Glade to Theater Square," *Soviet Anthropology and Archeology* 29: 2 (Fall 1990).

_____. "Chaos and Cosmos in the Structure of Mass Popular Movements," *Soviet Anthropology & Archeology* 29: 2 (Fall 1990).

Serge Afanasyan, "The Demographic Evolution in Azerbaijan SSR, 1959–1979," *Asbarez*, 13 August 1988.

Paruir Airikyan (Hairikyan), "Solving Nationality Problems: Some Words of Democratic Wisdom," *Glasnost*, no. 16–18.

Ludmilla Alexeyeva, *Soviet Dissent: Contemporary Movements for National, Religious, and Human Rights* (Middletown, CT: Wesleyan University Press, 1985).

_____. "Unrest in the Soviet Union," *The Washington Quarterly* (Winter 1990).

Audrey L. Altstadt, *The Azerbaijani Turks: Power and Identity under Russian Rule* (Stanford: Hoover Institution Press, 1992).

Artsakhyan Taregrutiun (Artsakh Annals) (Los Angeles: Asbarez, 1988).

V. B. Arutiunyan, *Sobytiya b Nagornom Karabakhe* (Events in Mountainous Karabagh) (Yerevan: Armenian Academy of Sciences, Institute of History, 1990).

Stepan H. Astourian, "On the Rise of Azerbaijani National Identity and Armeno–Azerbaijani Relations," *Armenian Review* 40: 3 (Fall 1987).

Viken Berberian, "Regional Rivals," *AIM* (April 1992).

George A. Bournoutian, *Eastern Armenia in the Last Decades of Persian Rule: 1807–1828* (Malibu, CA: Undena Publications, 1982).

_____. "Karabagh in Political Perspective," *Asbarez*, 18 February 1989.

_____. *A History of the Armenian People, Volume II: 1500 A.D. to the Present* (Costa Mesa, CA: Mazda Publishers, 1994).

Steven L. Burg, "Nationality Elites and Political Change in the Soviet Union," in *The Nationalities Factor in Soviet Politics and Society*, eds. Lubomyr Hajda and Mark Beissinger (Boulder, CO: Westview Press, 1990).

Andrea Chandler and Charles F. Furtado, Jr., eds. *Perestroika in the Soviet Repub-*

lics: Documents on the National Question (Boulder, CO: Westview Press, 1992).

Levon Chorbajian, *Karabakh and the U.S. Press: A Study in Mythmaking* (Cambridge: Zoryan Institute, 1988).

Robert Cullen, "Roots," *New Yorker*, 15 April 1991

Matthew Der Manuelian, "Chronology of July Events in Yerevan," *Armenian Weekly*, 27 August and 3 September 1988.

Nadia Diuk and Adrian Karatnycky, *The Hidden Nations: The People Challenge the Soviet Union* (New York: William Morrow and Company, 1990).

Tamara Dragadze, "The Armenian–Azerbaijani Conflict: Structure and Sentiment," *Third World Quarterly* 11: 1 (January 1989).

Nora Dudwick, "The Karabagh Movement: An Old Scenario Gets Rewritten," *Armenian Review* 42: 3 (Autumn 1989).

_____. "The Case of the Caucasian Albanians: Ethnohistory and Ethnic Politics," *Cahiers du Monde russe et sovietique* (April–September 1990).

G. A. Galoyan and K. S. Khudazerdyan, eds., *Nagornyi Karabakh: Istoricheskaia Spravka* (Mountainous Karabakh: Historical Note) (Yerevan: The Academy of Sciences of the Armenian SSR).

Haroutiun Gayayan, "The Disappearance of Rugs from Armenian Artzakh–Karabagh: A Cultural Robbery," *Armenian Review* 41: 2 (Summer 1988).

Rafael Ghazaryan, "Open Letter to General Secretary Mikhail Gorbachev" (Yerevan, 17 December 1988). (Photocopied.)

Tony Halpin, "Disaster and Recovery," *AIM* (January 1991).

Helsinki Watch Report, *USSR: Human Rights under Glasnost, December 1988–March 1989* (New York: Helsinki Watch, 1989).

Edmund M. Herzig, "Armenians," in *The Nationalities Question in the Soviet Union*, ed. Graham Smith (London: Longman, 1990).

Robert H. Hewsen, "Ethno-History and the Armenian Influence upon the Caucasian Albanians," in *Classical Armenian Culture: Influences and Creativity*, ed. Thomas J. Samuelian (Philadelphia: Scholars Press, 1982)

Richard G. Hovannisian, *Armenia on the Road to Independence, 1918* (Berkeley: University of California Press, 1967).

_____. "The Armeno–Azerbaijani Conflict over Mountainous Karabagh, 1918–1919," *Armenian Review* 24:2 (Summer 1971).

_____. "Nationalist Ferment in Armenia," *Freedom at Issue* (November–December 1988).

Silva Kaputikyan, "An Open Letter," *Asbarez*, 11 June 1988.

Firuz Kazemzadeh, *The Struggle for Transcaucasia* (New York: Philosophical Library, 1951).

Philip P. Ketchian, "Nayirit: Politics, History, Environmental Impact," *Asbarez*, 10 and 17 August 1991.

_____. "Air Pollution in Yerevan: Causes and Effects," *Armenian Mirror–Spectator*, 1 August 1992; 8 August 1992.

Vladimir Y. Khojabekyan, *Artsakhe Portsutyan Zhamin* (Artsakh in the Time of Trial) (Yerevan: Haiastan, 1991).

Gerard J. Libaridian, ed., *The Karabagh File* (Cambridge: Zoryan Institute, 1988).

_____. *The Question of Karabagh: An Overview* (Cambridge: Zoryan Institute, 1988).

_____. *Armenia at the Crossroads: Democracy and Nationhood in the Post-Soviet Era* (Watertown, MA: Blue Crane Books, 1991)

Corbin Lyday, "A Commitment to Truth-Telling: Behind the Scenes in Soviet Armenia," 1988. (Typewritten.)

Mark Malkasian, "A Report from Armenia," *Armenian Weekly*, 16, 23, 30 July, and 6 August 1988.

_____. "Yerevan School Takes Perestroika to the Limits," *Armenian Mirror–Spectator*, 24 September 1988.

Ashot Manucharyan, "Inchpes Yeghav" (How It Happened) (Yerevan, December 1988). (Photocopied.)

B. S. Mirzoian, "Nagornyi Karabakh: Statistical Considerations," *Soviet Anthropology and Archeology* 29: 2 (Fall 1990).

Romuald J. Misiunas, "The Baltic Republics: Stagnation and Strivings for Sovereignty," in *The Nationalities Factor in Soviet Politics and Society*, eds. Lubomyr Hajda and Mark Beissinger (Boulder, CO: Westview Press, 1990).

Shahen Mkrtchian, "Witnesses to History," *AIM* (June 1992).

Claire Mouradian, "The Mountainous Karabagh Question: An Inter-Ethnic Conflict or Decolonization Crisis?" *Armenian Review* 43: 2–3 (Summer/Autumn 1990).

Mouradian, "The Mountainous Karabagh Question: An Interethnic Conflict or Decolonization Crisis?" *Armenian Review* 32: 1 (Winter 1991),

Igor Muradyan, "Glasnost and Nagorno–Karabakh: The Public Speaks," *Glasnost* no. 16–18.

Bohdan Nahaylo and Victor Swoboda, *Soviet Disunion: A History of Nationalities Problems in the USSR* (New York: The Free Press, 1990).

Martha B. Olcott, ed., *The Soviet Multinational State: Readings and Documents* (Armonk, NY: M. E. Sharpe, 1990)

Pashdpanutyan Khorhurd (Defense Council), "Khachik Vardanovich Stamboltsyan: Biograficheskie Svedeniya" (Biographical Information) (Yerevan, 1989).

Marcus D. Pohlmann, "Socialism in Armenia," *Asbarez*, 26 December 1987.

Teresa Rakowska–Harmstone, "Nationalities and the Soviet Military," in *The Nationalities Factor in Soviet Politics and Society*, eds. Lubomyr Hajda and Mark Beissinger (Boulder, CO: Westview Press, 1990).

Yuri Rost, *Armenian Tragedy* (New York: St. Martin's Press, 1990).

Andrei Sakharov, "An Open Letter to Mikhail Gorbachev," *Glasnost*, no. 16–18.

Thomas J. Samuelian, "Cultural Ecology and Gorbachev's Restructured Union," *Harvard International Law Journal* 32: 1 (Winter 1991).

Avedis K. Sanjian, *Colophons of Armenian Manuscripts, 1301–1480* (Cambridge: Harvard University Press, 1969).

Mark Saroyan, "The 'Karabagh Syndrome' and Azerbaijani Politics," *Problems of Communism* (September–October 1990).

Gertrude E. Schroeder, "Nationalities and the Soviet Economy," in *The Nationalities Factor in Soviet Politics and Society*, eds. Lubomyr Hajda and Mark Beissinger (Boulder, CO: Westview Press, 1990).

Alfred Erich Senn, *Lithuania Awakening* (Berkeley: University of California Press, 1990).

Theodore Shabad, *Basic Industrial Resources of the USSR* (New York: Columbia University Press, 1969).

Samvel Shahmuratian, ed., *The Sumgait Tragedy: Pogroms against Armenians in Azerbaijan*, trans. Steven Jones (New Rochelle, NY: Aristide D. Caratzas for the Zoryan Institute, 1990).

Louise Manoogian Simone, "A Discussion with Vasken Manoukian," *AGBU News* (June 1991).

Hedrick Smith, *The New Russians* (New York: Avon Books, 1990).

Ronald Grigor Suny, *The Baku Commune 1917–1918: Class and Nationality in the Russian Revolution* (Princeton: Princeton University Press, 1972).

_____. "Modernization Soviet Style: The Case of Armenia," *Armenian Review* 36: 1 (Spring 1983).

_____. "Nationalism and Democracy in Gorbachev's Soviet Union: The Case of Karabagh," *Michigan Quarterly Review* 28: 4 (Fall 1989).

_____. "Nationalist and Ethnic Unrest in the Soviet Union: Gorbachev's Search for Accommodation," *World Policy Journal* (Summer 1989).

_____. "Transcaucasia: Cultural Cohesion and Ethnic Revival in a Multinational Society," in *The Nationalities Factor in Soviet Politics and Society*, eds. Lubomyr Hajda and Mark Beissinger (Boulder, CO: Westview Press, 1990).

_____. "The Problematic Neighbor," *AIM* (August/September 1991).

_____. "The Soviet South: Nationalism and the Outside World," in *The Rise of Nations in the Soviet Union: American Foreign Policy and the Disintegration of the USSR*, ed. Michael Mandelbaum (New York: Council on Foreign Relations Press, 1991).

_____. *Looking toward Ararat: Armenia in Modern History* (Bloomington, IN: Indiana University Press, 1993).

Tadeusz Swietochowski, *Russian Azerbaijan, 1905-1920: The Shaping of National Identity in a Muslim Community* (Cambridge: Cambridge University Press, 1985).

_____. "Azerbaijan: Between Ethnic Conflict and Irredentism," *Armenian Review* 43: 2–3 (Summer/Autumn 1990)

Anahide Ter Minassian, "The Revolution of 1905 in Transcaucasia," *Armenian Review* 42: 2 (Summer 1989).

United States Department of State, *Soviet Nationalities Survey* 15 (22 August 1988).

Luigi Villari, *Fire and Sword in the Caucasus* (London: T. Fisher Unwin, 1906).

Taline Voskeritchian, "Looking in from the Inside," *AIM* (October 1994).

Christopher J. Walker, ed., *Armenia and Karabagh: The Struggle for Unity* (London: Minority Rights Publications, 1991)

Christopher J. Walker, *Armenia: The Survival of a Nation* (New York: St. Martin's Press, 1980).

Index

Abbas, Shah, 9
Abkhazians, 131, 148
Abovyan, 33, 160–61
Adrianople, Treaty of, 11
Aganbegyan, Abel, 28, 156
Aghdam, 52, 123, 144, 146
Alaverdi, 109, 160
Alexander II, Tsar, 13
Alexandropol. *See* Leninakan
Aliyarov, Suleiman, 156
Aliyev, Haidar, 41, 156, 164, 211n.
Andropov, Yuri, 122
Arakelyan, Yuri, 60
Ararat, 71
Ararat, Mount, 24, 38, 134
Ararktsyan, Babgen, 76, 108, 130, 186, 202, 214n., 225n.
Armenia: ancient and medieval history of, 6–10, 18–21, 154; Azerbaijani blockade of, 192–93; conversion to Christianity, 7–8; dissidence in, 135–38; impact of Karabagh movement on, 1–4, 33–50, 64–66, 71, 83–86, 92–93, 95, 100–105, 121–22, 125, 127–30, 142, 144–45, 172–76, 184, 189–91, 194–96, 205–7; independent republic of 1918–20 in, 17–18, 22; intelligentsia of, 49, 89–90; minorities in, 53, 130, 176–77; Ottoman rule in, 15–17; *perestroika* in, 88, 102, 119–20, 127, 132–33, 160; pollution in, 133–35; Russian rule in, 10–15, 112, 150; secession

from Soviet Union of, 202–4; sovietization of, 18, 23–25; Supreme Soviet of, 31, 39, 59, 64, 77, 84–86, 90–93, 104, 106, 116, 129–30, 144–45, 159–61, 173–74, 186, 189, 194, 196–202; transformation under Soviet rule in, 44–45, 69, 97–98, 108–12, 131–35, 177–79
Armenian Academy of Sciences, 28, 42, 70, 133
Armenian Apostolic Church, 8, 11, 13, 19, 20, 76, 105, 108, 128, 157
Armenian–Azerbaijani relations, 17, 22–24, 26–28, 57–58, 93, 146–53, 156–58, 176–77, 192–95; conflict of 1905–6, 14–15, 177
Armenian National Army (ANA), 199, 201–2
Armenian National Council, 193
Armenian National Movement (ANM), 127–30, 132–33, 142, 160, 191, 194–95, 197–203, 206
Armenian Revolutionary Federation (ARF), 12–15, 65, 138–39, 152, 155
Arshakuni dynasty, 18, 180
Artsarkh. *See* Mountainous Karabagh
Arzumanyan, Robert, 41–42
Askeran, 52, 169
Association for the Defense of the Armenian Cause, 133
Association in Support of Perestroika, 132
Avan Yuzbashi, 20–21

230